BRIAN L. KACHELMEIER

READING
ISAIAH
WITH
LUTHER

CONCORDIA PUBLISHING HOUSE • SAINT LOUIS

ENDORSEMENTS

Reading Isaiah with Luther may appear to only be a journey back in time—not so! Brian Kachelmeier's stellar work is for the here and now. Wonderfully organized around the theme of conscience, this book exudes with pastoral concern for God's people. The idea of conscience was ubiquitous in Luther's time, but not so much in ours. Kachelmeier helps us recover what we have lost—a robust way of confronting counterfeit catechesis by pointing the baptized to God's gift of a new conscience that is Christ-centered and Gospel-saturated.
REED LESSING, SENIOR PASTOR, ST. MICHAEL LUTHERAN CHURCH, FORT WAYNE, AUTHOR, *CONCORDIA COMMENTARY: ISAIAH*

Martin Luther read Isaiah with the confidence that the prophet spoke of Christ, particularly His proper work of consoling terrified consciences with the evangelical and liberating word of forgiveness. Brian Kachelmeier has provided a guide into Luther's lectures on Isaiah that is not only accessible but rich with pastoral insights. Pastors will gain substantial insights for preaching and the care of souls while laity will be enriched in their understanding of Christian doctrine and life.
JOHN T. PLESS, MDIV, DLITT, ASSISTANT PROFESSOR OF PASTORAL MINISTRY AND MISSIONS/DIRECTOR OF FIELD EDUCATION, CONCORDIA THEOLOGICAL SEMINARY

With the Book of Isaiah in one hand and Luther's Works in the other, Pastor Kachelmeier goes to work like a true doctor of souls. He unfolds the preaching and teaching of Isaiah and Luther for us, bringing fresh understanding, new insight, and the true comfort of the Gospel. Pastor Kachelmeier, like Pastor Luther and Pastor Isaiah, focuses on the conscience and the cleanness and comfort that Jesus wants to bring to the Christian's conscience. For anyone looking for a better understanding of the Scriptures and Luther's teaching, this is your book.

PASTOR BRYAN WOLFMUELLER, AUTHOR, *HAS AMERICAN CHRISTIANITY FAILED?*

How misunderstood the role of conscience is in our culture today! How underappreciated also in the church! Here is a book that provides a powerful remedy. With Isaiah as the terrain and Luther's commentary in hand as a trusty map, Pastor Kachelmeier leads us on an adventure into the realm of conscience, exposing its malformation by the pressures of society and Satan and its reformation by the grace of the Holy Spirit operative in the Word of God. It's a much-needed trip from fear and uncertainty to faith's joyful conviction. I know that the readers of this work will join me in acknowledging our debt of gratitude to Pastor Kachelmeier for inviting us to travel along the contours of Isaiah with him!

WILLIAM WEEDON, CHAPLAIN, LCMS DIRECTOR OF WORSHIP, AUTHOR, *THANK, PRAISE, SERVE, AND OBEY*, AND *CELEBRATING THE SAINTS*

Published by Concordia Publishing House
3558 S. Jefferson Avenue, St. Louis, MO 63118-3968
1-800-325-3040 • cph.org

Copyright © 2018 Brian L. Kachelmeier

No part of this publication may be reproduced, stored in a retrieval system, or transmitted, in any form or by any means, electronic, mechanical, photocopying, recording, or otherwise, without the prior written permission of Concordia Publishing House.

Except for Scripture quotations within Luther's text and those otherwise indicated, Scripture quotations are from the ESV® Bible (The Holy Bible, English Standard Version®), copyright © 2001 by Crossway, a publishing ministry of Good News Publishers. Used by permission. All rights reserved.

Quotations from Luther's Works in this publication are from the American Edition: vol. 1 © 1958, vol. 16 © 1969, vol. 17 © 1972, vol. 25, © 1999 by Concordia Publishing House. All rights reserved.

Quotations from vol. 32 of Luther's Works, American Edition © 1958 by Augsburg Fortress. All rights reserved. Used by permission of the publisher.

Quotations marked *LSB* are from *Lutheran Service Book*, copyright © 2006 Concordia Publishing House. All rights reserved.

Small Catechism quotations are from *Luther's Small Catechism with Explanation*, copyright © 1986, 2017 Concordia Publishing House. All rights reserved.

Backgrounds: © Sweet Art / Shutterstock

Manufactured in the United States of America

LIBRARY OF CONGRESS CATALOGING-IN-PUBLICATION DATA

Names: Kachelmeier, Brian, author.
Title: Reading Isaiah with Luther / Brian L Kachelmeier.
Description: Saint Louis : Concordia Publishing House, 2018.

Identifiers: LCCN 2018018904 (print) | LCCN 2018032274 (ebook) | ISBN 9780758660121 | ISBN 9780758660060

Subjects: LCSH: Bible. Isaiah--Criticism, interpretation, etc. | Luther, Martin, 1483-1546.

Classification: LCC BS1515.52 (ebook) | LCC BS1515.52 .K33 2018 (print) | DDC 224/.106--dc23

LC record available at https://lccn.loc.gov/2018018904

1 2 3 4 5 6 7 8 9 10   27 26 25 24 23 22 21 20 19 18

CONTENTS

Introduction	7
Chapter 1: Cultural Cultivation of the Conscience	14
Chapter 2: The Role of the Prophet and the Conscience	40
Chapter 3: Idolatry and the Conscience	65
Chapter 4: When the Conscience Is Alarmed	94
Chapter 5: Satan Attacks the Conscience like a City	122
Chapter 6: The New Creation	150
Chapter 7: Isaiah at the Foundation of the Reformation	186
Chapter 8: The God Who Quenches the Thirsty Conscience	221

INTRODUCTION

> Let your conscience be your guide.
> —WALT DISNEY'S *PINOCCHIO*

In 1521, the Catholic Church excommunicated Dr. Martin Luther for challenging the authority of Pope Leo X. Later that year, he stood before Emperor Charles V and declared,

> My conscience is captive to the Word of God. I cannot and will not retract anything, since it is neither safe nor right to go against conscience. I cannot do otherwise, here I stand, may God help me. Amen. (32:112–13)

With these simple words, Luther summarized the common understanding of the role of the conscience in his day.

In his lectures on the prophet Isaiah's writings, Luther states,

> This is the single endeavor of Satan, to snatch away our faith and make the conscience unsure. (17:349)

We are fighting a spiritual battle in this world—a war of words in which the devil does not want our consciences to be sure. The tempter tempts us to doubt God's promises and fall into despair or ignore God's threats and become falsely secure in our sin.

> The most honest consciences experience this tribulation. Therefore they must always withstand Satan by means of the Word. (17:214)

The only way to properly shape the conscience is by the Word of God. The Lord desires to give us a good conscience and a clean heart.

Through the mouth of the prophet Isaiah, we hear the voice of the Lord:

> Strengthen the weak hands, and make firm the feeble knees. Say to those who have an anxious heart, "Be strong; fear not! Behold, your God will come with vengeance, with the recompense of God. He will come and save you." (Isaiah 35:3–4)

> For thus says the One who is high and lifted up, who inhabits eternity, whose name is Holy: "I dwell in the high and holy place, and also with him who is of a contrite and lowly spirit, to revive the spirit of the lowly, and to revive the heart of the contrite." (Isaiah 57:15)

Today, we don't typically talk about conscience. In fact, the devil would like us to ignore the subject altogether. The slogan of Satan is "If it feels good, do it." The motto of the world is "If it doesn't hurt others, do it." In many cases, we refer to these slogans and mottos when raising children. It is a culturally acceptable practice to raise children in doing the right thing. When I was a young boy, I thought and acted like a boy. After all, I was a real boy, because I had a conscience! At least, that's what I learned from Walt Disney's 1940 film *Pinocchio*, which tells the tale of a puppet who wanted to become a real boy.

As the story goes, Pinocchio the puppet needs a conscience to become a real boy. Jiminy Cricket is appointed to be his conscience; that's right, a cricket with a badge. After all, the cricket is the one who identified the conscience as the "still, small voice that people won't listen to." A fairy deems Jiminy Cricket the "lord high keeper of the knowledge of right and wrong, counselor in moments of temptation, and guide along the straight and narrow path," and then Pinocchio is taught to always let his conscience be his guide. Granted, this movie is fueled by fantasy: dreams come true when one wishes upon a star, a fairy grants wishes with the swish of a magic wand, and magical kingdoms are the realm of happiness.

But according to this fairy tale, the conscience is given to Pinocchio so that he can learn to choose between right and wrong, proving himself to be brave, truthful, and unselfish. Once he accomplishes this task, he can become a real boy. However, the task is not easy. The temptations to skip school, go to the theater, smoke cigars, drink beer, and play pool are difficult to resist. Jiminy Cricket is not an assertive character. Pinocchio perpetually ignores his conscience and covers up his moral behavior with lies, justifying his actions. The more he fibs, the longer his nose grows. Rather than becoming a real boy, Pinocchio ends up being a lost boy. He does not heed the fairy's warning: "A boy who won't be good might just as well be made of wood." By his actions, he becomes a (literal) stubborn jackass. However, in the realm of make-believe, "If your heart is in your dream / No request is too extreme / When you wish upon a star." Therefore, after trial and error, the puppet who brags about having no strings to hold him down proves himself to be brave, truthful, and unselfish. By his good behavior, he becomes a real boy.

Of course, we do not obtain our theology from fairy tales and cartoons. Nevertheless, as a child, I thought like a child. As a child, I learned about the role of a conscience from a film. Yet, as an adult, I still watch animated movies. The film industry caters to adults who do not want to let their childhood go. We do not want to grow up. We would rather escape reality and live in the realm of fantasy. We do not want to be real boys and girls, let alone real men and women. In our day, the corrupted culture catechizes the consciences of all people—children and adults. Our consciences are being instructed in what is right and wrong or what is good and evil. The still, small voice is enticed and coerced to sing to a different tune.

The conscience is a gift from God given to each human being. It resides in the realm of the soul, spirit, heart, and mind. When the conscience is at peace, we say that the soul, spirit, heart, or mind is at peace. When the conscience is troubled, we say that the soul, spirit, heart, or mind is troubled. Our thoughts, words, and deeds affect the conscience, which is the faculty of the heart that determines what is right or wrong in God's sight. It is an instrument to help us follow moral norms and convict us when we violate them. To have a conscience means that you know, see, perceive, and understand with others. That which we know and see (because of, for example, experiences, family, friends, acquaintances, society, or God) shapes and forms our consciences.

To be clear, the conscience is not the inner voice of God; the conscience is a tool that attests to the natural law written on the heart. "Natural law" is a term used to describe a universal objective moral code. For example, one does not have to be a Christian to understand that such actions as murder, adultery, and stealing are wrong. This is understood by natural reason, not divine revelation.

However, since the fall into sin caused by Adam and Eve, the natural mind is inclined to suppress the truth. Since the natural law is written on the heart, it can easily be edited and erased. The conscience is constantly being updated and upgraded. Ever since the Garden of Eden, we have been seduced by Satan to do whatever we please.

Unlike the fairy in *Pinocchio*, God does not give us a conscience to coach us into being brave, truthful, and unselfish. Far be it from that, the conscience bears testimony of our sin. Because of original sin, brought on by Adam and Eve, by nature, we are terrified, untruthful, and selfish. The conscience alarms us of our guilt before God, jolting us to recognize His judgment and wrath. But make no mistake, the solution to sin does not rest in allowing the conscience to be our guide. Our own efforts can never free us from the spiritual strings that enslave us as puppets of sin and Satan. Only Christ redeems lost boys and girls by making us real boys and girls, that is, children of God. He is the real boy who was brave, truthful, and unselfish. He emptied Himself to become a servant obedient to the point of death on the cross. Satan has pulled the strings on the conscience ever since the beginning. However, Christ has persistently cut the cords of slavery to sin and liberated the conscience from the bondage of the old evil foe with His promise. Through the mouth of the prophet Isaiah, Jesus says,

> The Spirit of the Lord GOD is upon Me, because the LORD has anointed Me to bring good news to the poor; He has sent Me to bind up the brokenhearted, to proclaim liberty to the captives, and the opening of the prison to those who are bound. (Isaiah 61:1)

In this life, there is a spiritual battle for the right to shape and mold us. The world wants us to conform to its ways. However, through God's Word, the Holy Spirit works faith in our hearts. Satan tries to deform our consciences with sin; Jesus comes to reform our consciences with forgiveness. Whereas the media of this age dishes out fake news and a false narrative, the preaching of the Gospel feeds us the Good News and the true narrative, that is, the message about the person and work of Christ. He is the truth. He gives us the correct editorial on life. Whereas the music of this culture hypnotizes us with a sick fresh beat and bumper-sticker theology, the hymns of the Church sung throughout the ages place the sweet sound of the Gospel in our ears and on our lips. Whereas movies grant us glimpses of fantastic realms, the God-breathed Scriptures reveal to us the mysteries of the kingdom of God.

In this book, we will learn from the lectures of Dr. Martin Luther on the prophet Isaiah, as published in the American Edition of Luther's Works. Each quote from Luther is followed by a citation of the appropriate volume number and page number(s) where the quote can be found in the American Edition. Keep in mind, there are sixty-six chapters in the Book of Isaiah and two volumes containing Luther's lectures. These books have many wonderful words to digest, but we will not be able to talk about everything. Thus, we will focus on the issues of the conscience. In Luther's day, the understanding of the role and function of the conscience was commonplace. Therefore, as a professor at the University of Wittenberg, he trained future pastors in the proper pastoral care of the conscience. In our day, we have neglected the seriousness of this role and function. Throughout this book, we will look at the examples of the crisis of conscience as found in the lives of Isaiah, King Ahaz, King Hezekiah, the people of Israel during the Babylonian captivity, and even Martin Luther.

Although Luther typically warns against the misuse and abuse of allegorical interpretation, you will find he does utilize it as he lectures on the Book of Isaiah to help embellish the teaching on faith and the conscience. He instructs his students to handle the allegorical interpretation wisely in the way of the Holy Spirit. He even gives the example of St. Paul's allegorical interpretation of Isaiah 54 as found in Galatians 4:22–31.

When you read Isaiah with Luther, I want you to see the reformer's unique contribution regarding the topic of the conscience. In fact, this topic is at the root of the Reformation, in which the article of justification through faith alone gives all glory to Jesus and brings comfort to the troubled heart. The role and function of the conscience in the days of Isaiah during the seventh and eighth centuries BC and in the days of Luther in the sixteenth century AD is no different from our days. The more things change, the more they stay the same. The corrupted culture constantly cultivates the conscience without the Word of God. Even American Christianity has confused matters by Americanizing the conscience.

When we hear Isaiah and Luther, we will hear the voice in the wilderness of our land, preparing the way of the Lord. Luther instructs us:

> To be a Christian . . . means to be moved by neither good works nor bad works. If you have done ill, commit it to Christ. If you have done well, commit it to the state. Therefore we must oppose the devil and his attacks in Christ alone. (17:214–15)

In the kingdom of God, God reigns as king when our crushed conscience finds comfort in Christ. Through the mouth of the prophet Isaiah, the Lord assures us,

> But this is the one to whom I will look: he who is humble and contrite in spirit and trembles at My word. (Isaiah 66:2)

Commenting on this passage, the blessed reformer teaches,

> The hypocrites despise all of God's commandments and go their way smugly in their own traditions, as it were, trampling all of God's commandments with their feet and boots. The godly man, however, knows that he is not fulfilling the law of God. Then follows a restless conscience, a constant evil which must not be treated by any human help but only by God's help. Summary: The Christians' poverty is the despair of conscience because of sin and death, but in such a way that we may know fully that this is God's workshop and place of operation. Given these materials, God begins to work. This is our Lord God's workshop, to make something out of nothing, to provide comfort where there is no comfort. Let this be our certainty and faith and hope, that we may know we must not despair in such spiritual poverty. (17:399)

In harmony with the prophet Isaiah, Luther sings like a swan, filling our ears with the comfort of Christ to calm our conflicted consciences. Through the power of the Gospel, Christ comes to assure us that for His sake, we have life, salvation, and the forgiveness of sins. Being justified by faith, we now have peace with God in our hearts through our Lord Jesus Christ.

CHAPTER 1

CULTURAL CULTIVATION OF THE CONSCIENCE

Before we learn from Luther and Isaiah about the conscience, we need to understand that our consciences are synced with society. The world around us forms and conforms our consciences just like it did in the days of Isaiah and Luther. The only difference in our circumstance is that the religious teachers have taken a back seat to the secular leaders who boast in the wisdom of the world. Such influential leaders shape and bind consciences by laws. Let's establish a clear distinction between these two different matters of the conscience.

The Culture Cultivates the Conscience by Convincing

The first way our culture forms our consciences is by convincing us to see that certain things are good or bad. Our culture constantly cultivates every one of us through media, movies, and music. The media (in all forms of mass communication) broadcasts running commentary on how we should process current events in our thoughts, words, and deeds. In person, on TV, or online, the loudest reflections and notions shape and mold our own perceptions. While our consciences testify that we should not despise the instituted authorities of God, the media amplifies the sound of sin, which breaks down the institutions of God. It disseminates disorder and disgust for the things of God. Sound bites ring throughout the land, drowning out the troubled consciences. The more the conscience becomes worried, the louder the sound grows. Thus, all that can be heard is "Resist!" "Pro-choice!" "Same-sex marriage!" The way of the world is to normalize wickedness and promote self-identity. The media diverts our attention away from our lives before God to a comparison game of our lives versus the lives of other people. It takes control of our minds. It makes us want to escape from all the problems in society.

Movies and TV shows project an alternative reality. On the screen, the camera operator invites us to look through his eyes. The director directs us to dwell in a different realm than the one in which we live. There, sensuality and the pleasures of the flesh are magnified and glorified. There, the depravity of humanity is etched in our minds. There, fallen creation comes into focus. There, the view of the world becomes our perspective on what life is all about. There, the dreams and fantasies of others are inserted in our minds. Movies entertain us with the experiences of others as if they were our own. Nevertheless, such events are fake. They are fabricated with props, lights, makeup, costumes, and special effects. Actors pretend to live out fictional lives for us to behold on artificial sets. Yet, the images captured on film captivate our eyes. The accompanying soundtracks overpower us and influence emotions of sadness and gladness.

Music perpetually changes as it changes us. The songs of our teenage years become the sweet-sounding themes for the rest of our lives. Music induces emotional responses to our daily experiences. It is as if each one of us stars in a self-made movie, swaying to the sound of the self-chosen jam. We give our ears to musical artists as if they are life coaches. The lyrics of the secular artist become words of wisdom to our hearts, inspiring us to live by the teachings of bumper-sticker slogans. Thoughts of the self-appointed worship leaders praising the practices of our society fill our minds. As a form of catharsis, the songwriters confess the troubles of their hearts. Like group therapy, the groupies gobble up every word. Music makes us feel miserable together, and at the same time, it makes us feel good about ourselves. Pop music plays as the accompaniment to pop culture. Fallen creation is in direct rebellion against the kingdom of God.

The Culture Cultivates the Conscience by Catechizing

This counterfeit catechesis instructs our hearts beginning at a young age. The reconditioned conscience becomes disconnected from God's Word. Now, the conscience of culture asserts itself to rule over our thoughts, words, and deeds. It guides us to be perpetual Peter Pans, who boast in being lost boys and girls who never want to grow up. In this world, we are enticed to escape to Neverland. Like Walt Disney, we dream of making a magical kingdom filled with fun and fantasy. The teachings of our culture come from the corrupted heart. The way of the world is to call evil good and good evil. The prophet Isaiah confronted the counterfeit catechesis in his day, saying,

> Woe to those who call evil good and good evil, who put darkness for light and light for darkness, who put bitter for sweet and sweet for bitter! Woe to those who are wise in their own eyes, and shrewd in their own sight! (Isaiah 5:20–21)

The conscience of culture was similar in Luther's day. Luther spoke out against the teachers who warped hearts in the ways of the world. He chided them, saying,

> Not only are you smug in luxury and abandon the Word of God, but you also blaspheme openly, you scoff at both promises and threats, you stubbornly persist in sinning, you are arrogant in the righteousness of the flesh. (16:64)

Then Luther went on to explain,

> Just as horses hitched to a wagon always pull even when they are tired, so also we. Hosea 10:11 says: "Ephraim was a trained heifer that loved to thresh." The teachers drive the people as teamsters do, and so they remain in a state of ungodliness. They do not actually question the Lord's power, but they do not believe what is proclaimed through Isaiah. They do not disdain the Lord in Himself but maintain Him in the Word and in preachers and in displays of the Law, yet they proceed from stubbornness to blasphemy. So it is impossible to refute a hypocrite. Therefore they do not draw righteousness but iniquity. . . .

They regard themselves as thoroughly holy, but they speak up against the prophet and do not fear for themselves. The cry of all the ungodly is: "Peace and safety" (1 Thess. 5:3). They say: We know what the Holy One of Israel has in mind, and we think the devil is speaking out of Isaiah. Disregard of the Word of God is certainly a great enough crime, but to attribute it to the devil, this puts an end to the game, this makes the earth quake, either as about to fall into ruin or as about to be reshaped with great loss of life.

The work and purpose of the Lord is His Word. The blasphemy against Christ is immediately followed by a counterfeit of reality. . . .

This is the way all ungodly and all men of the flesh act. But the prophet is here speaking not of matters subject to the senses but of the Word, which is good and useful, a light brightening and guiding on all ways, teaching right things, restoring consciences, etc. Therefore he accuses the pestilent teachers through the Word of God; they blaspheme and rail at it but proclaim their own ungodly ideas and the wisdom of the flesh, things which are never good. Creatures are indeed at times put to good use. A lie is always evil. God can put up with sins, and when sins have been acknowledged, God can easily take care of them. God cannot put up with the blasphemer. . . .

Solomon says (Prov. 3:5, 7): "Do not rely on your own insight. . . . Be not wise in your own eyes." This, too, refers to blasphemers, and we include both teachers and disciples. Their excessive wisdom makes them oppose the Word of God. Christ performed many miracles, but He never made folly look like wisdom. This unquestionably most difficult work and burdensome task He has left for us to carry out together with those who love themselves, so that they might become wise. Whatever is said to them, this they fight against and disparage. One must certainly walk in fear and humility, and we must first give up our own ideas. Then let us see whether what we have heard conforms to the faith. Let our wisdom be brought low and let us walk in fear. (16:64, 65)

Since the teachers in Isaiah's day did not subject themselves to the wisdom of God, they viewed his message as evil. The same thing happened in the days of Luther, and we should expect a similar reaction in our day. We must keep in mind that morality is a pattern of behavior that is conformed to accepted notions of right and wrong. Again, note that the conscience is a shared seeing and knowing of the difference between good and evil. When Luther refers to the ungodly, he means unrepentant unbelievers. The world warps their moral compasses. When he refers to the godly, he means repentant believers. God's Word forms their moral faculties. The ungodly parade around in their pride, for all to see and know their actions. The godly walk in the light of Christ, seeing and knowing His actions, which cleanse them from their sins.

> For the look on their faces bears witness against them; they proclaim their sin like Sodom; they do not hide it. Woe to them! For they have brought evil on themselves. (Isaiah 3:9)

Luther expounds on this passage from Isaiah by commenting that sinners "make no secret of it" (16:44). He then continues,

> It is as if [Isaiah] were saying that their sin is manifest and that one cannot say that they are going astray and sinning against Christ out of ignorance. Thus our own wickedness is manifest and is exposed to the view of all, so that it would be pure and incorrigible maliciousness for anyone to deny it. One realizes clearly how evil the bishops are. Recognition is taken in a passive sense for what is recognized, and the face shows clearly what they are.
>
> *Their sin like Sodom, etc.*, as if they commanded the people to do things in this way. They defend their sins as the Sodomites did, saying (Gen. 19:9): "This fellow came to sojourn, and he would play the judge!" They themselves wanted to be judges, just as today they command and command again out of pure malice. Therefore we can conclude from this, too, that all the bishops will perish; for they sin openly, and during the former rebellion some saw how they would perish.
>
> *They do not hide it*, like the Jews in Acts (5:28): "We strictly charged you not to teach in this name." No disgrace is greater

than this. Therefore he compares this wickedness with that of Sodom, a passion for sinning. I think the sin of our countrymen is greater than the sin of Sodom was. Who has ever heard more horrible blasphemies, etc.?

Woe to them! For they have brought evil upon themselves. There is force in the word "evil." For left in rebellion, they are in a ruinous life. They do not know by what kind of death they will perish. (16:44)

When Luther refers above to the bishops, he is talking about the accepted teachers of the conscience in his day. Likewise, when Luther refers to the Jews, he means the Jewish rabbis who rejected Jesus and taught others to abandon the messianic promises. Thus, in the days of Isaiah, this would include the Levitical priests who failed to direct the people to the visible means through which God bestowed His promised favor (e.g., the ritual cleansings, animal sacrifices, food offerings, circumcision, etc.). Even if the recognized teachers and idols of the day tell us that an evil action is good and convince us that we have a good conscience, before God, sin makes a conscience guilty. A bad conscience bears testimony to a bad action. A bad conscience is terrified when it hears the voice of God.

When Adam and Eve sinned in the garden, their consciences testified that they had done a bad thing before God. They felt naked and ashamed. Thus, they covered their bodies with fig leaves, trying to ease their bad consciences with this "good" action. However, when they heard the voice of God, they hid from Him. Their bad consciences were terrified. Their consciences deceived them by convincing them that God came to accuse and judge them as guilty. They concluded that God was not a friend; He was an enemy. However, the Word of God came to seek and to save the lost; Jesus is the Word of God who was in the beginning, creating all things. Before the incarnation, the preincarnate Christ came to bring them the Gospel promise and peace. The Seed of the woman would crush the serpent's head. In the words of the prophet Isaiah, "Behold, the virgin shall conceive and bear a son, and shall call His name Immanuel" (Isaiah 7:14). Jesus is the Seed of the woman, the Son born of Mary. Jesus is Immanuel, that is, God with us. Yet, in order to bring us back to God, the heel of the promised Seed would be

The Gospel... proclaims forgiveness and sanctification free of charge. In this God delights, that the Gospel is preached in its wisdom.

— MARTIN LUTHER

bruised by the serpent. In other words, Jesus had to die for our sins in order to make us right with God. The Holy Spirit teaches us, "Since therefore the children share in flesh and blood, He Himself likewise partook of the same things, that through death He might destroy the one who has the power of death, that is, the devil, and deliver all those who through fear of death were subject to lifelong slavery" (Hebrews 2:14–15). Without the Word of God, there is no life. Without the Word of the Lord, the conscience will remain deceived by Satan and deceiving to the soul. The Gospel alone gives us a good conscience that is certain and confident before God. The Gospel is the good news that Jesus was born to bear our sin and to be our Savior.

The Culture Cultivates the Conscience by Coercing

The second way our culture forms our consciences is by coercion. The words of the world cannot make a conscience good before God. The teaching of the corrupted culture can only create a bad conscience. There is a big difference between having a bad conscience and creating a bad conscience. The fall of Adam and Eve (original sin) makes our consciences inherently bad. False sins create a bad conscience. In other words, we are made to feel bad about doing the right things.

Our society—oftentimes through media, movies, and music—sets forth the standards of right and wrong, good and bad. It codifies and legislates its own morality. As Christians, we have become strangers in a land where the murder of an unwanted baby in the womb or an elderly person who is one step away from the tomb is a good deed. We are obligated to accept same-sex marriages, to bake cakes for them, to take pictures of them, and to fake our approval of them. If we have children, we are told how to parent according to the norms of society. Such standards compel parents to refrain from assigning their own children a gender, to provide sex-reassignment surgery when desired, and to accept men sharing restrooms with our daughters. Society attempts to bind consciences with laws and rules that ultimately force us to share the same views and perspectives on what is right and wrong. For, society says that anyone who opposes abortion or assisted suicide must surely be against the rights of women and against mercy for senior citizens. And whether these laws are unofficially adopted or officially legislated, society replaces the universal principles as found in natural law with personal preferences originating from individual hearts.

The Culture Cultivates the Church

Today, the American culture has Americanized some churches. We hear preachers teach the Bible as man's word that can be manipulated to the changing perspectives of the age. It is no coincidence that many of the voices advocating for political correctness, tolerance, and diversity come from the pulpits of mainline liberal Protestant denominations (e.g., the American Baptist Churches, the Episcopal Church, the Evangelical Lutheran Church in America, the Presbyterian Church [USA], the United Methodist Church, etc.). The contemporary views on social justice, feminism, marriage, sexual intimacy, gender identity, and abortion are seen in such churches. They boast that their consciences have been bound to their own views on life. On the other end of the spectrum, we see legalistic systems interwoven in the conservative American Christian culture that also create bad consciences when Christians are told to not drink alcohol, smoke, dance, chew tobacco, attend the movies, watch television, purchase merchandise from particular stores, eat at certain restaurants, or drink from specific coffeehouses.

The Culturally Conditioned Church Creates Bad Consciences

In Luther's day, the church created bad consciences in the lives of Christians through monastic vows, relics, pilgrimages, and canon law. Again, a bad conscience develops when invented laws create pretend piety and produce imaginary iniquity, that is, sin that God does not call sin. A bad conscience condemns and leaves the individual in sadness. In Isaiah's day, the temple bound consciences to new ways of worship in the style of their contemporaries. Such new methods of holiness did not have the promise of God pointing to the Messiah and His kingdom; instead, the people were taught to look at the prosperity of the earthly kingdoms. Thus, through the prophet Isaiah, God confronted the teachers:

> Hear, you deaf, and look, you blind, that you may see! Who is blind but My servant, or deaf as My messenger whom I

send? Who is blind as My dedicated one, or blind as the servant of the LORD? He sees many things, but does not observe them; his ears are open, but he does not hear. (Isaiah 42:18–20)

Here the prophet directs his attack at the righteousness of the Jews. All evangelists and prophets fought most fiercely with the Scriptures against the exceedingly stubborn presumption of the Jews. Therefore he says *Hear, you deaf.* "You are deaf because you do not hear the Word of God, and you are blind because you look around with your own ideas." *Hear.* Our skill is in hearing, through which faith comes. *And look, you blind*, that is, you must give attention to the Word. This rebuke belongs to the ungodly. But it applies in part also to us to the extent that we, too, are somewhat blind.

Who is blind but My servant? Beautifully he employs the metaphor with respect to the blind who do not want to be blind but say, "Are we blind, we who are bishops and princes and God's elect? Surely we can see." Christ replies (John 9:41): "If you were blind, you would have no guilt; but now that you say, 'We see,' your guilt remains." So here, *Who is blind but My servant, or deaf as My messenger whom I send?* "My servants are the blind and deaf ones." He is speaking of the popes and bishops. Here the prophet confesses: "The ones who were in charge of teaching were blind." This they could not put up with, and those very teachers of the synagogue accused the saints and servants of God of being blind. I myself would have been ready to help them throw stones. Thus here God does not condemn the office but the blind persons. Similarly we do not rebuke the office of bishop but the blind bishops and leaders of the blind. In this way we must admonish the evil incumbents of government and correct the office, while preserving the government and the office. This requires real skill. Hence it does not follow to say, "I am a bishop and a doctor, therefore I teach correctly." Here the messengers are called deaf. *Who is blind as My dedicated one?* He repeats these words which have much to criticize in the person who sits in the highest rank and in a loftier position. Therefore they boast that they teach more truly. It is these people whom the prophet here calls

> more blind, as if He were saying: "Others are blind too, but none are so blind as My servants, who do not want to hear Me, but insist on establishing their own affairs and relying on their own holiness." . . .
>
> *You see many things, etc.* It is as if He were saying: "Idle prattlers they are. They see many things and hear others, but they refuse to hear Me." They only admitted that faith is justification, but then, moving farther, they admitted the confusion of all the self-righteous.
>
> *Ears are open*, but they do not hear. "They hear other things but not Me. There is much to see but nothing to preserve. My light they do not see, Me they do not hear." (17:78–79)

Again, Luther refers to the teachers of the people. The Jews are the Jewish rabbis who reject Jesus and the messianic promises. The bishops are the teachers of the church who lord it over the people like earthly princes. Thus, the people perish, and their consciences become corrupted with a different image of God. Luther does not despise the preaching office; he has a distaste for those who are blind and deaf to God's vision and Word.

In the days of Isaiah, the prophet spoke out against the false teachers who led the people to see a false image of God and to hear a false message. Their teachings came from the imagination of their corrupted hearts. In chapters 40 and 41, Isaiah mocks the false gods made by fallen humanity. Then, in chapter 42, Isaiah sets the ears of the people on the true image of God and the true Word of God. Through the mouth of the prophet Isaiah, the Father declares,

> Behold My servant, whom I uphold, My chosen, in whom My soul delights; I have put My Spirit upon Him; He will bring forth justice to the nations. (Isaiah 42:1)

And again,

> Hear, you deaf, and look, you blind, that you may see! Who is blind but My servant, or deaf as My messenger whom I send? Who is blind as My dedicated one, or blind as the servant of the LORD? He sees many things, but does not

observe them; his ears are open, but he does not hear. The LORD was pleased, for His righteousness' sake, to magnify His law and make it glorious. (Isaiah 42:18–21)

We have heard how the prophet railed at those who are blind and do not want to be blind, those who have open ears but do not hear and are blind, that is, they listen to all other teachings except this one. This one teaching they do not hear. They are talkative and quarrelsome but contribute nothing to the matter in hand. There is much to see, to hear, yet they neither see nor hear. "To see" is the same as being a prophet. Here the prophet is called a "seeing one." This is a Hebrew idiom. So he says here, "There is much to see. There is a lot of talk, but they are idle prattlers who teach their own ideas." "Not to hear" means to teach one's own doctrine and not Christ's, always teaching but never arriving at understanding, as Paul says (cf. 1 Cor. 1:18ff.). This is what happened to our Enthusiasts, who shouted nothing but "Spirit, Spirit." They confused everyone and strengthened and taught no one. . . .

God accomplished all of this in order to destroy our own devices. *The Lord was pleased* thus to bring human wisdom to naught, and as Paul says (1 Cor. 1:21), "Since, in the wisdom of God, the world did not know God through wisdom, it pleased God through the folly of what we preach to save those who believe." Note that this passage of Paul's agrees with the statement before us. He extols and exalts this righteousness and wisdom, which is foolish and weak, to confound the wise and the mighty. Why this? *The Lord was pleased.* He did not do it, however, in order to take pleasure in the blindness and folly of men. No, He did it to delight in His own righteousness. Therefore He says, *The Lord was pleased for His righteousness' sake.* This is experienced in the Gospel, which proclaims forgiveness and sanctification free of charge. In this God delights, that the Gospel is preached in its wisdom. The proud repudiate and withstand this righteousness, and therefore God turns to the lowly, the unlettered, and the foolish. They are the ones who accept this righteousness. Therefore Jesus says (Matt. 9:13): "I came not to call the righteous, but sinners." It is as if He were saying: "I am not an idol accepting a strange righteousness, but I take pleasure in My own goods and give them to others." For this reason Paul says (Rom. 1:17): "The righteousness of God is revealed through faith."

Righteousness is grace itself, it is the gift itself without our merits. In this righteousness the Lord takes pleasure. Hence this passage deals with repudiating the righteousness of men and with delighting in the righteousness of God. I should think that you know well enough what the righteousness of God is.

To magnify His law, that is, to make His law great. Some can understand this as referring to the law of Moses, for all human presumption boasts of the law of Moses, but from ignorance. The righteousness of God, however, boasts in a different way, as St. Paul shows in Rom. 8:3: "God has done what the Law, weakened by the flesh, could not do." For the work of the Law is to reveal our sins and to show itself to be far superior to our powers of accomplishment. But when Christ would come, He would clarify and extol that Law, and this spiritual understanding of the Law put away the veil of Moses and that outward cover which externally confines man. In this work the people of the world are engaged, because it sanctifies men who outwardly live in the Law. The flesh likes this very much. This is the veil of Moses. Then follows the Gospel, which preaches the righteousness of God. To do this it is necessary to extol the law of Moses and its work. Another interpretation is to refer this passage to the law of faith. So Paul says, "Through the Law I died to the Law" (cf. Rom. 7:4ff.). For faith is the new law through which we die to the old law. I leave it to the judgment of my hearers whether the prophet is speaking of the law of Moses or of the law of faith. I hold with the latter view concerning the new law of faith, by which the righteousness of God is extolled. Therefore he seems here to be speaking about the new law of faith, abolishing the old, as if to say, "The Lord will make a new and admirable law, because it pleased the Lord in His righteousness to magnify and extol this law, abolishing the old law which offers nothing admirable and grand." Thus the

> Christian life is a wonderful life because it puts all holiness of the Law to shame. We see this in the example of the malefactor (Luke 23:42), who is saved through one plea, while the most showy saints in the world are rejected. Magnificent is this law, which glorifies in sin, death, and disgrace.
>
> *The Lord was pleased, for His righteousness' sake.* He takes no pleasure in our blindness, but because He delights in His own righteousness in order to magnify His law, He puts wisdom to shame. (17:80–81)

The Enthusiasts were those who claimed to have extrabiblical visions. Their teachings came from the imagination of their hearts. They claimed that the Bible was a dead letter without the Holy Spirit. Therefore, they despised the preaching office and the external Word. However, the written Scriptures were inspired by the Holy Spirit. The Church was given the Sacred Scriptures so that we could be certain that when we hear the voice of a preacher, we are listening to the voice of God. Thus, we study the written word of Isaiah. As a prophet, Isaiah saw the proper vision of God and heard the clear voice of the Lord. He directed the priests in his day to go back to the written words of Moses.

Ever since the days of Aaron, the first high priest, the priests of God were obligated to teach the Word of God in accordance with the Torah, that is, the first five books of the Bible. Through the office of prophet and priest, the people were given a picture of the coming true Prophet and true Priest, that is, Jesus, the incarnate Word of God. When the teachers of Israel failed to do their duty, the Lord sent a prophet to correct their teachings. However, if the teachers or the people resisted the work of the Holy Spirit, He handed them over to the spirits of the age. In every age, humanity develops its own wisdom, discernment, counsel, and knowledge regarding the reality of life. Such thoughts and values guide the culture and influence the conscience in moral behavior. These choices are prompted by the devil, who is actively involved in promoting a continuous rebellion against God.

The apostle Paul warns the baptized in Ephesus not to walk according to "the course of this world, following the prince of the power of the air" (Ephesians 2:1–2). Likewise, he alerts the baptized in Colossae to the allurement of "philosophy and empty deceit . . . according to the elemental spirits of the world," which are in opposition to Christ (Colossians 2:8, 20–23). Such human precepts and regulations may seem to have the appearance of wisdom, but they cannot overcome the power of sin or appease the wrath of God provoked by sin.

In our own age, we have seen a shift in thinking regarding the institution of marriage. In the past, our Western culture held the belief that the union of a man and woman in holy matrimony was the foundation of society. Husbands and wives learned to love the neighbor in good times and in bad. The fruit of this union was the gift of life found in the conception and birth of a child. Sexual activity outside of marriage was understood as sin.

Now, however, we live in the times of the sexual revolution. Our culture views sexual activity as the fruit of the desire for an emotional union—it is called "making love." Thus, the spirits of this age teach that if a man and a man or a woman and a woman love each other, then they should have the right to marry. Furthermore, these new human precepts and regulations penalize anyone who opposes such a view as a hater who is against love.

> But this is a people plundered and looted; they are all of them trapped in holes and hidden in prisons; they have become plunder with none to rescue, spoil with none to say, "Restore!" Who among you will give ear to this, will attend and listen for the time to come? Who gave up Jacob to the looter, and Israel to the plunderers? Was it not the LORD, against whom we have sinned, in whose ways they would not walk, and whose law they would not obey? So He poured on him the heat of His anger and the might of battle; it set him on fire all around, but he did not understand; it burned him up, but he did not take it to heart. (Isaiah 42:22–25)

But this is a people robbed and plundered. This is Moses' own people, exposed to robbers and ungodly teachers. Those, however, who cling to Christ will not easily err but will remain on target, Christ. If we should lose this target, an endless string of errors would result, as we experienced under the papacy. We were as sheep without a shepherd, exposed to all kinds of robbers. Whatever was taught, that we accepted. This happened to the cold Enthusiasts, who wavered this way and that and could teach nothing with conviction, because, having lost sight of the target, they were exposed to the robber, and they in turn exposed others. Thus, error brings error, and sin brings sin. So it happens to all ungodly teachers who ravage and plunder all their hearers. . . .

All of these words are spoken concerning the innocent's plunder, by means of which they expose the hearers. . . . They are robbed and deprived of the faith and then, having been deprived, they are imprisoned and bound in chains. The godly, however, are free from bonds. They do not permit the bonds to be placed on their conscience through laws but are certain in Christ alone. The others, however, are caught in endless traps and held in caves, imprisoned by their own teachings and opinions. So it happened to the Enthusiasts, who see the plainest words of Christ with their eyes and yet are held captive in their traps and caves. . . .

These prisons are the laws and established rules that imprison their conscience, as Paul says (Gal. 3:23f.): "We were confined under the Law, kept under restraint until faith should be revealed." Here the law of Moses is called a prison. Summary: All toil and sweat caused by outward works prescribed by any law is a prison. . . .

Because they trusted in their own righteousnesses and powers, they did not walk in the way and righteousness of God.

So He poured upon him the heat of His anger and the might of battle. They refused grace, which was again withdrawn, and so God's wrath does not fall in drops but is poured upon them for living in blasphemies and ungodly activities against God. These are the waterfalls and rains of God's wrath, so that they are manifestly sinning in a most shameful way, because it is the wrath of God. *The might of battle.* God goes to war against them. With what weapons? With robbers and wolves, who draw them from one error into another, coming at them as with an army. (17:82–83)

Those, however, who cling to Christ will not easily err but will remain on target, Christ.

— MARTIN LUTHER

The Culturally Cultivated Church Invites the Government into the Conscience

When the teachers refuse to teach God's Word and scratch the itching ears of the people, the Lord eventually hands them over to the delusions of their hearts. When the institution of the church fails to correct the conscience with God's Word, the institution of the government steps in and tries to legislate conscience-binding. The clearest example of such a power group was seen in the controversial move of the United States government to mandate birth control as part of the restricted health-care plans. On February 16, 2012, the Rev. Dr. Matthew C. Harrison, President of The Lutheran Church—Missouri Synod, gave his testimony at the House Committee on Oversight and Government Reform's hearing:

> We fought for a free conscience in this country, and we won't give it up without a fight. To paraphrase Martin Luther, the heart and conscience has room only for God, not for God and the federal government. The bed is too narrow, the blanket is too short. We must obey God rather than men, and we will. Please get the federal government, Mr. Chairman, out of our consciences. Thank you.[*]

In his speech, Rev. Harrison stated clearly that the role of the Church is to proclaim the Gospel message of the blood of Jesus, which cleanses us from sin. The authority of the Church rests in the Word of God. In addition, the Church does not have the task of Christianizing the government. The American government is to be governed by natural law, reason, and the Constitution, which establishes religious freedom in our land. Thus, the government should not force Christians to fund abortion-causing drugs, which violates their consciences. The Christian instructed with God's Word knows that abortion is murder and evil in God's sight.

---

[*] Quoted by Vicki Biggs, "Missouri Synod President tells House Committee: *LCMS 'religiously opposed to supporting abortion-causing drugs,'*" The Lutheran Church—Missouri Synod (website), February 16, 2012, https://www.lcms.org/?pid=1374. For the full transcript, see "Lines Crossed: Separation of Church and State. Has the Obama Administration Trampled on Freedom of Religion and Freedom of Conscience?," Oversight and Government Reform (website), February 16, 2012, https://oversight.house.gov/hearing/lines-crossed-separation-of-church-and-state-has-the-obama-administration-trampled-on-freedom-of-religion-and-freedom-of-conscience.

The realm of the conscience does not belong to the government. Earthly kingdoms step outside of their jurisdiction when they try to rule conscience. It is the sole role of the Church on earth to correct the conscience. Christ alone reigns over the conscience. His kingdom frees bound consciences with the forgiveness of sins. Thus, Isaiah was sent to free the captives with the promise of Christ's kingdom. He shared what he saw and knew from God. However beneficial the laws of the land may seem to be for the well-being of the society, they should not burden our consciences. In Christ's kingdom, no laws, whether human or divine, are to enslave the conscience. Yet, because of sin, the Law rules and reigns in oppression and condemnation, leaving the conscience terrified and troubled—far from free. However, the Gospel comforts and consoles the conscience. Whereas the Law shows God as a judge without Jesus, the Gospel shows Jesus as the one who fulfilled the righteous requirements of the Law in our stead. The Gospel does not free us *to* sin, it frees us *from* sin. To see Christ crucified for your sins is to gain a good conscience before God. To know Christ is to obtain a joyful conscience. And it is the Gospel, the Good Word, that strengthens our conscience.

In the days of the prophet Isaiah, the teachers of the people would not heed the warning of God's judgment. Thus, they were handed over to the Babylonians. (Babylon was an ancient kingdom centered in Mesopotamia and located in modern-day Iraq.) In the New Testament Scriptures, Babylon is the epitome of the darkened dominion of the devil deceiving the earth and deafening people to God's voice (see Revelation 14:8; 16:19; 17:5; 18:2–8). The kingdoms of the earth try to reign over the conscience, plundering and looting the people of the treasure of God's Word. Yet, in the midst of physical distress and pressure, the Word of the Lord comes to bring peace and joy. God sends Isaiah to free the captives with the promise of Christ's kingdom, the message of the Gospel. Isaiah shares what he sees and knows from God:

> The people who walked in darkness have seen a great light; those who dwelt in a land of deep darkness, on them has light shone. You have multiplied the nation; You have increased its joy; they rejoice before You as with joy at the harvest, as they are glad when they divide the spoil. For the yoke of his burden, and the staff for his shoulder, the rod

of his oppressor, You have broken as on the day of Midian. For every boot of the tramping warrior in battle tumult and every garment rolled in blood will be burned as fuel for the fire. (Isaiah 9:2–5)

Yoke means death, *staff* means a prod, sin. *Rod* is the Law, "the power of sin" (1 Cor. 15:56). This description is certainly contrary to all experience, since all laws ought to be the power and motivation of righteousness. But without the Law sin is dead and weaponless. The Law brings it about that there is sin, that it has power, and that it acts (Rom. 7:8). What does it accomplish? Death. There are therefore three strong tyrants: the Law, sin, and death. Sin is twofold: known and unknown. The latter is original sin, the former the sin of outward acts. This needs to be disclosed by the Holy Spirit through a spiritual understanding of the Law. Then the conscience, frightened by the judgment of God, is alarmed: Even though you may not be an adulterer, a thief, a robber, etc., you are born in sins and you are altogether buried in sins, if you do not have Christ. Paul did not know that desire was sin, as he says in Rom. 7:7. The prophet inverts the order. Paul lists it directly. Therefore there is joy because we have been set free from these tyrants. Joy is a skin-deep tickle, it annoys and is unreliable, for it does not remove death, the fear of death, and sin. (16:98)

Luther describes the tools of Satan's tyranny as the Law, sin, and death. The Law troubles us with its demands not to sin, its exposure of our wickedness, and its accusations of our guilt. Sin encumbers our thinking, speaking, and acting to be self-centered. It brings isolation, alienation from others, and separation from God. It produces death in our bodies. Death loads us down with the fear of temporary and eternal punishment before God. Suffering, pain, and even getting old is the assault of death on our individual freedom. These three instruments of Satan's oppression bind and burden the conscience. Yet, Christ delivers us from the oppressors of the conscience that terrify us of God's judgment. Christ comes to free us from the burden of the yoke, staff, and rod. Christ fulfills the Law in our stead. Without the Law, sin is dead and weaponless. Sin empowers the Law to bring death. Christ dies for our sin. Without sin, we are not condemned before God. Christ overcomes death itself, giving to us the victory over the grave. Without death, we are free to live. Christ purifies our consciences from dead works to serve the living God in His kingdom.

> The most oppressive tyrant is the Law, which the prophet here calls our judge and king. It dictates: "You shall love God," etc. But no one is without evil desire. By nature all hate God and the things that are of God. This is not felt except in temptation. The whipped son is angry with his parent. No one likes discipline, not even God's. Natural man would prefer that there be no law, because he is not able to perform what it demands. The sin that has been committed is the second tyrant, and it brings forth the third, namely, death and damnation. Who could be happy when he is answerable to these three? But now they have been vanquished, the Law is fulfilled by Christ and then also by us who have been endowed by the Holy Spirit. He adds the courage so that we may glory even in our sufferings (Rom. 5:3), and thus the Law is no longer outrageous in its dictates but an agreeable companion. The Law itself indeed is not changed, but we are. Obviously this is Christian liberty, when the Law is voluntarily fulfilled, so that it cannot accuse, demand, and render guilty. Where the conscience is not guilty, where there is no sin because it is forgiven, there is no power of death but peace of conscience, the certainty of eternal life. (16:98–99)

Being Acculturated by the Messiah

For the baptized believer, Christ is the king who reigns and rules over the heart in comfort and peace. He delivers us from the tyranny of the Law. He is not the angry judge who comes to condemn us; rather, He is the merciful judge who brings justice to the oppressed. The Father sends forth His Son in the flesh and condemns sin in His flesh. Jesus sets us free from the curse of the Law by becoming a curse for us on the tree. In Christ, we are a new creation, and there is no condemnation. In Christ, the Law cannot condemn. He takes our sin away and pardons our guilt. Instead of a guilty conscience, we have a peaceful conscience before God. The Law is no longer an outrageous dictator, but rather a friend and agreeable companion. Yet, the

Law has not changed; instead, we have been changed by the renewal of the Holy Spirit. The Gospel sets our consciences free. The prophet Isaiah uses the example of the liberation from the oppression of the Midianites as a picture of the liberating work of Christ, the true Gideon.

> The people of Midian had destroyed everything. So the tyrants condemn all our endeavors and works and wisdom, etc. The torch of Gideon is the light of the Gospel, so is the sound of the trumpet, and the clash of jars is Christ's crucifixion (cf. Judges 7:16). These are the things that overcome those enemies: the Word and the Holy Spirit in the Word preaching Christ as having died for us, etc. We draw no sword, but we only shout, hear, believe, confess: Christ died for us, etc. "Thanks be to God, who gives us the victory, etc." (1 Cor. 15:57). The Law, sin, and death have attacked the sinless Christ, they converged upon Him; but they were themselves made culpable and guilty, they were condemned and rendered powerless by Christ, and this was for us. This is our joy and the reaping of the harvest.
>
> *For every violent taking of spoils.* This sheds light and is added for the sake of explanation. For in the kingdom of the church the highest peace and safety will follow after deliverance from sin, the Law, and death. There will be no war. He says (Is. 11:9): "They shall not hurt or destroy in all My holy mountain." The end of righteousness is peace. (16:99)

The prophet Isaiah compares the temporary tyranny experienced by the people of God to the oppression of the Midianites recorded in Judges 6–7. After Joshua led the Israelites into the Promised Land, they refused to hear the Word of God and resisted the work of the Holy Spirit. They began to listen to the voices of the darkened wasteland and engaged in the worship styles of their contemporaries. They embraced the idolatry of Baal. Therefore, God handed them into the hands of the Midianites. The Midianites oppressed the Israelites and devoured their food and devastated their land. But they called out to Yahweh for deliverance from their oppressors. Gideon was the judge sent by God to liberate them. He was not a judge to bring condemnation; rather, he came to bring justice to the oppressed. First, he broke down the altar of Baal. He freed them from the slavery to idolatry. Second, he took a band of three hundred men equipped with torches that were encased in jars. Then, in the middle of the night, they broke the jars and the light scattered the darkness of the land. He freed them from the tyranny of the Midianites.

In this picture of liberation, we see the mystery of the incarnation. God sends forth His only-begotten Son to deliver us from our oppressors, namely, the Law, sin, and death. The Son is not sent to condemn us. He is sent to bring us light and life. The Holy Spirit enlightens our conscience with the Gospel, which frees us from the oppression of the Law, sin, and death. In Christ, our warfare is ended and our iniquity is pardoned. We are justified by faith, which brings peace in our conscience before God. Our King comes to deliver us from the tyrants of the conscience. Throughout our lives, oppression comes in many shapes and forms. For example, our consciences are assaulted when leaders in society tell us to walk in their laws in opposition to God, when teachers in the church tell us to follow their methods to gain victory over sin, or when medical professionals tell us that death is a friend and an act of mercy.

> For to us a child is born, to us a son is given; and the government shall be upon His shoulder, and His name shall be called Wonderful Counselor, Mighty God, Everlasting Father, Prince of Peace. Of the increase of His government and of peace there will be no end, on the throne of David and over His kingdom, to establish it and to uphold it with justice and with righteousness from this time forth and forevermore. The zeal of the LORD of hosts will do this. (Isaiah 9:6–7)

In our culture, most people are familiar with one of Handel's most famous oratorios, the *Messiah*. Well, at least they are familiar with the *Hallelujah Chorus*, which opens with the word *Hallelujah* repeated five times in a row. Commonly, this piece is used as background music for a "eureka moment" in movies or television episodes. However, the real reason for singing "Hallelujah" is the epiphany of Christ's kingdom. In fact, Handel's canticle proclaims, "And He shall reign for ever and ever." Of course, this exclamation comes after singing the words from Isaiah 9, "For unto us a child is born," earlier in the oratorio. These words are a well-known Christmas passage in our day, thanks to Handel. Yet, in the days of Isaiah, no one listened to Handel's oratorio of the *Messiah*. It would have been new news to them.

The prophet Isaiah sees the coming kingdom of Christ in the mystery of the incarnation. A child is born for us. A Son is given to us. Through the birth of this baby boy, we are filled with joy. He is the promised Seed who crushes the serpent's head. Christ is the great light who takes us out of darkness and places us in His light. When we walk in His light, His blood cleanses us from all sins. He is the Prince of Peace, and His kingdom brings eternal peace with God in the conscience. He lifts us up out of sadness and increases our gladness in our hearts. This gift grants us cheerful consciences that have been set free from all forms of bondage.

> Here you see the prophet speaking about the kingdom of peace, because he boasts about a Child born and a Son given, who will be the Head and King of this kingdom. And therefore it will be a kingdom of peace, not of strife. All these words are strong and intense. Above he spoke of the greatest affliction, of darkness and the shadow of death. Likewise of the Law, of sin, and of death, the most oppressive tyrants. Against them he now places the King born and given to us, who is to set us free from them and implant us into His peaceful and happy reign. He now proceeds to explain what kind of reign that is. . . .
>
> The government of Christ are we, whom He carries on His shoulders. Other kings are carried like rods by their subjects. All kingdoms of the world are carried and are burdens on our neck, and they reduce bodies and possessions to slavery. Therefore in the manner of ruling in the kingdom of the world and in that of Christ there is a difference. In the kingdom of the world the prince or king alone is free, all others are servants. But in Christ's kingdom Christ alone is a servant, and we are free. . . . So to the present day it is with Christ, once for all, however, in His cross and death. He commanded His ministers and all His members to bear one another. He Himself is the Cornerstone and the Foundation. Thus in the kingdom of Christ those who serve rule, and those who rule serve. . . .

The kingdom of Christ is beyond grasp, reason, and experience. Here the flesh must be put to death with all its wisdom and judgment, and it must be grasped only by faith. We must believe that Christ's righteousness is ours. Reason wants to lean only on its own righteousness, not on someone else's. We *believe* life, glory, righteousness, and peace but on the contrary *feel* death, shame, sin, and trouble. . . .

Lest we come short in the matter of faith He gives us counsel, that is, the Word, so that we may abide in so wonderful a government of His kingdom. This is truly not a simple word, but it is a word that is able to save in dangers. . . .

In the kingdom of Christ there is grace, comfort, forgiveness of sins, joy, peace. He does not deal with the transgressor in sternness, but as a father. The forgiveness of sins is justification, and peace follows justification. . . .

Therefore David's reign over the Jews was physical, but at length Christ has begun the spiritual reign over the people which will last forever. Hence there will be a resurrection of the dead. Christ is indeed a King different from David, and the government of His kingdom is different, and yet it is a reign over the same people. To believe in life everlasting is the last article and the greatest. However, Christ prepares, establishes, and strengthens this kingdom in the world through the Word and faith, and He does this in a hidden way. . . .

In the kingdom of Christ the ungodly are condemned, the godly are justified, saved, and set free from sin and death. A happy reign in which mercy flourishes. (16:100–102)

In our day, the government tries to Americanize the conscience. Political agendas push the conformity of moral scruples to match current cultural trends. Let us be clear: the duty of the Church is not to Christianize America; rather, pastors are given the task of Christianizing the conscience. In other words, the message of Christ and His kingdom brings Christian freedom, that is, the liberty of the conscience. Jesus frees us from the tyranny of the Law, sin, and death. When the accusation of unfulfilled laws accuses us, Jesus assures us that He fulfilled all the requirements of God's Law. When the guilt of sin weighs us down, Jesus reminds us that He bears our sin and takes it away. When the fear of death terrifies us, Jesus comforts us, proclaiming His victory over the grave. The one who believes in Him, even though he dies, yet he will live (see John 11:25). Christ's kingdom is a kingdom of comfort and peace in the heart.

CHAPTER 2

THE ROLE OF THE PROPHET AND THE CONSCIENCE

Whether we realize it or not, the media, music, and movies that entertain us also teach and preach to our hearts. These three instruments of the culture lead us to embrace a distorted truth and reality. They lead us to embrace the world's perception of right and wrong. When we welcome these voices for our entertainment, our consciences are slowly muffled, silenced, or changed. We are trained to hit the snooze button and even pull the plug on the alarms ringing in our hearts. We are led to decide what is right in our own sight, much like the time of the judges (see Judges 21:25). We tell our souls that all is well, when it is not. However, although our culture shapes our behaviors and beliefs, there is nothing new under the sun. The more things change, the more they stay the same.

In the days of the prophet Isaiah, the contemporary culture formed the people of Jerusalem, just as our culture forms us. The people of God were lulled into accepting the ways of the world, but they didn't even realize it. When people remain in the dark, their eyes become accustomed to it, and eventually they do not even notice the lack of light. The people of God, too, did not see clearly. They saw what they wanted to see. They heard what they wanted to hear. Thus, Isaiah was called to speak the voice of God in the wilderness—a place barren and desolate, a place without God's Word.

Ever since the beginning of sin, the prophets of God have instructed us, saying, "Trust in the LORD with all your heart, and do not lean on your own understanding. In all your ways acknowledge Him, and He will make straight your paths. Be not wise in your own eyes; fear the LORD, and turn away from evil" (Proverbs 3:5–7). The role of the prophet is to be the mouthpiece of God in order to lead us into truth. God is truth. Jesus is incarnate truth, who gives to us the Spirit of truth. The prophet's voice, then, comes to destroy any false images of God that a misinformed conscience projects. The power of the Word of God opens eyes to see, ears to hear, and hearts to understand.

God's Prophet Opens Eyes and Ears and Hearts

In chapter 6, Isaiah recalls the day he was placed into the prophetic office.

> And I heard the voice of the Lord saying, "Whom shall I send, and who will go for Us?" Then I said, "Here I am! Send me." And He said, "Go, and say to this people: 'Keep on hearing, but do not understand; keep on seeing, but do not perceive.' Make the heart of this people dull, and their ears heavy, and blind their eyes; lest they see with their eyes, and hear with their ears, and understand with their hearts, and turn and be healed." (Isaiah 6:8–10)

Almost all the prophets were accustomed to contend with these saintlets and wiseacres who always resist the Holy Spirit, blaspheme the Word and grace of God, and boast of their own righteousness, their own works, and their own ideas. And especially when the carnal man begins to learn the things that pertain to faith while his reason has not yet been mortified and has not yet been taught its beliefs, this is a situation to be deplored. The Word of God does not always have humble hearers; on the contrary, the great majority of hearers are proud and presumptuous. . . .

Go and say to this people. The emphasis lies on His saying "this," not "My," as if He were saying "rejected," "accursed." We do not here wish anxiously to torture ourselves regarding the secret will of God, but only to set forth those matters concerning the mood of God and of His preachers. For God is justly angry with the stubborn who please themselves and have no desire to learn to know themselves and to deny themselves. It is to them that this must be said with displeasure. . . .

They must at last be abandoned. The prophet's words, *make the heart fat, heavy, shut, etc.*, mean that by his preaching the prophet would insult them and inflame them to greater hardness. . . . The meaning briefly is this, that there exists a righteousness different from that of which the Jews boasted, that is to say, not an external but an internal one. But the fact that the Jews would not hear this shows that this is the time when Christ preached and also performed many miracles. The words and deeds of Christ were against the Jews, and they were so embittered against Him that they would not have received Him, even if He had created a new heaven and a new earth, simply because He condemned their works. Solomon says in Prov. 18:2: "A fool receiveth not the words of prudence, unless thou say those things which are in his heart." But if they are unwilling to hear Him, there will nevertheless be those who will hear. He says (Deut. 32:21): "I will stir them to jealousy with those who are no people; I will provoke them with a foolish nation." The ungodly are irked by much preaching, especially by the preaching of faith in opposition to works, but this preaching must nevertheless not be omitted because of them. . . .

This is a clear prophecy of the devastation of the kingdom of the Jews by the Romans, as if to say: The people are obstinate and cannot be healed until they are abandoned. It must not be thought here that their descendants would be healed, but this is a frequent way of speaking in Scripture. Cf. Gen. 8:22; Ps. 110:1; Matt. 1:25. Thus we say: You will not be reformed until death has snatched you away, that is, never. (16:73–75)

Isaiah was sent to a people who refused to listen to God's voice, much less rejoice in hearing it. They resisted the work of the Holy Spirit in their hearts. They kept on seeing but would not see the truth. They kept on hearing but would not hear the truth. Their eyes, ears, and hearts were sealed shut. There was no understanding in their hearts. Luther calls them "the ungodly" because of their unbelief. To him, unbelief is the worst kind of godlessness, worse even than bad moral behavior. This, too, is the fault Luther finds with "the Jews" whom he mentions in this passage. In Luther's thinking, anyone who does not believe God's Word is in error, not just one particular race. Luther connects the unbelief in Isaiah 6 to people's responses of unbelief in Jesus, the Messiah, in all times and places.

Isaiah proclaimed that Israel's unbelief meant their teachers were blind watchmen, silent watchdogs, and shepherds who scattered the sheep (see Isaiah 56:10–11). The blind were leading the blind. Still, God sent forth His Word through the mouth of the prophet to open eyes to see, ears to hear, and hearts to understand. God spoke light where there was night.

And I will lead the blind in a way that they do not know, in paths that they have not known I will guide them. I will turn the darkness before them into light, the rough places into level ground. These are the things I do, and I do not forsake them. They are turned back and utterly put to shame, who trust in carved idols, who say to metal images, "You are our gods." (Isaiah 42:16–17)

The kingdom of Christ is such that He leads the blind on a way he does not know and on a path of which he is ignorant. This is the way of life. There the Lord demands of us not to obey Him with closed eyes and ears, as He says, John 9:41: "If you were blind, you would have no guilt." Human wisdom, however, looks around with endless deliberation, but with all that looking around it succeeds in nothing and loses everything. All of their deliberation is in vain and ends in failure. Have we not seen this in our own experience? But here He teaches us to close our eyes and ears, as if to say, "I will stand firmly enough to protect you in the depths of the sea, as I protected Jonah, who was in the belly of the fish and did not see where he was or whether he was alive or dead." Here God saw and watched and preserved him. Thus we go on in weakness, blindness, and deafness. Those who are sighted with a hundred eyes are swallowed up, just as it happened to our enemies. This, then, is the fast rule: "You must walk on a path you do not know. How will you do that? Follow Me. I will fix My eyes on you. Just close your eyes and follow Me. On this path Abraham walked when he was about to sacrifice his son. In his blindness he did not look to the former promise, he did not struggle with his own ideas, but he simply went his way with eyes closed, saying: 'I commend myself to my Lord. I will slay my son for His sake. Let Him give me back my living seed.'" This is what it means to walk on unknown ways. This is the nature of faith to walk in such danger where reason always argues, "Where will this end?" But faith closes its eyes and commits the manner and the way and the method of preserving to God. Thus, in all perils, Christian wisdom walks with closed eyes and does not take offense. Just so we must carry on against the seeing Enthusiasts. Thus Israel everywhere was in the midst of death and had death before its eyes, and yet the Israelites went blindly on their way, through the most turbulent sea.

Summary: The Christian way is to despair of all counsels and wisdom, to commit everything to God alone, and to walk the unknown way. God could have guarded Israel in a far different manner if He had wanted to use another way, and thus He devoured Mount Pharaoh and led His own out on their way like blind people.

I will turn the darkness before them into light. They have darkness and death before them. Just close your eyes and suffer a little pain, then we have completed the crossing to Christ the Comforter. This is what it means to turn the darkness into light, when in contemplation we place the Word as a lantern for our feet; as Peter says (2 Peter 1:19), the Word is "a lamp shining in a dark place." This is an outstanding verse containing a grand promise. "Thy Word is a lamp to my feet and a light to my path" (Ps. 119:105). Here God promises us the light and lamp of His Word, so that we may see in the midst of impenetrable darkness. When we have despaired of any counsel and help, this one Sun and Lamp, the Word, remains there for us.

The rough places into level ground. "I will not lead them on twisting and winding roads, but on a straight and level way. Only

> believe. I will guide you to the end on a straight course. If you want to follow your own ideas, your way will be nothing but curves. One idea will follow another. Follow Me; I will put a lantern in place of the darkness, a straight path instead of the crooked. This is what I will do and nothing else. Therefore commit the business to Me in all articles of faith." Leave your reason and wisdom behind and cling to the Word and the seeing God, who will bring you through on an unknown way. The world does not do this. The people of the world open their eyes wide and would like to have 20 eyes. For them everything depends on their own resources. (17:76–77)

Israel's blind teachers, leading their people by the ways of the world, did not realize they were blind. They thought they could lead the people, but they only led them into deception. The teachers' eyes were wide open. But they were still blind. Thus, Luther says that the people should not look with their eyes. In fact, they should close their eyes and walk not by sight, but by faith. The people should see with their ears. They will not be blind, even though their eyes are closed, if they hear the Word of God and trust it.

The wisdom of the world leaves the heart in darkness, doubt, and despair. The wisdom of God leads the heart into light, faith, and hope. However, the corrupted human nature desires to remain in the darkness. Therefore, even when the true light came in the flesh, His own people would not receive Him. They would not believe in Him. Even when the light is present, we refuse to see it. Therefore, the Lord sends His prophets to speak His Word and bring light so that we may see Him as the true light.

God's Prophet Sees Even When God's People Are Blind

> The word that Isaiah the son of Amoz saw concerning Judah and Jerusalem. It shall come to pass in the latter days that the mountain of the house of the Lord shall be established as the highest of the mountains, and shall be lifted up above the hills; and all the nations shall flow to it, and many peoples shall come, and say: "Come, let us go up to the mountain of the Lord, to the house of the God of Jacob, that He may teach us His ways and that we may

Wherever this Gospel is proclaimed with sincerity, there this kingdom of Christ is.

—MARTIN LUTHER

walk in His paths." For out of Zion shall go forth the law, and the word of the LORD from Jerusalem. He shall judge between the nations, and shall decide disputes for many peoples; and they shall beat their swords into plowshares, and their spears into pruning hooks; nation shall not lift up sword against nation, neither shall they learn war anymore. O house of Jacob, come, let us walk in the light of the LORD. (Isaiah 2:1–5)

Isaiah describes kings and their kingdoms as mountains. While earthly kingdoms will fade away, the kingdom of God will last forever. His kingdom is a spiritual kingdom that comes through the hearing of His Word, bringing life and light. Jesus Himself said, "I am the light of the world. Whoever follows Me will not walk in darkness, but will have the light of life" (John 8:12). Jesus is the only true light who gives light to all humanity; there is no light apart from Him. Therefore, unlike Israel's blind teachers, God's prophet sees. Ironically, prophets are even sometimes called seers in the Old Testament. God's prophet sees rightly because he speaks God's Word, bringing the light to the darkness, testifying to the truth.

Now follows the prophecy concerning the kingdom of Christ that is to come after the return from the captivity. But these words must be carefully noted, because the prophet speaks spiritually when he describes the church of Christ and skillfully depicts it, namely, that this kingdom is ruled by one scepter, which is the Gospel. Wherever this Gospel is proclaimed with sincerity, there this kingdom of Christ is. The Word does not deceive. Works can deceive. The Holy Spirit accompanies the Word. . . .

That mountain, He says, will be most highly praised, because from it the church receives its name and will be called Mt. Zion. Out of a physical mountain the prophet makes one that is spiritual and a kingdom that is spiritual. Therefore the church, or the kingdom of Christ, is an exalted mountain, the house of the Lord in a spiritual sense, because there it had its beginning in a physical way. *Established* is a Hebraism and means confirmed, attested, made stable. Scripture is also wont to speak this way elsewhere. In 1 Kings 2:46 we read:

"So the kingdom was established in the hand of Solomon." Thus this kingdom will also be lifted up beyond all hills, all other kingdoms, principalities, and whatever is lofty on earth. No matter how much the church is sure to be harassed and trampled underfoot by death, sins, Satan, tyranny, and heretics, yet in this trampling underfoot it shall be exalted above all mountains. For no other kingdom is so firmly established, and compared with it all other kingdoms are filthy: the Assyrians, the Greeks, the Chaldeans, the Romans, etc. For that kingdom endures, overcomes, and triumphs over death, devil, and heresies. No other kingdom can do this. But this takes place by the Word alone. Very many kingdoms have been laid waste. The church remains victorious over all kingdoms and the gates of hell (Matt. 16:18). . . .

The others are set up by force of arms in such a way that the nations are subjugated against their will. This kingdom, however, is not established by force, and here men are not compelled against their will. But because it will be raised up, they will flow to it; that is, the virtues of the church will attract the nations so that they come of their own free will. The kingdom of Christ has been put in progress because it is placed in public view with its powers and gifts. Here one sees truth, pure doctrine, safety, peace; the Gospel is heard, and nothing can give greater joy. For it promises an abundance of things and salvation both here and hereafter, and a man stands safe in this Word against everything that opposes him, even against the gates of hell (Matt. 16:18). . . . The Gospel will be published among all nations, and some will be converted everywhere. For the Gospel sanctifies in every place and bears fruit, as Paul says in Col. 1:6 and as Isaiah says below in ch. 55:11: "My Word . . . shall not return to me empty." Therefore all nations shall come to this mountain, that is, to the church, which is called a mountain. To this place the souls gather through faith; for when the Gospel is heard, hearts grow soft, rejoice, and come running. . . .

The flesh, sin, death, and the world assail us. Not for even one moment are we safe from spiritual adultery. This is how it is because sins surround us on all sides and weaken

> godly feelings. Besides, the world persecutes us. Hence it is necessary to hear the Word of God constantly, to proclaim the death of Christ constantly, and to ponder constantly, in order that our feelings may be enlightened. At another place He says (Matt. 7:13): "And lead us not into temptation, but deliver, etc." For no one is safe for even one hour, but all are daily in a most precarious state. Now they stand, now they fall, etc., and now an evil conscience, etc., is immediately associated with sin. (16:27–30)

Because of our sinful nature, we love darkness rather than light (see John 3:19). The devil also is at work in this world, holding humanity captive by deception. He blinds eyes, deafens ears, and hardens hearts (see 2 Corinthians 4:3–6). When God's prophet calls us to walk in the light, he is not merely calling us to follow what God says is right and wrong. More important, God's prophet invites us to believe in Jesus, the great light (see Isaiah 9:2). When we walk in His light, when we trust in Him, His blood cleanses us from all sin (see 1 John 1:5–7). The Holy Spirit speaks through God's prophet to call people out of darkness by the Gospel (see 1 Peter 2:9–10).

God's Prophet Nourishes Consciences with Both Law and Gospel

As we said at the beginning of the chapter, the conscience is always formed by something. Likewise, the conscience is always fed by something. Many people gorge their consciences on junk food. Only the Word of the Lord can feed the conscience what it actually needs and make it spiritually healthy. The Law part of God's Word is given as a gift to form and shape the conscience with heavenly wisdom. God alone gets to decide what is right in His sight. When our consciences are spiritually healthy, fed with God's Law, God's will, our consciences inevitably bring awareness of sin, death, and God's judgment. The Law instructs the conscience and condemns the accused conscience before God. The Gospel part of God's Word gives a clean conscience before God. God's prophets speak both God's word of Law and God's word of Gospel.

Yet, in this life, sin still remains in the believer. Thus, a conscience fed by God's Law, God's wisdom, continues to bring awareness of sin, death, and judgment throughout a person's life. A healthy conscience keeps revealing to a person his or her failure to keep the Law of God perfectly. For this reason, the prophets perpetually remind the believers of the promises of God. For a believer, the Law shapes but does not reign over the conscience; instead, Jesus reigns as king in His kingdom of comfort and peace. When a spiritually healthy conscience accuses the guilty believer of sin, God's Holy Spirit gives the forgiveness won by Jesus and peace and comfort in Him through the power of the Gospel.

> O house of Jacob, come, let us walk in the light of the LORD. (Isaiah 2:5)

Come, let us go up. They have a taste of the Word of God. Therefore they have a greater desire to hear the mountain of the Lord. He will teach, etc. All the words are emphatic. For Christians live every day by the Word as the body lives by food. He who does not have the Word or ponder it soon becomes a sorry wretch. If I do not reflect on a verse of a psalm or a statement of the Gospel, my heart is completely full of sins. A return to the Word guards against sins. The heart should always grind, if not something else, then at least itself. If the grain, namely, the Word of God, is good, the flour will be good, and the bread will be good. This life of ours is certainly most wretched. There is no rest, and therefore Christianity is most truly a hearing or pondering of the Word, in order that Christ may speak to us at all times. Therefore when anyone has trials that torture him in body or in soul, it is a sign that Christ is not at home, that is, is not in that person's heart. But he who wants to be set free should place Christ before him—Christ who says in Matt. 11:28: "Come to Me, all who labor," and in John 11:25: "I am the resurrection and the life." When Christ speaks he is set free and is not afraid. But when Christ is absent, the trial returns. Then the slaughter and the misfortunes of men begin, and those thoughts terrify the heart. Then return to Christ, who says (John 6:37): "Him who comes to Me I will not cast out." Behold, you hear the joyful and saving Word.

His ways. The ways of the Lord are His works, especially the

> works He does in us, namely, that He destroys the works of the devil, sin, death, sadness, fear, trembling, and all evils, then also our daily lapses; and He works the opposite in us: hope, righteousness, patience, joy, peace, etc. These are the ways of the Lord which His Word brings when it is heard and believed. When the Word is missing, we begin to be offended, to judge and accuse others. But when the Word is present, I say: "God has forgiven you your sins. You, too, must likewise forgive that person his sin and pray for him." In this way the heart is filled with new thoughts through the Word and is put at rest. Then we walk in the paths of the Lord; for Christ works and rules more and more in us—Christ, who is the Word of God and King over all. Good-bye to all other paths, for they are false. (16:30–31)

It is as if the world's ways of living are candy, made with artificial colors and sweeteners. One of the jobs of God's prophet is to proclaim that, though they taste sweet at first, such false paths eventually lead the consumer to a condition of a sick or even dead conscience. The conscience cannot live very long on malnutrition.

Satan's strategy is to seduce the children of God with this candy. He lures them with the sweetness of hearing that they are fine on their own, that they don't need God. He says there is peace when there is no peace with God. He lies; but his lies masquerade as truth.

On the contrary, the Lord is the truth. He cannot lie. Therefore, He sends His prophets to make His truth known to us. To fallen humanity, God's Word does not taste good at first. It is bitter, increasing the troubles of the conscience by showing the bitterness of sin and death. But the pure sweetness of the Gospel follows, bringing the sustenance of healing, reconciliation, and forgiveness that gives life. He sends His teachers to call people to become His people by the power of the Gospel. Only Christ can console the troubled conscience and reign in the heart as the true king.

God's Prophet Sounds an Alarm to Shake Consciences Awake

> The vision of Isaiah the son of Amoz, which he saw concerning Judah and Jerusalem in the days of Uzziah, Jotham, Ahaz, and Hezekiah, kings of Judah. Hear, O heavens, and give ear, O earth; for the LORD has spoken: "Children have I reared and brought up, but they have rebelled against Me. The ox knows its owner, and the donkey its master's crib, but Israel does not know, My people do not understand." (Isaiah 1:1–3)

The Book of Isaiah is not an account of Isaiah's own hopes or dreams for the future of God's people. God gave Isaiah the visions that he relayed as a prophet. God restored His people's consciences—He gave them a shared seeing and knowing with Himself—through the visions Isaiah received. Even though the people of God had the written Scriptures and the preached Word of God among them, they had covered their eyes, plugged their ears, and hardened their hearts. Their consciences had become numb and cloudy. And instead of being formed by God's Word, they thought their self-chosen forms of piety would be acceptable to God.

Nevertheless, God sent His prophet Isaiah to speak God's Word and bring life where there was death. The Word of God does what it sets out to do. It creates and re-creates. It opens eyes to see and ears to hear. It afflicts the comfortable and comforts the afflicted. Isaiah's first order of business is to expose the people's pretend piety as sin. God's prophet comes to diagnose the broken consciences by sounding the alarm.

The prophets condemn sins; they praise righteous deeds and point out future rewards for both. And in this respect they excel other historians.

But this whole prophecy is summed up above all in three parts, namely, the prediction of the coming captivity in Babylonia, secondly, the return from this captivity, and thirdly, what it says about Christ.

Vision. We correctly explain a vision as a prophecy, for the prophets used to be called "seers" (1 Sam. 9:9), certainly a word denoting weakness and humility, as if the prophet were saying: "I come to proclaim the things I have seen." Thus Christ says (John 3:11): "We bear witness to what we have seen." The prophet sees; the people hear.

. . . This is an imitation of Moses (cf. Deut. 32:1) and an intense and fiery exclamation and appeal. For Isaiah is an exceedingly eloquent prophet, endowed with a rich supply of words; he is a man who speaks with great earnestness. But this is Scripture's way: first to terrify, to reveal sins, to bring on the recognition of oneself, to humble hearts. Then, when they have been driven to despair, its second office follows, namely, the buoying up and consolation of consciences, the promises. This is how the Holy Spirit teaches. Satan, on the other hand, worms his way in by means of sweet speeches and flattering words until he infects innocent hearts. Then he leaves behind horrible terror and despair without consolation. For this reason the prophet, speaking in the Holy Spirit, moves in on the people with a loud and powerful exclamation. (16:5–6)

Through the proclamation of the Word of God, people receive ears to hear and eyes to see. When God opens the eyes and ears, then the heart can be converted. Note, this is not a generic faith in faith itself. It is specifically faith in the person and work of Christ, who saves us from our sins.

Here the Lord certainly speaks plainly, for He should rather have said: "My people are foolish. They have no knowledge or understanding. They are more stupid than an ox and an ass. But what will happen?" "My people," He says at another time, "are destroyed for lack of knowledge; because you have rejected knowledge. . . . And since you have forgotten the Law of your God, etc." (Hos. 4:6). Here, therefore, you understand what is the wisdom and godliness of men who depart from God. Certainly there is nothing they think they do not know. He who would call them ignorant would be very hard of hearing. But here the prophet proceeds especially against those very people and says that they are more uncouth than an ass. Nevertheless, they think they know everything, and the prophet calls their wisdom and knowledge sheer

> stupidity and ignorance. But is it not foolhardy so to open the mouth and rail at the saintly people and condemn their wisdom and light? But who listened to this? No one except him who was of God. He confesses and deprecates his guilt in terror. Other hearts are not touched. (16:8–9)

Without the proper preaching of the Word of God in its purity, consciences cannot work properly. There were many pseudo-preachers in Isaiah's day, peddling false comfort. Most of the population was won over by the feel-good message they were sold with pretend piety. The only way to make things right in God's sight was to expose the people's sin. First, Isaiah had to shake their consciences awake with God's word of warning, God's word of Law. Isaiah broke down the people's false sense of security by showing them God's perspective on all that was happening. Only then could God's word of promise, God's word of Gospel begin to restore their consciences.

God's Prophet Reveals How Things Really Stand between God and His People

> Ah, sinful nation, a people laden with iniquity, offspring of evildoers, children who deal corruptly! They have forsaken the LORD, they have despised the Holy One of Israel, they are utterly estranged. (Isaiah 1:4)

As a seer, the prophet Isaiah reveals God's perspective for the people of Jerusalem. Isaiah describes to the people how God sees them. They are corrupt and estranged. Their sins are scarlet. Jerusalem looks no different from Sodom and Gomorrah (see Isaiah 1:10; 3:9). The once faithful city has become a whore (see 1:21). Their silver is dross in His sight (see 1:22). He sees the land desolate and overthrown by foreigners because the people have forsaken Him (see 1:7). He sees Jerusalem fallen (see 3:8). Yet, the people do not see it that way. They see their silver as a sign of prosperity and the Lord's blessing. They think they are being faithful. They think they are honored above the other nations. They think God will be pleased with their offerings and worship. But God does not delight in all the blood of bulls, lambs, and goats that they offer Him (see 1:11). Rather, He says His people are an oak with withered leaves and a garden without water (see 1:30). Only by hearing God's Word will the people understand the truth of who they are and who God is.

> But give heed to the ability of the prophet; he strips those people of every mask. Above he said that they were ungodly and foolish; now he robs them of the glory because of which they boasted of being the people of God, a holy nation, a royal priesthood (1 Peter 2:9), the seed of Abraham, the children of God whom He led out of Egypt and to whom He gave the Law. All this the prophet overturns and says that they are indeed a nation, but a sinful one which ought to have been holy, a people chosen indeed by God and one that ought to be borne up above the stars but now lies on the ground crushed with sins. Therefore their god and prince is the devil. A seed they are indeed, but an evil one and of evil parentage, not of godly Abraham. Children they are indeed, but of corrupt parents, not of God; sons of the damned, not of salvation, whose every effort is directed toward evil. This, you see, is the distinction of the Jews and of the ungodly among us too. Certainly they were not all like this; yet the great majority were, and they were involved in both gross and internal sins to such an extent that they did not accept the rebuke, namely, that they are lost and hopeless people who must be chastised by the executioner, since they refuse to be chastised by their Father. But this is their sin. (16:9–10)

In our day, there will be leaders and teachers of the Church who also lead people astray. There will also be many non-Christians—whom Luther calls "the ungodly"—who will reject the Word of God and resist the work of the Spirit.

God's Prophet Humbles the Heart with God's Threats

When the conscience works properly, it feels guilt when sin is committed. When something other than the Word of God forms the conscience, it becomes numb to iniquity. The self-chosen methods of holiness that Luther talks about are the heart's false antidote when something other than God's Word forms the conscience. People's inventive righteousness does not please God. Such holy acts are centered on the people involved, rather than on God. People want to decide for themselves what

We neglect [the fruit of faith], and meanwhile we busy ourselves in vain with various religions. Nobody considers how great the demand of faith and love is.

—MARTIN LUTHER

is righteous and what is not. But even what looks good on the outside is not pleasing to God. Only what is done out of fear, love, and trust in Him, according to His Word, pleases Him. Therefore, it is impossible to please God without faith.

As He said through Isaiah,

> When you spread out your hands, I will hide My eyes from you; even though you make many prayers, I will not listen; your hands are full of blood. (Isaiah 1:15)

Here the prophet says that they are all murderers. By the hands are meant the works which should be done for the needy neighbor. But he who does not help his neighbor destroys him. 1 John 3:15 states: "Anyone who hates his brother is a murderer." Ambrose says: "Feed your starving brother. If you have not fed him, you have killed him." We read (Matt. 25:42): "I was hungry, and you gave Me no food." Again (1 John 3:17): "If anyone has the world's goods, etc." In short, he who does not practice love toward his neighbor is regarded by God as a murderer; for even though he is able to help, yet he does not do so. So far as he is concerned, he lets his brother perish. In brief, the meaning is this: "You have hands full of blood. Therefore your prayers and all your efforts are ungodly." Thus with one word he involves them in all sins and proves them guilty of damnation. . . . We do everything except what love demands; we give much for monstrous and godless religions but nothing for the need of the poor. Clean before men, but unclean, cruel, and murderers before God. Who could rest when thinking of these things? God grant that these things do not come to mind in the last hour! James says: "Come now, you rich, weep, etc." (James 5:1). One aspect of ungodliness is unfaithfulness. Another is bloodiness; that is, a lack of love, which is the fruit of faith. We neglect these, and meanwhile we busy ourselves in vain with various religions. Nobody considers how great the demand of faith and love is. (16:17–18)

True love issues from a pure heart and a good conscience and a genuine faith (see 1 Timothy 1:5). Israel's self-chosen methods of holiness caused them to rejoice in the works of their hands while the Lord lamented all the sin they committed against their neighbors with those same hands. While the people preached their own prosperity, they oppressed the widows and the orphans among them. God's people would not listen to His voice, so He would not listen to their prayers.

> Wash yourselves; make yourselves clean; remove the evil of your deeds from before My eyes; cease to do evil, learn to do good; seek justice, correct oppression; bring justice to the fatherless, plead the widow's cause. (Isaiah 1:16–17)

What, then, is to be done? Now he sets forth a command in an affirmative manner. . . .

He mentions two parts. One is to put aside filth, unfaithfulness, hatred, and all ungodliness. The other is to do good. Thus David says (Ps. 37:27): "Depart from evil and do good." The filth is removed by a bath. Cleanness is a new kind of life. Therefore wash yourselves from ungodliness; cleanse yourselves through godliness. Put an end to the unclean blindness and the bloody hand. . . .

"The evil of your thoughts," that is, of your plans, blindness, ungodliness, hypocrisy. Keep quiet, stop acting spitefully and doing evil to your neighbors contrary to love. Do no harm; do not offend them. . . .

The defense of an orphan consists in bringing it about that he is not oppressed. When there is no defender in the world, then a poor man lies exposed everywhere to every act of robbery. Consider the dealings of guardians and those who draw up wills, whether they are guilty of blood. Widows have been bereft of a defender. Here there is sinning in an extraordinary manner. Many live for themselves. Meanwhile they neglect the poor, devote themselves to prayer, and consider themselves saints. Yet it is not enough not to have harmed one's neighbor; God also demands positive uplifting of the needy through love, and one's whole substance and life must be expended for the brethren, as John 3:17 says. Would that we only realized that this is our duty! For it is evil for us to think smugly that we are living a good life. (16:18–19)

God does not listen to the prayers of those with blood on their hands, but He hears the voices of the ones who have been afflicted by those hands. God's prophets in the Bible regularly speak up for those who suffer but to whom no one pays attention: the widows, the orphans, the poor, and the foreigners. Some theologians in our day have interpreted this to mean they sufficiently speak on behalf of God if they merely advocate for social justice. Many such liberation theologians become so overly concerned about the outsiders in society who are burdened in thoughts, words, or deeds that they reduce the Gospel to freedom from earthly oppression, rather than robust and eternal forgiveness of sinners' sins. This social gospel is a popular form of Christianity in our culture.

Those who make the Gospel solely a message of anti-oppression don't realize that the biblical prophets were not concerned about oppression simply for oppression's sake. Biblical prophets were concerned about sin. Though sin was manifest in God's people's oppression of the weak and vulnerable among them, the biblical prophets also spoke out against all sin of any kind. Failing to love one's neighbor was just as abominable in God's eyes as murder, fornication, homosexuality, rape, adultery, and idolatry. God's purpose for His prophets was to correct His people's consciences according to His Word, because they had become misshaped by the corrupted creation. As we can see from Isaiah, God's prophets spoke in exactly the opposite direction of the people's felt needs in most cases.

Our culture wants to champion freedom without truly knowing what is good or evil, right or wrong. Love and tolerance are touted without any idea of what true love is. Yet, the more we tune into the voices of our culture, the more those voices form our consciences, making our consciences numb to what God says is good and evil—and numb to sin. The same thing happened in Judah and Jerusalem in Isaiah's day.

Therefore, God instructed Isaiah:

> Cry aloud; do not hold back; lift up your voice like a trumpet; declare to My people their transgression, to the house of Jacob their sins. Yet they seek Me daily and delight to know My ways, as if they were a nation that did righteousness and did not forsake the judgment of their God; they ask of Me righteous judgments; they delight to draw near

> to God. "Why have we fasted, and You see it not? Why have we humbled ourselves, and You take no knowledge of it?" Behold, in the day of your fast you seek your own pleasure, and oppress all your workers. (Isaiah 58:1–3)

Now he condemns their works and life. This is the content of the preaching: Faith and works. First he chides them for being unbelieving and puffed up, and now he also repudiates their remaining manner of life and attacks it as being of no use to them. . . .

Cry aloud, because they refuse to hear and because their sins are worse than those of beasts. *Lift up your voice.* Here he is referring to the ceremonies of the Law. The trumpet denotes preaching, and this must be shouted forth most boldly.

Declare to My people their transgression. "Go down and show how shamefully they live, even though their appearance is most attractive." One who can do that has real ability. He can despise those grand sins, even if meanwhile every hypocrite walks about with an oversupply of religion. There is nothing else there but the grossest and most repulsive sins. This is so because the Holy Spirit is not there. In fact, nothing is there but pride, lust, harm, and these sins are neither corrected nor regarded by the common people. Fasting and making gloomy faces draws attention. Hence all of our good habits are esteemed as nothing, simply because we do not fast. Now he lists the sins. . . .

"Not only do they forsake the commandments of God and all His ceremonies, but they want this too, that while they keep their own ceremonies intact, they would like to fight with Me. In their affliction they murmur against Me like people innocently afflicted. They want to know why I act the way I do." So "wisdom is justified by her children" (Matt. 11:19), and (Ps. 51:4) says, "So that Thou art justified in Thy sentence." They want to know the will of God, why God does thus and so, and they want to argue with God. "They want to know the reason why I do not justify them, why I condemn and blame them, because they say, 'Why do You afflict me, since I fast twice on the Sabbath and give the tithe?'" (cf. Luke 18:12). So today the enemies of the Gospel pass judgment on God as if He were not God. They want to get control of God; they want to determine what is our job, to ask why God should choose and cast off. . . .

They go about, thoroughly hardened, as if they were without sins: "We are a righteous nation." Here you see that the prophets were concerned about making accusations against the morals of the holiest men. . . .

But just the same, they reject God when He speaks to them in His sermons, because they condemn this Word and its servants, and meanwhile they say in words that they are imitating God, while in their actions they deny and condemn the wisdom of God. For that reason God says here, "They want to defend their own and condemn My Word." (17:282–83)

> Is not this the fast that I choose: to loose the bonds of wickedness, to undo the straps of the yoke, to let the oppressed go free, and to break every yoke? Is it not to share your bread with the hungry and bring the homeless poor into your house; when you see the naked, to cover him, and not to hide yourself from your own flesh? (Isaiah 58:6–7)

He is here not condemning fasting as such, but the fact that it is used as a cover. Even so He does not condemn food, but He does condemn gluttony. So here He condemns fasting as a cover for ungodliness. It is inevitable for the ungodly man who fasts that he does not achieve righteousness on the basis of it, but regards it as a sacrifice, a necessary matter, a cover for sins. God loves an ungodly harlot more than such a person. . . .

Undo the thongs of the yoke, that is, get rid of all grievances by which you oppress your neighbor. Put it off so that you do not injure the neighbor. Summary: If you want to fast, put on mercy and love for the neighbor, so that you may do good to him. . . .

We have heard that in this general proclamation the prophet first attacks unbelief and then also the outward customs which

> [are used as a cover] for the heart's ungodliness. A bad tree cannot bear good fruits (Matt. 7:18). The ungodly are unfit for every good work. Meanwhile they occupy themselves with works of their own choosing and wear themselves out with labors, and yet they produce no good work. As you see here, they humble their souls in sackcloth and ashes and do no one any good. They cannot please God because they cannot help the neighbor. Yet this is the rule prescribed for them: Feed the hungry, love your neighbor as yourself. This they cannot do. Now the prophet proceeds to urge them on to works of mercy and to love for the neighbor. (17:286–87)

When people try to brag to God about all the good works they have done, He sees all the evil works they have done and the good works they have neglected. Self-chosen works of piety do not cover sin. Instead of boasting about expertise in fasting, one should feed the hungry. Instead of displaying sackcloth and ashes to impress others with one's humility, one should clothe the naked. As Christ loved and had mercy on us, we are to love and have mercy on others.

God's Prophet Consoles the Conscience with God's Promises

Our God is the God of the needy.

On God's behalf, Isaiah declares in one of the most beautiful passages,

> Come now, let us reason together, says the LORD: though your sins are like scarlet, they shall be as white as snow; though they are red like crimson, they shall become like wool. (Isaiah 1:18)

> Come, and let us have a discussion. It is as if He were saying: "I will enter into judgment with you. If I do not do good and am not gracious to those who do these things, believe, are washed and clean, then accuse Me and charge falsely that I am not God. Indeed, it is God's inward feeling and His preponderant desire. How much He would want us to be good! . . .

Though your sins are like scarlet, etc. . . . This is a new and strange way of speaking. Why did He not rather say black sins? Black denotes sadness, but red denotes bloodguiltiness. Sins are red when we are guilty of blood. "Deliver me," he says, "from bloodguiltiness" (Ps. 51:14), that is, from the guilt of death and of punishments. White is the sign of innocence and justice. Therefore the angels, as innocent spirits, appeared mostly in white garments. For Oriental kings, namely, for those who were rather mild, the special attire was white. But bloodthirsty Rome conducted itself as worthy of purple. Therefore the meaning here is this: "Though your sins are in the highest degree deserving of punishments and death, they will be worthy of righteousness and faith; and though they are worms, they will not bite you." Certainly the fullest, finest, and sweetest consolation. Although we have very many sins, yet they will be as if they did not exist. Nor will they frighten us, even if they are present; for they are white. (16:19–20)

In Isaiah 1:15, the Lord declares that He will not hear the people's prayers. But after humbling their hearts, God assures them in Isaiah 58 that He *will* listen. He calls the prophet to console the people's consciences with His promises.

Then shall your light break forth like the dawn, and your healing shall spring up speedily; your righteousness shall go before you; the glory of the LORD shall be your rear guard. Then you shall call, and the LORD will answer; you shall cry, and He will say, "Here I am." If you take away the yoke from your midst, the pointing of the finger, and speaking wickedness, if you pour yourself out for the hungry and satisfy the desire of the afflicted, then shall your light rise in the darkness and your gloom be as the noonday. (Isaiah 58:8–10)

These are excellent and golden consolations for the conscience. These are testimonies that bring joy to our conscience, as Peter says (2 Peter 1:10), "Be the more zealous to confirm your call," and Paul says (2 Cor. 1:12), "The testimony of our conscience." Although we must not rely on this, yet, since we are justified, it puts my conscience at peace, that I do evil to no one, and thus I walk safely in God. This is what it means for righteousness to go before, when we boast before the world and against Satan that because the fruits of faith are there, I have not lived in vain. *And the glory of the Lord shall be your rear guard.* Now comes the confidence in the Lord that on the basis of this conduct we can be certain that God is well disposed toward us. This is the true glory of God, when I have proved my faith to believe that God is well disposed toward me and that what I do is not the result of my effort but is by the goodness of God. These are the testimonies of our conscience, if anyone lived properly in his calling and did his duty. These things cannot perform the duties of one's calling. Although they have an office, they cannot produce the works that belong to it. But the godly who exercise themselves in their faith are to have all good things in abundance and have a joyful conscience before the world to such an extent that they can even boast in the presence of the Lord. Such a passage is this one: "He who finds a wife finds a good thing, and obtains favor from the Lord" (Prov. 18:22), that is, he knows that God is well disposed toward him. Thus all who do good to their neighbor know that they are pleasing to God, since this is the testimony of our conscience, that we are conducting ourselves before the world in a holy manner. Yet you must carefully distinguish the glory of faith, which justifies, from the glory of works, which assures us of God's favor. When we concern ourselves with things that please God, this is the meaning of the glory of the Lord. (17:288–89)

The role of the prophet is to instruct the conscience on God's behalf. By speaking the Word of the Lord, the prophet enlightens those dwelling in darkness and enlivens those languishing in death. The prophet clearly proclaims how to be made right in God's eyes: trust in Jesus. He reveals what is good and what is evil, according to God's standards. He forms and feeds the conscience with God's Law and God's Gospel. The Gospel of Christ then reveals a definition of what is "good" that we could never have known on our own. "Good" is being loved by Christ and made holy in Him and then living in that holiness by loving our neighbor as Christ has loved us.

CHAPTER 3

IDOLATRY AND THE CONSCIENCE

There is a common misconception regarding idolatry. In general, people tend to think that idolatry is statue worship practiced by ancient people who didn't know any better. Therefore, even in the Church, people are led to believe that since we don't worship statues, these words don't apply to us. We assume that idolatry was an Old Testament problem. However, even in the New Testament Scriptures, we are told, "Little children, keep yourselves from idols" (1 John 5:21). In this chapter, we will consider more thoughtfully what idolatry is and the depth of the problem for the conscience.

Making God in Our Own Image and Likeness

Originally, Adam and Eve were made in the image and likeness of God. That was an incredible gift and honor that God bestowed on humanity, something that set them apart from the rest of God's creation. However, Adam and Eve committed the first sin when they wanted to make their own image of themselves. They decided what God made and what God gave them was not enough. They wanted to be like God and decide for themselves what was good and evil. And by their rebellion, sin came into the world. From then on, all humans after Adam and Eve have been born in the image and likeness of their parents: their human nature is in rebellion against God.

Our corrupted human nature causes us to be born into the darkness of not knowing the true God who made us and loves us. Yet, humans throughout history have sensed that something is wrong and needs to be fixed in their lives and experiences.

Instead of being formed and shaped by God through His Word, corrupted humanity desires to form and shape God in its own image and likeness.

> Because of images and idolatry human thinking is perverted; it fashions a god for itself and does so according to its own whim and the suggestion of Satan. A knowledge of God is implanted in all men, and therefore they think that God is to be worshiped. In this they certainly make no mistake, but they do err in the manner of their worship if they worship Him not simply according to His Word and will but rather according to their own ideas. (16:160)

For Luther, idolatry is not statue worship in and of itself. It is false worship. It is any worship without God's Word. Idolatry is a self-chosen method of making one right in the sight of God. It is an attempt at self-justifying, that is, pardoning oneself from one's own iniquity by one's own effort. It is a false faith in the nature and work of sinful humanity. Thus, as idolatry is false worship without God's Word, an idol is a false image of God that proceeds from the imagination of the sinful heart.

> An ungodly man shapes his own god, does not have a true knowledge of God, and contrary to the will of God, invents a religion to suit his own opinion. What a person fears, loves, worships, trusts—this is his god. Our God has no regard for our works, but only for the race and for His glory in us. Therefore every ungodly man bows down to the work of his own hands. And the heretics have their own idea, which they themselves have fashioned, and a fictitious Christ. It is not man's business to determine what pleases God; it is the business of God alone. (16:35)

As Luther says, idolatry occurs whenever we fear, love, worship, and trust anything other than the true God. This is why Luther's explanation of the First Commandment is "We should fear, love, and trust in God above all things" (Small Catechism, Explanation of the First Commandment). To do anything else is idolatry. Luther notes that to do anything other than worship the true God is to worship the *work* of our hands. He emphasizes the *work* that goes into making an idol, because the statue in and of itself is not the issue; rather, the *work* that is done in forming the idol is the idolatry. The idol-maker thinks he is doing a *work* to please God. But anyone who trusts in the *work* of his or her own hands makes a false image of God. Instead of a statue, an idol is the false image of God in the heart. An idolater refuses to let God be God. In this state of rebellion, God becomes the beggar and the idolater becomes the giver.

Idolatry in Isaiah's Day

We noted that humans by nature create false gods because their nature is corrupt and they are born into the darkness of not knowing the true God. And yet, even ancient Israel, who had God's revelation of Himself, fell into idolatry.

God freed the Israelites from a land full of idols when He brought them out of Egypt, and God warned them through Moses about the temptation to worship other gods that awaited them in the land of Canaan. Thus, when they entered Canaan, the Israelites were to tear down the pagan altars, dash their pillars into pieces, and chop up the carved images—lest Israel try to worship God in the way of their contemporaries (see Deuteronomy 12).

God's instructions for His people also included giving the priests the job of teaching the Torah, that is, the Five Books of Moses, and carrying out the sacrificial system God created to cleanse the people of their sin. God gave the priests the task of properly instructing the people's consciences with what is right in His sight.

God's instructions for His people also designated Jerusalem as the place where His name would dwell for the benefit of humanity. His people were to worship Him there because He chose to put His name there. God promised to be found where the ark of the covenant was located. He gave His people the image of His Mercy Seat, where He is enthroned above the wings of the cherubim on the covering of the ark. The ark was housed at first in the tabernacle and then later at the temple. The people of Israel were invited to meet God at the specific, tangible, visible place of His promised presence (see Exodus 25:20–22).

Despite all of this, Israel became idolatrous. While Moses

received the instructions for worship from God, Aaron made a golden calf. Neither Aaron nor the people thought the calf was their God; rather, they thought they were worshiping God by means of the calf. It was as if the invisible presence of God was enthroned above the golden calf (see Exodus 32:4–6). They were worshiping God without His Word.

Later, when they entered the land of Canaan, the temptation to fall into idolatry became even more alluring. Perhaps they were intrigued by the religious practices of the cultures around them. Perhaps the worship practices they saw among their neighbors simply made more sense according to human logic. After all, it would have been more exciting, exhilarating, and extravagant to worship God in the way their neighbors did. The Moabites' worship was emotional. The fertility cults of Baal of Peor were appealing to their sexual desires. The one-to-one correspondence of acts of worship to visible results in Israel's neighbors' worship would also have made sense to human logic. If God provides rain and abundant harvest to the pagans, then He must be pleased with their worship.

The message that shaped Israel's false image of God was something like this: "If you feel guilty because of your sin, offer up as many sacrifices as you can. The more, the better. If your conscience is still in conflict, keep offering up blood until God's anger is appeased. If it does not work at this location, try another place. If it does not work in this style, try another method. Continue sacrificing until you feel blessed. Feed the appetite of God. The more you do, the happier the Lord will be with you. When you are happy, then He must be happy with you." A god who can be leveraged by your actions is much safer than an almighty God over whom you have no control.

The man-made methods of holiness were also more flexible than Yahweh's instructions for the people. Why should all of Israel have to travel to Jerusalem to make sacrifices and engage in worship? So Israel created other holy places. In Isaiah's day, Ahaz, king of Judah, made high places in every city of Judah. Ahaz also decided to change the Jerusalem temple to his own liking. He wanted to modernize it. He removed the altar of Yahweh and built a bigger and better altar like the one he saw in front of the pagan temple of Damascus. He removed the water basin from being upon the bronze oxen and placed it on a pedestal. He even closed the doors to the temple of Yahweh.

There was also the inflexibility of priests being the intercessors for Israel's king and people. So another king of Judah in Isaiah's day, Uzziah, decided he should be able to offer up incense to God, even though he was not a Levitical priest ordained to serve in the temple.

> They did everything with great zeal and at great expense. They established new kinds of worship in opposition to God after forsaking the temple in imitation of their fathers and of the Gentiles. They sought piety according to their own feelings. (16:26)
>
> The prophet [Isaiah] is speaking of his own time or also concerning their various forms of worship, later in groves, on mountains, etc. Then at the time of Christ they were also divided into various kinds of worship, as Matt. 23:20 says, "He who swears by the altar," also Matt. 5:34ff. (16:35)

By the time of Isaiah, the priests in Jerusalem consistently mimicked the doctrine and practice of the pagan priests in the religions of Israel's neighbors. Though these rituals and practices went beyond God's Word or were even in blatant contradiction to God's Word, the priests and the people were doing what was right in their own eyes.

When the Levitical priests failed to follow Yahweh's Torah in ritual ceremonies as well as acts of justice, God sent the prophets to correct the teaching of the priests and the practices of the people with His Word. As we talked about in chapter 2, the job of a prophet like Isaiah was to sound the alarm, calling sin sin because the people's consciences had been lulled to sleep through their negligence in hearing and attending to God's Word.

Isaiah proclaimed, addressing God,

> For You have rejected Your people, the house of Jacob, because they are full of things from the east and of fortune-tellers like the Philistines, and they strike hands with the children of foreigners. Their land is filled with silver and gold, and there is no end to their treasures; their land is filled with horses, and there is no end to their chariots. Their land is filled with idols; they bow down to the work of their hands, to what their own fingers have made. (Isaiah 2:6–8)

"All their idolatries may be put to shame, one after the other. The Word of God abides forever."

—MARTIN LUTHER

The Nonsense of Idols

A significant part of Isaiah's proclamation was that the idols the people of Israel had become so attracted to and did not think were a problem were deeply offensive to God. It was as if they had forgotten the First Commandment entirely. Through Isaiah's proclamation, God challenged the nonsense of what they were doing: fearing, loving, and trusting in something made by their own hands, rather than in the God who made them. God's prophets then served as idol mockers of the idol makers.

> All who fashion idols are nothing, and the things they delight in do not profit. Their witnesses neither see nor know, that they may be put to shame. Who fashions a god or casts an idol that is profitable for nothing? (Isaiah 44:9–10)

The images are like those who make them. As their god is, such is their teaching and their religion. Their god is nothing, he is a manufactured object. What sort of worship could they have? This must be applied as a general truth to all kinds of idolatry, which might look different today and yet are the same in kind. Work righteousness is the fountain and source of all outward idols. The same abomination in the heart appears in a variety of idols and images. Therefore this text must be applied to all rites that originate with work righteousness, because this idol is opposed to faith in Christ. . . .

That they may be put to shame, that is, that all their idolatries may be put to shame, one after the other. The Word of God abides forever.

Who fashions a god or casts an image? It is as if he were saying: "Who is so stupid and crazy as to fashion a god and cast a useless image?" This is indignation. "What do you think you are doing, you mortal creatures, fashioning the true God for yourself?" The sects make a god for themselves by their rites, and yet they do not believe but say, "It is not true, our God is in heaven." (17:107–8, 109)

> The ironsmith takes a cutting tool and works it over the coals. He fashions it with hammers and works it with his strong arm. He becomes hungry, and his strength fails; he drinks no water and is faint. The carpenter stretches a line; he marks it out with a pencil. He shapes it with planes and marks it with a compass. He shapes it into the figure of a man, with the beauty of a man, to dwell in a house. He cuts down cedars, or he chooses a cypress tree or an oak and lets it grow strong among the trees of the forest. He plants a cedar and the rain nourishes it. Then it becomes fuel for a man. He takes a part of it and warms himself; he kindles a fire and bakes bread. Also he makes a god and worships it; he makes it an idol and falls down before it. Half of it he burns in the fire. Over the half he eats meat; he roasts it and is satisfied. Also he warms himself and says, "Aha, I am warm, I have seen the fire!" And the rest of it he makes into a god, his idol, and falls down to it and worships it. He prays to it and says, "Deliver me, for you are my god!" (Isaiah 44:12–17)

In the ancient world, people chose designated locations to gather and to pray before the images of their deities. These images were considered a portal to the invisible spiritual realm. When the biblical prophets confronted such practices done without the Word of God, they mocked such silly behavior. Since God did not promise to be present for their benefit at these sites, they worshiped nothing behind the image. It was not an access point to the true God. Thus, their worship before the idol was directed to the work of their hands. Therefore, the prophets taunted them as worshiping wood.

> Here the prophet shows fully how foolish that man is. It is as if he were saying: "Is he not an outstanding fool? He knows that he has used the same wood for cooking." (17:113)

Isaiah says on God's behalf,

> To whom will you liken Me and make Me equal, and compare Me, that we may be alike? Those who lavish gold from the purse, and weigh out silver in the scales, hire a goldsmith, and he makes it into a god; then they fall down and worship! They lift it to their shoulders, they carry it, they set it in its place, and it stands there; it cannot move from its

place. If one cries to it, it does not answer or save him from his trouble. (Isaiah 46:5–7)

He is ridiculing their folly. They themselves hire a man who makes a god for them. The god is himself carried, and he cannot move from the spot. . . .
This is a word of rebuke. They thought they were worshiping the true God, and they made this image to represent Him. But these were ideas apart from the Word. So we expected help through our activity and our endeavors. They say, "I do not expect anything from my works, but I trust that God will look upon these merits of mine." So you imagine a god according to your merit, you set up and fashion an image for yourself which is unable to help you. (17:141)

Idolatry in Luther's Day

When Luther reflected on Isaiah's words to the people of Israel, Luther saw the same sin of idolatry in some of the practices, ideas, and beliefs of his day.

Speaking again about this Isaiah passage,

All who fashion idols are nothing, and the things they delight in do not profit. Their witnesses neither see nor know, that they may be put to shame. Who fashions a god or casts an idol that is profitable for nothing? (Isaiah 44:9–10),

Luther says,

It is just as ridiculous, and even more so, to revere cowls and cords as it is to adore a pagan image. Idolaters are all teachers who teach something apart from God, teachers who are not shaped and formed by God but who shape and form Him, as the Franciscan imagines God: "On this way and in this manner of life I will serve my God by this ritual, this food." By this mode of a chosen life he strives and believes he is pleasing God and attaining to the forgiveness of sins, so that he even presumes to save and help others. And day by day that idolatry increases, and always he thinks, "God is the kind that needs my work." But this text says, "There is no such God as is produced by human thought." In our nature we look at God as through painted glass, and we see God in conformity with our thought. So the self-righteous look at God through a glass. . . . However, one who looks at God by faith knows that God does not regard him because of his righteousness but for the sake of His own grace. . . . We are shaped by the Word to the righteousness of God. But the manufacturers and inventors of a teaching for life shape and form God. Thus the pope is an idol-maker who neglects the teaching about faith and sets up various sects and forms of self-righteousness. Therefore it is well for you to know what makes one an image-maker: a shaper, an idolater, that is, every ungodly religion or thought which does not believe that sins are forgiven for Christ's sake and therefore is quick to take up with endless works and monstrosities in a search for righteousness. . . . The self-righteous, however, begin to appease God with works and ceremonies and then undertake to obtain faith. This is making an idol. He who truly knows sins and the free forgiveness of God does not seek his own satisfactions, he does not shape God but is shaped by Him. Know therefore that all other teachers outside of faith are nothing. The papacy is nothing. Ecclesiastical colleges are nothing. . . .

"Beware, all that is dearest and most precious to them, what they cherish most, their best teachings and works to which they attribute righteousness, is worth nothing. Their desirable and praiseworthy teachings and endeavors, their holy orders, rules, and statutes, in which they seek righteousness, do not profit. Hosea says the same thing (cf. 9:16). The things they delight in are nothing. . . .

Summary: He who is deceived in faith and in the free grace of God errs everywhere, and nothing but error that puts forward more error will be applied to him. Therefore let those who will remain certain in the catholic religion remain certain in the righteousness of faith without all works. Where this article is preserved, the Holy Spirit is present to preserve you. Where this article is lost, we soon fall. (17:108–9)

Luther names a specific monastic order here, the Franciscans, whose religious order was founded in 1209 by St. Francis of Assisi. Having been a monk in the Augustinian order, Luther criticizes the idea that monks were more holy than laypeople because they gained God's favor through certain acts and rituals. These practices were self-chosen ways of worship that went beyond God's Word. Luther decries any means of obtaining self-justification as idolatry.

Isaiah wrote of the ridiculousness of man-made idols:

> To whom then will you liken God, or what likeness compare with Him? An idol! A craftsman casts it, and a goldsmith overlays it with gold and casts for it silver chains. He who is too impoverished for an offering chooses wood that will not rot; he seeks out a skillful craftsman to set up an idol that will not move. (Isaiah 40:18–20)

As the heathen thought he was appeasing God with his image, so the Carthusian seeks justification by means of his cowl and his righteousness. Thus both are engaged in the same plan, attitude, and works, although the material of the idolatry is not the same. Both seek justification by works. The heathen were not so foolish as to adore the wood as such, but they shaped the wood into a figure of God and worshiped this work. So the Carthusian does not simply adore his cowl and his fasting, but he acts under the pretext and in the name of God, he adores his work as a god formed in the name of God. (17:23)

The Carthusians were another monastic order, known in particular for their extreme dedication. This order was founded in 1084 by St. Bruno. Again, Luther criticizes any self-chosen means of sanctification that then draw one's trust away from God to oneself. As the idolaters in Isaiah's day did not actually worship the wood, the idolaters in Luther's day did not actually worship the monk's garments. Yet, both the wood and the cowl represented how they worshiped God with their own works.

Instead of looking to the written Scriptures, inspired by the Holy Spirit, to learn and follow what God has declared pleasing to Him, monastic orders followed a way of life that was pious according to human wisdom. It was a pretend piety no different from pagan piety in the days of Isaiah. Rather than receiving God's grace as a gift, they reversed the roles and gave God their self-chosen gifts as if God needed their good works.

Luther sees the ridiculousness of idolatry in monasticism. Commenting on Isaiah 44:15–20, Luther states,

> It is too bad to take this material [the wood] for an idol when it can be used for more common purposes. They use these perishable things which they themselves observe being consumed by fire. This is certainly a folly which is to be ridiculed. The same thing happens to us. Thomas writes that the wood of the cross should be adored by means of hyperdulia, that is, a lesser worship. Therefore the prophet rebukes these idolaters. So in our time the idolaters adore perishable things: "Do not touch, do not handle, do not drink." Isn't this true? Hence cowl, tonsure, rope, and scapular are idolatry, as if we could not be saved without them. They are human works and external things which are used up, and yet they become a god whom men worship. Here they make a god out of a vestment, a girdle, a rope, things which the farmer uses for an amulet. He says, "I do not worship this as god, but I worship my God in this girdle." Yes, you have made a girdle for your god, a girdle manufactured by the ropemaker. Summary: Our eyes must look to faith and lay hold of God's grace and freely let all these external things go. Forget about cowl, tonsure, rope, etc., and consider grace alone. The ungodly go their way and make a bewitched god out of a girdle, something sealed with a bull, or something placed into a shrine. A barefoot monk's god is the contemplation of God in heaven who might have regard for his rope. Another does something else, and each one fashions God according to his own ideas. I therefore admonish you that in all such places of idolatry you pay close attention, because all religion that is the product of one's thought arises from this ungodliness. Before God this alone is religion: the forgiveness of sins. Outside of this He knows nothing. . . .
>
> This is what a Franciscan does. He buys ropes to tie up his wagon, and what is left he uses for a belt. Here is the rope. It is the same rope for the wagon and for the belt, but the

ropemaker made it in one piece. God did something else. He made his brain. Therefore we know surely that all the self-righteous who make use of external and perishable things have established righteousness by things that pass away. They govern their consciences by these things and attribute divinity to them, because rope, foods, and tonsures justify and condemn. So the pagan Romans forced their people to adore stone and wooden idols even to martyrdom, and so our idols are cords and cakes. Therefore beware that you cling to grace alone and to faith, and do not ascribe righteousness to external creatures. . . .

Therefore the prophet draws the final conclusion: Whatever is outside of faith, however attractive and toilsome it may be, is idolatry, because the opinion that we are justified by works apart from faith is the source of all idolatry. Therefore if you have one notion of idolatry, you must apply it to all idolatry. This is the rule of faith, that we are justified by the grace and mercy of God. All self-righteousness must depart. (17:112–13, 114)

Luther connects the rope wrapped around the monk to the kind of idolatry practiced with statues of gold and silver. Both are ridiculous in comparison to the living and active, true God. The Lord never commanded that wearing a rope would make satisfaction for sins. Thus, the "rope" ties the conscience to a false system of justifying and condemning. In a quest for hyper piety, the monks in Luther's day sought ways to serve God outside of the institutions where God calls us to serve our neighbor. It was a lifestyle of self-chosen crosses and burdens, promised to bring eternal rewards apart from the Word of God. On the contrary, Christians are called in Baptism to take up their crosses and follow Jesus. In their stations in life, they are to serve their neighbors even in difficult times. God Himself places custom-made crosses on their shoulders—not self-inflicted ones. Self-inflicted sorrow and pain are not the same as suffering for the name of Christ or sacrificially loving one's neighbor. In the end, the monks in Luther's day focused on their own works to serve God instead of rejoicing in the person and work of Christ for our salvation. Thus, they robbed God of His glory and stole true gladness from their consciences.

When Luther criticized the common practice of idolatry in monasticism, there were some who felt he did not go far enough. The radical reformers accused him of being inconsistent, because he simultaneously said such things while upholding that Baptism does save. Luther's opponents argued that Baptism was no different from a monk's cowl. Specifically, the Anabaptists called Luther's understanding of Baptism idolatry, because they perceived he was saying water can save a person.

Luther clarified that idolatry is not simply trusting in anything external, but rather trusting in something external apart from God's Word:

> In addition, I admonish you not to be deceived by the fallacies of the Anabaptists, who say that Baptism is external water and nothing but water, since they omit the words of God connected with the water. They are indeed perishable signs, but they are conjoined with the divine Word. Therefore reply to those who teach these things: "Behold, you cling to externals and do not simply reject them. I say to you that we reject also your internal righteousnesses." But we must make this distinction: Physical things are of two kinds, some in themselves and some connected with the imperishable Word. So in the case of Baptism, the Eucharist, and the honor due to parents, external things are linked with the imperishable Word. (17:113)

God's Word clearly promises that Baptism does bring salvation (see 1 Peter 3:21), because it is water combined with the Word—a life-giving water and a washing of regeneration and renewal by the Holy Spirit (see Titus 3:4–7). Luther railed against any work that is apart from God's Word.

As Isaiah wrote,

> And the Lord said: "Because this people draw near with their mouth and honor Me with their lips, while their hearts are far from Me, and their fear of Me is a commandment taught by men, therefore, behold, I will again do wonderful things with this people, with wonder upon wonder; and the wisdom of their wise men shall perish, and the discernment of their discerning men shall be hidden." (Isaiah 29:13–14)

Luther applied these words to other instances in which he witnessed God's people serving the wisdom and commands of men rather than the commands of God.

Christ cites this passage in Matt. 15:8, where He adds the word "in vain." With this single word He embraces this whole chapter and every attempt of the ungodly, who have zealously crucified themselves with their labors, who exercise themselves with vigils, "who draw near to Me in order to obtain Me," and yet they are blinded. Why? Because they are hypocrites and self-righteous. *Draw near* properly refers to the state of mind of those who are externally zealous and glittering in appearance and boast that they are next to Christ. But they "draw near to Me" in this way that "they honor Me with their mouth and lips." Is not this most terrible that the pope, the bishops, and all the papists, sweating with strenuous efforts, even with the Word of God, are in position nearest to God, but with their heart least of all? Thus we make a concession to the adversaries, who boast that they are nearest to God. I say: "It's true. With your mouth and lips you are closest to God, preaching that Christ suffered, was born, and died for us." This is what the papists have said with their mouth. This is the approach of the mouth. But when I say: "If Christ died for us, we toil in vain with our endeavors," there they oppose us while they rely on their own boasting, and therefore in their heart they are far from God. . . .

This is what the Hebrew says. "What they practice toward Me is called *fear*, that is, worship of God, or piety, and religion, and that has gone directly off into manmade teachings, so that they are more afraid of, and have more respect for, the teachings of men than of God." This we see in the Decretal, where there is such stern adherence to this teaching that they lift their own rules above the commandments of God, where fornication, robbery, usury, and murder are far less important than the eating of meats and eggs on a fast day. We saw this in the monasteries, where pride reigns in the highest degree, where the hood, scapulars, and other observances are defended much more quickly than the commandment of God. They pay no attention to God and His Word in setting up their own rules. In this they decree the greatest sins and merits. But when they thus turn things upside down, God upsets and rejects them by a just judgment. For God wants His worship to surpass all others. The pope, however, extols his worship over all; he does not permit anyone to whisper one little word against him, but meanwhile he himself overlooks more than enough against Christ and His Word and, worst of all, he himself persecutes Christ, as we have hitherto seen by experience and still see. To listen to anyone saying anything against the pope was a greater sin than if it were against God; so has the fear of human traditions taken possession of us. This is indicated by these words, "with the mouth and lips they honor Me." For the ungodly seducers proceed in this way that they always come praising God with the mouth and the lips. For all evils and seductions are done under the guise of godliness. Every calamity begins in God's name. He says, moreover: They *honor Me*. What is this, that they even *honor Me?* The ungodly invent such a god for themselves as has regard for them and saves them on the basis of their works and merits, as our papists all believe in God and glorify Him, yet nevertheless everyone relies on Francis or Dominic and their respective party. He does not worship the true God, but by his perverted practice he thinks and boasts that he is worshiping God; yet he lies shamelessly and, as Paul says (2 Tim. 3:5), they indeed glorify God in appearance and words, but not at all in deed and in power. (16:244–45)

As much as Luther was incredulous about the idolatry he saw in his day, he also testified to the idolatry in his own life. He realized that he was not in any way immune to the temptation to trust in himself and to look to his own glory, rather than to the glory of God for all things.

> I am the LORD; that is My name; My glory I give to no other, nor My praise to carved idols. (Isaiah 42:8)

Even I, Martin Luther, harassed by conscience, by tyrants and Enthusiasts, so that I can hardly breathe, cannot be free of it. It is impossible for us, as Christ says, to believe and to cling to the Word while we stand in our own glory. And the

> more outstanding the talents are, the greater is the glory, as we experience in the case of our enemies. Therefore we must fight against that beast with prayer alone. Let us, then, break loose from our own religion, worship, and works. Let us turn away from our idol and turn to the glory of Christ. (17:71)

In the end, Luther is clear: anyone who clings to something other than the righteousness of faith in Christ is an idolater, because that person robs Christ of His glory.

Idolatry in Our Day

When we realize the definition of idolatry in God's eyes, we see that we are just as guilty of idolatry as the ancient people who worshiped false gods and as those in Luther's day who trusted in their works to make them righteous in God's sight.

Luther doesn't allow any of us to dismiss idolatry as something that doesn't apply to us because we don't worship statues:

> The rich man has long-lasting gold and silver, but the poor man is careful not to choose wood that will rot so that his god will not soon rot. This was customary in the prophet's time. Although we do not have this kind of idolatry, since the material of the heathen's idolatry is not the same as ours, yet the use and the attitude of both kinds of idolatry is the same. What the heathen had in their wood, we have in our opinions and our righteousness, and thus the attitude is the same. (17:22–23)

What does idolatry look like today, in our culture and in the Church? Perhaps some of the most prevalent forms of idolatry in our culture are agnosticism and atheism. That's right, agnosticism and atheism. Agnostics do not believe in a God who makes Himself known with certainty. Thus, one is free to make up concepts about God as he or she desires. Atheists do not believe in the true God revealed in the Bible. Those who consider themselves atheists or agnostics, in many ways, worship the idol of human reason, because they distrust what cannot be proven. In the end, they have made themselves to be the gods they worship. Remember, an idol is what we fear, love, and trust in above all things. Therefore, even agnostics and atheists have idols. Atheism and agnosticism tempt us to doubt God's Word.

For Christians who confess faith in the living, revealed Word of God, idolatry can be more subtle but still just as evil. Idolatry is the worship—in thoughts, words, or deeds—of the corrupted creation rather than the incorruptible Creator. Therefore, covetousness is idolatry. It is a symptom of a corrupted heart that loves creation more than the Creator—clinging to the world instead of the Word.

> There is always an abundance of ungodly teachers and of those who lead people away from sound doctrine, namely, belly worshipers (Phil. 3:19); and throughout Scripture they are charged with being greedy. Hence He describes not only the prophets who have been alienated from sound doctrine but also those who are addicted to lusts and riches. For whoever is turned away from the Holy Spirit does not seek the things that are above (Col. 3:1). Therefore he has a taste for nothing but earthly things (cf. Matt. 16:23), and they take pains to scrape gold and silver together. (16:34)

Even brief reflection makes clear that materialism drives our society and our own lives. What do we strive after? What shapes our goals and aspirations? What brings us joy when we have it and causes fear and anxiety when we don't have it? Often the answer is "stuff"—material things: a nice place to live, a car, money, vacations, technological devices. We always want more, and we are never satisfied. We become obsessed with our obsessions. We become possessed by our possessions. We want to have "stuff" because it provides temporary happiness. It makes our lives feel worthwhile and gives us something by which to identify ourselves. We idolize the rich and famous, such as athletes, movie stars, and singers. In fact, there is even a singing competition giving contestants a chance to become the next American Idol—a title that may be more indicative than we realize. Materialism tempts us to seek prosperity preachers who tell us about how God wants to unlock the inner millionaire and rain down blessings upon us.

Another current obsession in American culture is our identities as individuals. We strive to be defined by our job, our abilities, our connections, our productivity, our sexual orientation, the color of our skin, or our families. As Christians, we are tempted to acculturate to the trends around us and try to create an image of ourselves and for ourselves and others rather than be defined solely by what God says of us and what Jesus has done for us. This obsession with choosing our own identity tempts us to seek preachers who preach the Christian rather than preach Christ. They tell us what we want to hear about ourselves. They tell us how to worship God by our own means and without His Means of Grace—the Word, Baptism, and the Lord's Supper. As a result, these good gifts of God, His Means of Grace, are neglected and rejected. Then these preachers assure us that God is pleased with whatever we offer Him—our hearts, our love, our lives, our songs of praise, our words, our "spiritual" devotion. God is made into a beggar, and we become the givers.

Bound to Anything Other Than God's Word

Anytime we distort the Gospel, we make God into our own image. The Holy Spirit works in the heart through the Word. Without the Holy Spirit, the conscience can deceive and be deceived. This can take the form of reducing the Gospel to a liberation theology or a prosperity gospel, or the form of binding the Gospel with requiring works-righteousness.

When we consciously choose to reject God's Word and bind our conscience to anything else, we are enslaved to idolatry. Forming the conscience with anything other than the message of God reconciled to sinners through Christ Jesus is setting up God in our own image.

> Mark well that all idolaters worship God by means of their idols. For here He is saying, "You have fashioned for Me, you have shaped in imitation of Me." This is the origin of all idolatry, that people worship the true God, but when they lack the Word, they invent things in accordance with their own ideas. When I fashion a god outside of the Word, I soon fashion a god to suit my own opinion. Thus the Carthusian believes in the true God, but his own heart then imagines that God is pleased with his hooded way, and he thinks that thus he is gaining God's favor to be saved. This opinion is such a dark glass. No Scripture, however, says that God is such as to have regard for such works of a Carthusian. No, it sets Christ before us as the Son of God who is to be heard. The likeness is properly an opinion itself, thought up without the Word and outside of it, and from that opinion follow

> endless monsters. The soldier thinks, "I shall venerate Saint Barbara; she will preserve the sacraments for me three days." This is the basic idea: idolatry is nothing else but an opinion apart from the Word of God. Thus you read in Daniel about the people inquiring of the prophets what they should do, whether they should fast the fifth and the seventh months, etc., quite forgetful of the promises. But they thought they could obtain these things by means of sackcloths, hair shirts, and fasts. This is what misfortune does. It looks for endless places of refuge, but the godly man says, "Not on our account, Lord, not on our account, but because You have promised, since You make promises freely, without regard for works." (17:140–41)

Effects of Idolatry on the Conscience

Though rejecting what God says in favor of autonomy sounds like freedom, it is darkness and slavery. Instead of being a source of shared seeing with God, which gives life, freedom, and joy, the conscience becomes a source of poison when it is bound to anything idolatrous, anything other than God's Word. Without the promise of Christ and His atoning sacrifice, there is no forgiveness, mercy, salvation, pardon, or peace with God. Without God's promise, there is no true faith. It is impossible to please God without faith.

When the conscience is normed to a lie, to an idol, it proclaims loudly only what the proud heart wants to hear. The more the conscience asserts itself, the more the heart insists on its own worship and works and ways. So the conscience no longer works—it only confirms the heart in its own way. It is a self-perpetuating cycle that leads further away from God. The conscience does the opposite of what it is supposed to do.

As Luther says concerning the effect of idolatry on the conscience in his day,

> Where people have once forsaken the Word, it is inevitable that tradition will soon follow; or there is opinion, that is, error, on the part of those who erect their own idols according to their own ideas, and then error soon follows. Meanwhile, however, they always have their supreme boasting, also for these; for he says here "their fear." We experienced this

among the papists, who were terribly afraid where there was nothing to fear and were not afraid where they should have been afraid. This, then, is the nature of human traditions: They bring very great fear with them, but it is altogether perverted and opposed to God. . . .

Thus you see that they have no wisdom, no faith and understanding, no discernment of Scripture and the Word. The wise men are those who know the rule and analogy of faith. The understanding ones are those who test doctrines and adjudicate them by a keen judgment, those who in fear test all things according to the analogy of faith. The ungodly lack these gifts and have no understanding or faith but always snore away in their own smugness. . . . However, there has been nothing in them of the Word, of faith, of conscience, and of love. Always the heart has remained the same. Therefore they remain in their dream, possessing nothing of faith or of love, because they are neither wise nor understanding. And when they will be most wise, they will be most ungodly; and when they want to be most understanding, they are the most stupid. This is so because they do not have the Word but their own traditions. (16:245–46)

As Psalm 14:1 declares, "The fool says in his heart, 'There is no God.'" According to God's Word, the fool is one who lacks the wisdom of God, who says, "I am and there is no other. I decide what is right in my own sight." Satan is quite content to let the conscience perpetuate an idolater's distortion and deception. The idolater is falsely secure, because he has no concept of what is truly good and evil, yet he thinks he does. His conscience tells him everything is all right when it is not. Like the people in Isaiah's day, idolatry creates a conscience that does not even see its need for the true God or God's Word.

Isaiah proclaimed on God's behalf,

> What to Me is the multitude of your sacrifices? says the LORD; I have had enough of burnt offerings of rams and the fat of well-fed beasts; I do not delight in the blood of bulls, or of lambs, or of goats. When you come to appear before Me, who has required of you this trampling of My courts? Bring no more vain offerings; incense is an abomination to

He is a true Christian who neither is presumptuous in his works nor despairs in his sins, even though he avoids sins and does good works.

—MARTIN LUTHER

Me. New moon and Sabbath and the calling of convocations—I cannot endure iniquity and solemn assembly. Your new moons and your appointed feasts My soul hates; they have become a burden to Me; I am weary of bearing them. (Isaiah 1:11–14)

The people and the priests in Isaiah's day were so preoccupied with loving the Lord in the ways they thought were good, in the style of their contemporaries, they failed to see the needs of their neighbors. The people's consciences did not convict them of their sin against others because their consciences were not bound to God's Word. Simultaneously, they believed they were being truly pious, praising Yahweh with their offerings and incense. They wanted God to look down on all they were doing for Him and see the blood offered to Him.

What to Me is the multitude of your sacrifices? According to the judgment of the flesh, which does not understand the Holy Spirit, these words are indeed pure blasphemies. The prophet agrees with David in Ps. 40:6 and in Ps. 50:13, and with others who reject the sacrifices offered for the purpose of appeasing God, such as Jer. 7:22; Ezek. 20:25, although the offering of sacrifices was the supreme work and was commanded by God through Moses. And this is our doctrine of faith, that God is not appeased by our works and merits; for He neither needs nor wants them in order that we may have glory. But He Himself, who has regard for nothing else than His own goodness, has the glory. Therefore whoever wants to appease God by his own merits is worse than the Sodomites, namely, an idolater. Consequently, these people are reproached here in this way because they do not understand the Law. But when the godly bring sacrifices, they testify that they believe God; and by this faith they are justified. The ungodly disregard faith and consider sacrifice to be the supreme worship of God; that is, they despise the kernel and admire the husk. To them faith is worthless because they do not see it, but they do see the showiness of works and therefore admire them and make much of them. To be sure, sacrifices are not evil; but if on their account I wanted to boast that I am a righteous child of God, etc., then I would be misusing them. It is like this: If

I wanted to boast that I am an heir of heaven because of the bright eye God gave me, I would be misusing an otherwise good eye and would be making it only an idol and making a liar of God, who says that He will be gracious for His own sake, not for the sake of anything else whatever. Therefore we must do works only for the purpose of bearing witness to faith in God—the faith by which I acknowledge that He is merciful and freely pours out His mercy on my misery. And in the end he is a true Christian who neither is presumptuous in his works nor despairs in his sins, even though he avoids sins and does good works. Nevertheless, the affections of hope must be fixed on God alone, not on a creature or a work.

I have had enough of burnt offerings. This means that He is disgusted with them; that is, that they are useless to Him and that He has need neither of eating the flesh nor of drinking the blood for the purpose of being appeased but is nauseated by them, even though they were the most praiseworthy offerings in the Law, especially the fat, which, as He has particularly mentioned, was offered to Him. Does the prophet not forbid good works here? Not the works, but the attitude.

I did not delight. "I do not delight" is better, since he is speaking of the present status of the people before God. There was not the least praise even for the offering of blood, from which they abstained completely. They smeared and sprinkled the altars. Yet He condemns even this form of worship. What, then, is holy, when the best part of the religion is removed?

When you come to appear before Me. It is as if He were complaining of the insult that by their entrance into the court they have desecrated the place. He does not consider them worthy of entrance into the court, as if they were an unbearable burden for His court. It is as if He were saying: "You enter My court as filthy peasants going into a lovely creek with their muddy boots." . . . And surely such a religion handed down by God should not be despised. What God hands down is something great, even if it is physical, that men may know that they worship God through these things; for otherwise one seeks God here, another there, yet will find God nowhere except where He has bound Himself through His Word. On the other hand, however, it is insolent to condemn what Moses commanded and to say: *Who has required these things?* God requires our works, and He does not require them. How is this? I answer: He simply requires them, not as if they themselves were necessary or as if He wanted to be appeased by them. Thus, on the other hand, He does not require them. But consider the folly of men. We reverse the order and want to serve God with works and men with faith. Thus they say that what has been presented to the sacrificing priests has been given to God and must not be turned to profane uses. Of course, it has been given to them that they might serve God. But to serve and come to the aid of neighbors, to those who are needy, this they do not consider to be a service of God. For this reason they are taken to task here. . . .

Furthermore He says that they are not only useless but are even an abomination, since they had the idea that the more often a burnt offering was brought, the more praiseworthy it was. In sum, these are statements directed specifically against the efforts and works of men. And the works are not condemned, but only their misuse, that is, false trust in them. You should rather sing (cf. Ps. 51:1): "Be merciful to me, O God, not on account of the multitude of my burnt sacrifices, not on account of the holiness and purity of Mary and others, but on account of Thy great mercy." Scripture always proclaims the mercy of God and our sin. The majesty of God is supreme; we are completely worthless. Yet we must convince ourselves that God is merciful to us, because this is what He has promised. If only our faith were strong, this gracious disposition of God would make us fearless in all things. Fear indicates weakness on God's part. A faith undaunted defies all things, and because faith is such a great thing, it condemns our efforts and works, even the best of them, as sins, because they puff us up, etc. (16:14–17)

> Luther and Isaiah do not condemn works themselves; they condemn faith in works. If we think we can make God merciful, we are making an idol. Works do not make God merciful. God is merciful—that is who He is. Isaiah's condemnation of the people

(and us, by implication) reflects that God is merciful to us actually in spite of what we have done. God's mercy comes to us in the ways and places He has said: in His Word and Sacraments. But without God's Word, we think we can trust our works. When our conscience is bound to anything other than God's Word, the conscience is no help at all because it provides a distorted perception that only compounds our rebellion and sin.

The Outcome of Idols

As we have heard in some of the Isaiah texts in this chapter, God will not tolerate His glory being given to anything else—not to any false gods, and not to us when we trust in ourselves.

God's response to the rhetorical question He poses through the prophet Isaiah to His people in Isaiah 46:5 is to clarify for His people how completely different He is from idols. Unlike idols, He can and will act to carry out His purpose.

> To whom will you liken Me and make Me equal, and compare Me, that we may be alike? . . . Remember this and stand firm, recall it to mind, you transgressors, remember the former things of old; for I am God, and there is no other; I am God, and there is none like Me, declaring the end from the beginning and from ancient times things not yet done, saying, "My counsel shall stand, and I will accomplish all My purpose." (Isaiah 46:5, 8–10)

Luther notes God's insistent and repetitive tone in this passage:

> After a notion has been fixed in an ungodly man's mind, a great deal of admonition is required, because he sees nothing but his own idea and regards nothing but his own works while fasting, dressing, praying, etc. He believes that in this way he is pleasing God. He does not think otherwise: "God truly has regard for these things." While that idol stands in his mind, it is impossible for him to think about the promises of God. For that reason the prophet says *Recall it to mind*. (17:142)

Because He is the true God who is jealous for His people, He will not let them continue in their blind, deceived, idolatrous way. Their false security will be stripped away in the time of trouble.

Isaiah says of Israel's idolaters,

> Behold, all his companions shall be put to shame, and the craftsmen are only human. Let them all assemble, let them stand forth. They shall be terrified; they shall be put to shame together. (Isaiah 44:11)

> There is no stability in being a monk or in being self-righteous. Whatever righteousness there might be outside of the righteousness of grace, this will be put to shame. Why? Because *the craftsmen are but men.* Conclusion: Whatever is conceived and said by men does not justify. Whatever is not set forth by the Word of God is abominable. Therefore the Christian man should not walk anywhere except by the thoroughly reliable Word of God. With this teaching we make sport of all our adversaries. However, they do not want to forsake what is their own. When it comes to other things, external arrangements, crafts, buying, selling, building, rearing children, etc., we need reason and craftsmen, etc. But when it comes to faith, let reason and craftsmen desist. *Craftsmen,* that is, "ungodly teachers."
>
> *Let them all assemble,* as if to say, "Even if they should all gather together with all their resources." Even if they come together and stand together, they shall nevertheless be put to shame. Even if they should conspire and make plans, their conscience shall nevertheless at length be confounded and become alarmed. For those who are zealous of works shall finally be terrified. Those who believe in God shall not be put to shame. (17:110)

Isaiah promises that God will bring about the destruction of idols of any kind. All idols will come to an end. We will see this on the Last Day.

> And the haughtiness of man shall be humbled, and the lofty pride of men shall be brought low, and the LORD alone will be exalted in that day. And the idols shall utterly pass away. (Isaiah 2:17–18)

Luther considers what this passage means for his context.

> The idols shall be completely changed. "The heavens will perish, but Thou dost endure," as Ps. 102:26 says. And the same King is here. Not only will that which is lofty in matters of the state, with which he has dealt up to this point, be brought down, but also what is high in the spiritual administration. For the world is divided into these two things even among the Gentiles. For no nation has not had gods. In sum, every form of worship, both of the Jews and of the Gentiles, is dung in comparison with the worship of Christ. Therefore all those forms of worship will be changed and overthrown. Moreover, the idol denotes the culture, the religion, the ultimate witness, what men think and have in mind, etc. And now the idols are changed, that is, monks into laymen, etc., through the Gospel. Even so these spiritual people, will together with their worship, hide themselves in caves; that is, they will confess that everything of theirs, both their righteousness and their religion, are nothing in comparison with the glory of Christ. (16:37–38)

Saving Us from Our Idols

Humans have struggled with idolatry ever since Adam and Eve accepted the temptation to the first idolatry and fell into sin. Instead of rejoicing in the image of God in which we were created, we have wanted to create our own images for ourselves and to make God into our own image.

But God loves us enough not only to destroy our idols but also to send His Son, His very own image, in order to re-create us in His image once again. Because of our original sin, we do not want to be formed and shaped into the image and likeness of God's only-begotten Son. But God loves us so much that the Holy Spirit keeps drawing us to Christ, in spite of our rebellion. This is why God sent Isaiah to Israel.

> We have heard how the Spirit admonishes the unbelievers who strive to save themselves. This evil is inborn in us, that in times of need we run to all gods except the one God. Therefore God meets us with Scripture, where the contention is that all our toil and merits are cut out by the promises alone apart from the works of the Law, as Paul treats of it

> so richly in Gal. 3:15ff. There he says that God's covenant was in force out of pure mercy and promise a long time, 400 years in fact, before the Law. These arguments are unfailing: By grace alone all things come to us who merit nothing. Yet the flesh cannot keep silent in afflictions but always runs back to its own resources, and people look for help to their own prayers and merits. . . . So here Israel should be plucked out of the Babylonian captivity gratis, at no cost, absolutely free. Therefore the prophet meets this evil especially, since all of us, immersed in trials, forget the promises of God and have recourse to our own resources. (17:141–42)

Without the Word of the Lord, there is no life, salvation, or the forgiveness of sins. Without the voice of God, there is no Jesus. Without Jesus, there is no access to the Father.

And this is why God keeps sending His Word to us so faithfully. The prophetic voice sent from God leads us into the truth. Because God alone determines what is right and wrong, good and evil, life and death, only God's Word can govern the conscience so that we are not enslaved to idolatry. The best news that God's Word ever proclaims to our conscience is "You are forgiven, because Jesus atoned for your sin and cleansed you from iniquity." Only in Christ can we find what we truly need: forgiveness, mercy, salvation, and peace with God. Only in Christ is there a new creation in which we are formed once again into the image of our Savior and God. Christ is the true image of the invisible God. He is the only image by which the conscience can faithfully be formed. The prophetic voice brings this true image of God to us. The purpose of the prophetic voice is to establish us with a good conscience before God. Therefore, in the time of trouble and the day of death, the believer seeks to hear God's Word of Christ, because it alone gives true peace to the heart.

CHAPTER 4

WHEN THE CONSCIENCE IS ALARMED

An Alarmed Conscience

The role of an alarm helps us to understand the role of a conscience. For example, we set an alarm clock to wake us up from sleep. On the other hand, a smoke detector is an alarm that we can't set for a certain time; rather, it is set to go off at the threat of fire. When a smoke detector rings out in the middle of the night, it scares and startles us. Although we might ignore an alarm clock by hitting the snooze button, we cannot disregard a smoke detector. There actually could be a threatening fire. In haste, we quickly jump out of bed, ready to flee the flames. Just as a smoke detector alarms us when it detects smoke and warns us of the threat of fire, the conscience alarms us when we become conscious of sin and warns us of the threat of God's wrathful fire. Thus, the alarmed conscience causes us to flee from God's presence. In this chapter, we will consider examples of how people respond to the alarm of the conscience, including the people of Israel in Isaiah's day, King Ahaz, and the prophet Isaiah himself.

The Sinful Response to the Alarm

The conscience that is formed by God's Word alarms us when we sin. Sometimes it takes the voice of God's Law to frighten us when we realize that we have done what He forbids or failed to do what He requires. At other times, experiencing the day of trouble makes us hear God's judgment and our guilt. When the conscience is troubled, even the sound of a rustling leaf can alarm it.

When Adam and Eve transgressed God's will by eating fruit from the tree of the knowledge of good and evil, they had bad consciences. Their bad consciences drove them to try to cover up. They covered themselves with leaves, thinking they could make their consciences artificially good again. Death no longer seemed like a threat to their bad consciences. However, the sound of God alarmed and terrified their consciences. God's presence is made known through His voice. In the Hebrew language, the same word is used for voice and sound. Thus, Adam and Eve heard the presence of God in the sound/voice of Him walking in the garden, and they were startled. Like a smoke detector, their consciences sensed fire. They thought they heard God coming as the judge. And they knew the wages of sin is death. They knew that He knew what they had done. They knew the fig leaves could not hide their nakedness, so in haste, they fled from His presence. The simple question "Where are you?" accused them of their sin. They tried to hide from God. Of course, no one can hide from God. He knows all. Yet, a characteristic of an alarmed and terrified conscience is to flee from the presence of God.

Luther notes that a terrified conscience hastily flees the rustling of even a leaf. In his commentary on Genesis, Luther writes about Adam and Eve:

> After their conscience had been convicted by the Law, Adam and Eve were terrified by the rustling of a leaf (Lev. 26:36). We see it to be just so in the case of frightened human beings. When they hear the creaking of a beam, they are afraid that the entire house may collapse; when they hear a mouse, they are afraid that Satan is there and wants to kill them. By nature we have become so thoroughly frightened that we fear even the things that are safe.
>
> Therefore after their conscience has been convicted by the

Law and they feel their disgrace before God and themselves, Adam and Eve lose their confidence in God and are so filled with fear and terror that when they hear a breath or a wind, they immediately think God is approaching to punish them; and they hide. I, too, think that by the voice of the Lord, who was walking about, Moses means the wind or the sound of the wind, which preceded the appearance of the Lord. Similarly, in the Gospel Christ says of the wind (John 3:8): "You hear its sound." When they heard the leaves rustling as if they were being moved by the wind, they thought: "Behold, now the Lord is coming to demand punishment from us." . . . This fear, which overtook Adam and Eve in the very light of day after their sin, is a clear indication that they had fallen completely from the faith.

This I believe to be the true sense of this passage; it also agrees with the threat in Lev. 26:36, where Moses is speaking of the punishments that will follow sin, namely, that sinners will become frightened by the sound of a falling leaf and will take to flight as though from a sword. When the conscience is truly and thoroughly frightened, man is so overcome that he not only cannot act but is unable even to do any thinking. They say that such a thing happens in battle when soldiers who are overcome by fear cannot move a hand but permit themselves to be slain by the enemy. Such a terrible punishment follows sin that at the rustling of a leaf conscience is full of fear. (1:170–71)

Luther refers to the warning of Moses in Leviticus 26, where it is written, "And as for those of you who are left, I will send faintness into their hearts in the lands of their enemies. The sound of a driven leaf shall put them to flight, and they shall flee as one flees from the sword, and they shall fall when none pursues" (v. 36).

Moses taught the people the promises of God. If the people of God continued to walk in His light and rejoice in His voice, then the land would prosper with rain and grain. The sword of their enemies would not harm them. They would have no need to be afraid or fear their enemies, for the Lord promised to be with them. However, Moses warned the people about following other words and voices. If they did, the Lord would walk contrary to them, instead of with them. He would unsheathe the sword of their enemies against them.

Isaiah was sent to the people of Jerusalem to test their consciences like a fire inspector inspects a smoke detector. Thus, Isaiah threatened the people with the coming sword of their enemies, as Moses had warned. However, the people failed their smoke-detector test. Their leaders assured them it was a false alarm.

> Why will you still be struck down? Why will you continue to rebel? The whole head is sick, and the whole heart faint. From the sole of the foot even to the head, there is no soundness in it, but bruises and sores and raw wounds; they are not pressed out or bound up or softened with oil. (Isaiah 1:5–6)

When Luther comments on this passage, he uses the same ideas as found in his Genesis commentary on Adam and Eve. He writes,

> *The whole head is sick, etc.* Not a part or member remains that has not been smitten. To be sure, we deserve more smiting; but there is no room, because already the whole head has been smitten enough and is sick. Even now the whole heart is faint. Even though I could undoubtedly find a place to smite you, yet I still desist, because there is no physician to provide a cure. Nor do you want to be reformed. You promise yourselves the highest seats in heaven, etc. So it is with our hypocrites. But no matter how much we have sinned, there is no reason for us to despair, provided that we acknowledge our sins and have knowledge of our Lord Jesus Christ and of God's mercy in Him. If there is no light, there will be no room for a cure. Isaiah is a rhetorician in a wonderful manner, and he uses flowery language; for he almost always employs allegories and figures of speech. The people are the body; the head, the superiors; the heart, the sages and practitioners of justice. The remaining classes of the people are the other members. Therefore He wants to say that these people are smitten and abased as much in the upper classes as in the lower classes of men. Look at the histories. When the 10 tribes were led up,

> how the two tribes in the land of Judah and elsewhere feared for themselves! For the words of the prophet should not be pulled apart to apply only to this or that historical situation, but the prophet speaks in a general way except when he speaks of Christ. This is the hardness of the human heart, which is deep and inscrutable, since it has been impenitent. For even though all evils are inflicted on it, yet it remains hard like the trunk of a tree and like an anvil. This is the heart that deserves to be terrified by even a flying leaf (Lev. 26:36), since it does not have the promises by which it may be buoyed up and lacks the comfort of faith and help. It is smitten within by dread, blindness, and madness. Without there are disturbances of all classes: of princes, prophets, and priests of the people, since God smites all things. There is no physician with the obligation to cure this, that is, no prophet with the obligation to proclaim and teach this. Yet there are false prophets who presume to offer comfort of a sort, but as it is in Jeremiah, the people are worse off because of the cure offered by those men. (16:12)

Moses and Isaiah in unison warn the people that if they reject the promises of God, they will be left with the curses of God. The sound of even a flying leaf will terrify them and alarm their consciences, much less the sound of their enemies.

Befriending Death

One of the ways the people in Isaiah's day wrongly responded to the alarm of their consciences was to try to thwart death by making a covenant with death.

> You have said, "We have made a covenant with death, and with Sheol we have an agreement, when the overwhelming whip passes through it will not come to us, for we have made lies our refuge, and in falsehood we have taken shelter." (Isaiah 28:15)

The conscience is supposed to work like a smoke detector that sounds the alarm when smoke is detected. Where there is smoke, there is a fire. Where there is fire, there is the danger of death.

Yet the religious leaders in Isaiah's day convinced the people not to worry about the judgment of God, nor about death and the grave. They peddled a pact with death, making death a friend. They advertised an agreement with Sheol. They did not fear the grave, since they had an ongoing covenant with death. They promoted fireproof shelters and waterproof refuges. The false prophets pushed their faulty fire-insurance plans and lied about their life-insurance policies. These prosperity preachers persuaded the people to live their best lives now. They disarmed their consciences.

The false prophets painted over the fire alarms. They taught their followers to ignore signs that read, "Danger! Flammable!" However, flammable gas and dangerous vapors flowed out of their mouths and the imagination of their corrupt hearts.

Therefore, the prophet Isaiah mocked the false teachers' pride in pretend piety. As Adam and Eve were deceived by the devil into trying to hide behind leaves and trees, the people in Isaiah's day boasted in lies and falsehood as their refuge and shelter. Isaiah prophesied that when hail and floodwater came, their pitiful shelters would fall. The people had built their houses on sinking sand.

In our day, people do the same thing when they don't even contemplate the reality of death and just assume they will live forever. Unbelievers talk about death as a natural part of life. When a person dies, they say, "She has gone on to another place," or "He is at peace now," or "She is no longer suffering."

Isaiah wrote,

Stand fast in your enchantments and your many sorceries, with which you have labored from your youth; perhaps you may be able to succeed; perhaps you may inspire terror. You are wearied with your many counsels; let them stand forth and save you, those who divide the heavens, who gaze at the stars, who at the new moons make known what shall come upon you. Behold, they are like stubble; the fire consumes them; they cannot deliver themselves from the power of the flame. No coal for warming oneself is this, no fire to sit before! Such to you are those with whom you have labored, who have done business with you from your youth; they wander about, each in his own direction; there is no one to save you. (Isaiah 47:12–15)

The Word of God indeed proclaims things hidden and not manifest, and they are grasped only by faith.... Here it is enough to hear and to believe.

—MARTIN LUTHER

This oracle is spoken against the teachers in Babylon. But in the days of Isaiah, the people of Israel were mesmerized by similar false teachers who taught them to follow the wisdom of the world. Thus, when the people of God want to be like Babylon, like the pagan earthly kingdoms, the Lord threatens His own people with the same punishment. They will be consumed in the flames of God's wrath. We can disconnect the battery in a smoke detector, but it will do us no good when the fire comes. Likewise, a conscience that has been painted over to look pretty will be of no value in the time of trouble or the day of death. Such external experiences testify to the wrath of God provoked by sin. Sin has infected this whole creation, causing a rebellion against the Creator. By nature, we have been conceived and born as rebels who are at war with God.

> This is the general description of the ungodly in the Scriptures, where the ungodly are called stubble and dust snatched away by the wind. Here the prophet attacks their god Hur. Their god is the fire. The wise men of Babylon are stubble. This makes a fine combination. The mockery is truly ironical. He compares the wisest men to stubble, not to trees and woods, and then he places them into the fire. Like one stubble in a glowing oven, so the Babylonians, so insuperable and secure before the world, must be like one stubble over against Cyrus. So the Turk must be like stubble to the Christian. So the papacy is stubble. These are dramatic words that bring comfort to the weak. . . .
>
> Just as the stubble which is consumed by fire cannot protect itself against the flame, so the power of the Babylonians cannot save them from Cyrus. These are great words. . . .
>
> This refers to the coming destruction brought about by the king of the Persians. . . .
>
> This fire will not be a fire of live coals which lasts for some time. It is a fire that flares up quickly, before which people cannot warm themselves. This denotes a very easy and quick destruction, as if to say, "Before Me the most powerful kingdoms are just like a stubble fire. They must be consumed like stubble in the fire, so that no coal remains." . . .

> "So your priests and wise men will be situated, with whom you labored." . . .
>
> "All your counselors, who labored for you, will be scattered each in his own direction. Those who formerly sat firm in the kingdoms will be scattered into uncertainty." Such is the destruction of the Babylonian kingdom, written by apostrophe to them. Hence it is written for the sake of the Jews, so that they might not lose hope. He sends these dramatic words to them so that they might console themselves in their captivity and in the rest of their troubles. These words, however, are in force to the end of the world for all who are oppressed by tyrants because of the Word of God. For we today suffer things similar to what the upright Jews suffered. (17:153–54)

Luther notes that Isaiah 47 describes all of ungodly humanity, not just the Babylonians to whom it is most specifically addressed. By nature, we sinfully respond to the alarm of our consciences.

Without Christ, we are enemies of the kingdom of heaven. The passions of the fallen flesh rule our hearts, inciting us to rebel against the will of God. The devil deceives us into reconditioning our consciences. Instead of detecting sin, our consciences become a defense system. They alarm us of an invasion and identify God as the intruder. When the conscience is alarmed, we respond as if we are under attack, being assaulted by the kingdom of God. We are ready to fight for the kingdoms of the earth, desiring to dwell in the dominion of darkness and deception. We assume that if God's kingdom comes, we will be tried for treason.

Ahaz's Conscience

Another example of a sinful response to the alarm of the conscience is the response of King Ahaz of Judah.

> In the days of Ahaz the son of Jotham, son of Uzziah, king of Judah, Rezin the king of Syria and Pekah the son of Remaliah the king of Israel came up to Jerusalem to wage war against it, but could not yet mount an attack against it. When the house of David was told, "Syria is in league with Ephraim," the heart of Ahaz and the heart of his peo-

ple shook as the trees of the forest shake before the wind. (Isaiah 7:1–2)

Isaiah's ministry was contemporaneous with the reigns of four kings in Jerusalem: Uzziah, Jotham, Ahaz, and Hezekiah. During Ahaz's reign, the king of Syria and the king of Israel made an alliance and came to battle against Ahaz and Judah. Rumors of an imminent attack alarmed Ahaz's conscience.

> And the LORD said to Isaiah, "Go out to meet Ahaz, you and Shear-jashub your son, at the end of the conduit of the upper pool on the highway to the Washer's Field. And say to him, 'Be careful, be quiet, do not fear, and do not let your heart be faint because of these two smoldering stumps of firebrands, at the fierce anger of Rezin and Syria and the son of Remaliah.'" (Isaiah 7:3–4)

Notice that the smoke alarm of Ahaz's conscience is terrified by the coming fire of the two enemy kings. Here the external threat of doom and death terrifies Ahaz's heart. Yet, God assures him through the mouth of the prophet Isaiah that these small fires are about to be extinguished by God. Their plans will not come to fruition. Isaiah brings the promise of God, declaring,

> Because Syria, with Ephraim and the son of Remaliah, has devised evil against you, saying, "Let us go up against Judah and terrify it, and let us conquer it for ourselves, and set up the son of Tabeel as king in the midst of it," thus says the Lord GOD: "It shall not stand, and it shall not come to pass." (Isaiah 7:5–7)

There are four admonitions: *Take heed, be quiet, do not fear, and do not let your heart be faint*, that is, no longer let your heart quake like the trees, but let it be still. Who would not take courage in response to these exhortations? Who would not believe the words of the Supreme Majesty, who thus consoles and so promises? But they were offered to Ahaz in vain. And here you see how a wicked heart and promises agree together. This is an example for us that we may learn. Yet Isaiah believed, as well as his son, if not Ahaz.

Two smoldering stumps of firebrands. A remarkable personification set against the personification above, where the smug and the presumptuous who do not consider the power of the Word hiding in the small nation of Judah are described. God certainly speaks far more contemptuously of them than the enemies themselves do against us. He does not call them burning firebrands, but stumps of firebrands, that is, the leftovers of coals. They are coals no longer burning but extinguished, although they still smoke a little and are such as little boys play with to the present day. Who would here be afraid when God considers such great kings to be so worthless, if only one would believe it? They are indeed wrathful and raging, but they cannot accomplish what they wish. This is certainly a splendid promise of the kindness and protection of God even for the most ungodly king and idolater, that for him the wrath of those enemies should be minimized and the will of God to protect should be magnified, so that it is a shame that it fell on so unbelieving a heart. To him nevertheless, so that he could and should believe the more quickly and firmly, the prophet recounts the plan and attempt of these two kings. . . .

The prophet reports this so that Ahaz may have no doubt that the Lord knows what they had in mind. . . .

Now he discloses in what way they are smoldering firebrands, but it is without doubt a detailed and rich promise. Not any one of them will be head of Judah, but the house of David will. They will have to be satisfied with their own realm. Their own bounds have been set for all people. God is the one who transfers kingdoms, etc. (16:80–81)

"If you are not firm in faith, you will not be firm at all." Again the LORD spoke to Ahaz: "Ask a sign of the LORD your God; let it be deep as Sheol or high as heaven." But Ahaz said, "I will not ask, and I will not put the LORD to the test." And he said, "Hear then, O house of David! Is it too little for you to weary men, that you weary my God also?" (Isaiah 7:9–13)

If you will not believe. This indicates that the king showed signs of disbelief. Therefore he adds a threat to the promise. The king turns up his nose, sends the prophet away, and measures the matter according to the appearance of the flesh, namely, that the two kings are stronger than he, that many thousands of people will be lost, that cities will be lost, etc., as if he were saying: "You call them stumps of firebrands who are forest fires; you are talking contrary to reason and experience and truth." It was exactly as if someone were to say now: "Do not fear the Turks, etc." Therefore the king opposed reality. But the prophet insists that the Word of God is much more powerful than all the kings on earth, for He can also do what He says. The Word of God indeed proclaims things hidden and not manifest, and they are grasped only by faith. In other books and arts you must study and put all things to the test so that you may understand and grasp what is presented. Here it is enough to hear and to believe. Therefore the ancients explained this passage thus: If you do not believe, you do not understand. Certainly a good thought. But the prophet set given works against the Amen, that is, the truth against hypocrisy. He means to say: You will not prevail, and whatever you may have planned otherwise will not endure, it will not continue, it will not succeed. Therefore he condemns every religion, all endeavors, all plans of the king, unless he believes God, not only such things as belong to the external and physical man, but also such as pertain to the spiritual man and the ecclesiastic. Hence faith alone makes certain and has a solid foundation. But the promise becomes useless unless faith is added. Then this passage is also explained Hebraically in this way: If you do not believe, you will not be truthful. For those who believe God make and reckon Him to be true, which is giving glory to God, as Rom. 4:20 says, and they themselves also become truthful through faith. On the contrary, to the unbelieving all things become deceptive, unreliable, and unsure. With this conclusion the prophet said his final farewell to the king. This must be taught everywhere, because he who believes nothing accomplishes nothing. But whatever the godly man does will always prosper (Ps. 1:3). . . .

Again the Lord spoke. . . . *Ask a sign of the Lord.* Behold the great and overflowing goodness of God and His sublime patience. For even though disdained in His promise and threat, He still does not stop inciting to faith, as if to say: If you do not want to believe promises and threats, at least believe the signs and choose whatever you wish. Ahaz, in turn, rejects also the sign with the worst blasphemy and ingratitude. God offers a sign; this man cites Scripture. . . .

Always the ungodly become more hardened. Now, those are wrong who say that signs avail nothing for faith. God is almost always accustomed to add a sign to the Word, just as here, too, he would have added one, provided that the king would have accepted it. Paul also approves the use of signs in 2 Cor. 12:12. And signs do not make for distinguishing this person from that one. . . .

Ahaz pretends religion, as if from fear of God he did not wish to ask for a sign. Such is the nature of hypocrites, who display religiosity where it is not proper; on the other hand, where they should fear, they are most proud and stubborn, as Ps. 36:1 and Ps. 53:5 say. Both are extremely offensive to God and deceptive to the people.

To put God to the test is indeed evil when it is done without a word of God. He who is commanded to put God to the test and does not do so is sinning. God is not being tempted when He Himself orders it. It is not tempting God to believe in Christ, to love the neighbor, because God has commanded these things. However, he who desires to serve God short of His commandment is tempting Him, since he does not know whether it will please Him. Thus Ahaz multiplied the religions of the heathen in Judah, he tempted God and yet did not think he was tempting Him. He thought so, however, when he was ordered to do so. There are many such people, above all the false prophets. . . .

To weary men is certainly evil. But if anyone has sinned against God, who will pray for him? (16:82–84)

> Rather than responding to the alarm of his conscience by trusting in the comforting promises of Yahweh, King Ahaz flees to his own forms of idolatry.

To understand the prophet, one must first of all carefully ponder the historical situation. Jotham was godly; Ahaz, his son, was the most ungodly of all. Under Jotham Isaiah was silent for a while, under Ahaz he began to prophesy again. The latter established many kinds of idolatry and did it with a show of piety, because on every side he was pressed by the worst kind of evils, which he wished to counteract. Let him serve as an example for all people in the world so that they may see what faith in God can accomplish and, on the contrary, how works avail nothing before Him if any one trusts in them. Ahaz certainly did not worship trees but rather a divinity, only he did not do so with the right kind of worship. Idolatry consists in believing someone else rather than God alone. The Christian religion consists in believing in the mercy and goodness of God for Christ's sake. This religion is pure and sincere; everything else is idolatry, even though it uses the name of the true God as a cover. There are as many idols as there are sects. Because of the many new installations for the worship of God, Ahaz was proclaimed by the false prophets to be the holiest of all kings. David was nothing alongside him. The crowd goes after the outward form. And the holier and more zealous anyone is in a strange faith, the more destructive and deplorable he is. Such have they all been. Paul says of the Jews in Rom. 10:2: "They have a zeal for God, but it is not enlightened." They apply the terms God, the name of God, the work of God, and faith in God to that which is not God. They follow a shadow like that well-known dog and lose the truth. Therefore let this example scare us away from every pretense, let it open our eyes so that we may distinguish false religion from the true. (16:78)

Again, notice Luther clearly states that Ahaz attempted to worship the true God. Ahaz was a very spiritual man. He had a zeal for God but lacked the knowledge of salvation. Without God's Word, he was left without God, without the Son of God, and without the Spirit of God. Without the Spirit of God, he was blown to-and-fro by the wind and carried off with the spirits of the age. The creative king gathered visionary leaders around him to cast their dreams before his eyes. Such false prophets assured him of the success of his kingdom. His false security was built on the abundance of his silver and gold and his building projects. Thus, with the threat of his kingdom crumbling before his eyes and the loss of all his gathered goods, his heart shook as a tree in a windstorm.

> This is indeed a description of the condition of the ungodly, whom the Word of promise will not help unless despair is already driving them, so that it may be a Word of life providing aid in death, a Word of liberty giving relief in captivity. And indeed it can demonstrate its power in no other way than to come into straits of the kind that befell Ahaz. . . .
>
> Where there is no faith, there is no counsel. Now every form of divine worship that Ahaz had dared to set up beyond the Word of God broke down. No one is more scared in trouble than the top hypocrites. In peace they are unyielding and harder than flint; in distress they are shaken like trees at every breeze. But John the Baptist was not like that. The leaves of the trees are exposed to the gusts of wind, for there is no wall surrounding them to ward off the winds. So is the heart that is destitute of the Word of God and wide open to all calamities. Then works try to come to one's assistance instead of the Word, but these provide no protection. But God's wisdom does. Prov. 1:33 says: "He who listens to me will dwell secure and will be at ease, without dread of evil." Likewise (Prov. 28:1): "The wicked flee when no one pursues, but the righteous are bold as a lion." And in Ps. 112:6 we read: "The righteous will be remembered forever." Let us do the works that God has commanded, but let us not rely on them, but rather on the Word alone, that we may cling to it, letting go of works and all other things. (16:79–80)

In the ancient world, there were a variety of methods for managing troubled consciences. For example, babies were slaughtered as a sacrifice to stop the alarm of a frightened conscience. King Ahaz introduced child sacrifice to the Israelites. He burned his own sons and offered them in the way of his contemporaries. In our day, babies are also dismembered in the womb to pacify guilty consciences. In the self-chosen piety of religions in the ancient world, sexual services were encouraged as part of one's offering at temples in order to bring prosperity. In our day, sexual sin has been normalized to relieve troubled consciences and allow for promiscuity. Temporary happiness is promoted as a replacement for eternal joy in our day as well. It seems reasonable to live for the moment. Not only is the world preaching this message, but even some mainline churches also join in proclaiming as a right and good thing what God has said is evil: murdering a baby and indulging in sexual immorality.

Without the Word of God, people cannot listen to the voice of the true God. Without the true God, there can be no true faith and thus no true comfort. In our day, there are many people who call themselves spiritually Christian but not religious. Like Ahaz, they have moved past the old-time religion. They do many innovative things for God. They fund large building projects. They attend weekly worship services. They even call themselves followers of Jesus. But they are led by their own hearts, rather than by the Word of God in their vision of service to God. In the day of affliction, all the deeds they have done will not provide them peace in their consciences.

Isaiah's Conscience

However, the prophet Isaiah's response when he encounters God in His temple represents the correct response of a sinful human to the alarm of the conscience.

> In the year that King Uzziah died I saw the Lord sitting upon a throne, high and lifted up; and the train of His robe filled the temple. Above Him stood the seraphim. Each had six wings: with two he covered his face, and with two he covered his feet, and with two he flew. And one called to another and said: "Holy, holy, holy is the LORD of hosts; the whole earth is full of His glory!" And the foundations of the thresholds shook at the voice of him who called, and the house was filled with smoke. And I said: "Woe is me! For I am lost; for I am a man of unclean lips, and I dwell in the midst of a people of unclean lips; for my eyes have seen the King, the LORD of hosts!" (Isaiah 6:1–5)

This points to the shape of true religion, which is confession, praise, the proclamation of God. When this is known, man is terrified and humbled, and he gives up everything in which he formerly trusted and of which he made his boast. The preaching of grace confounds all self-assurance. . . .

Thus the prophet says that he was completely reduced to nothing, or reduced to silence, of which let nothing more be said.... [It is] as if the prophet were saying: "Formerly I, too, used to think that I was holy and that I could teach properly, but now I am found to be like the false prophets, because I have *unclean lips*. This is the distress and trial of conscience than which no other is more dreadful, namely, to be put on trial concerning the Word and doctrine. The ungodly and fanatics can think of everything except this, where they sin most. Isaiah feels this, and his conscience is tormented in final death, and he says that he is unworthy to teach. He confesses not that he has defiled hands, but defiled lips, that is, an unclean mouth, and he says that the entire nation is thus afflicted. No, this seems to be blasphemy, not only because he says he has seen God but also because he confesses that his teaching is useless and he thinks he must teach otherwise. And certainly reason, even when it teaches the Law and the Prophets in the very best way, is defiled. For the Law, as Paul says in Rom. 4:15; Heb. 7:19, justifies no one but rather makes him guilty. Therefore teaching the Law is not the same as cleansing man, neither hearer nor teacher, since also those who teach the true force of the Law are unclean. For by faith, says Peter (Acts 15:9), the hearts are cleansed, not by works or merits. Therefore saintly Isaiah, too, even to the extent that he taught the Law for the purpose of touching consciences, is defiled and dies as a defiled man. Hence the vision has this purpose, that the righteousness of the people may be condemned and they may aspire to the glory which the prophet saw, that is, move from Law to grace. The prophet is saying: We must become holier so that we may go to the Lord sitting on His lofty throne; we must hear the seraphim and the heavenly fires. You see, he brings charges against himself as well as the people. (16:71, 72)

With these words, Luther describes the distress and trial of Isaiah's own conscience. As a prophet, Isaiah preached and restored the consciences of the people by projecting the proper image of God—God as the judge who stands to judge peoples. Thus, he preached the warnings of the Law, such as,

> Woe to the wicked! It shall be ill with him, for what his hands have dealt out shall be done to him. (Isaiah 3:11)

He reset the people's smoke detectors, their consciences. However, now Isaiah sees God Himself, sitting on the throne, a consuming fire. Isaiah is no different from anyone else. He, too, is a sinner. He is speechless. He sees the smoke and hears the voice and sound of the cherubim. He knows God alone is holy.

Isaiah had not been sinning by preaching the Law. However, the preaching of the Law exposes all unholiness. The Law cannot justify; it can only bring the knowledge of sin. Isaiah had been touching the consciences of others with the Law, and now his own conscience is touched. He is terrified. "Woe to the wicked" sounds forth in his own heart, and his lips declare, "Woe to me!" He, too, is unclean, and He sees that He stands before the judge. He properly responds to the alarm of his conscience by confessing his sin.

With Isaiah's response in Isaiah 6, Luther shows that the purest form of devotion is to confess. To confess is to say the same thing as God. Before God, we confess that we are sinful and unclean. We are unholy. We cannot free ourselves from our sinful condition. We confess that He is holy. Yet, God responds to us in the same way He responded to Isaiah. When we confess our sins, seeing a vision of Christ on His throne, God shows us Christ's work that atones for our sin, cleanses us from iniquity, and bestows His holiness on us.

Christ Is the Only Answer for the Alarmed Conscience

When Adam and Eve heard the sound/voice of God walking toward them, they heard the Word of the Lord, sent to seek and save the lost. He did not come to judge; rather, He came that they might have life. He came to bring comfort by speaking the promise of the incarnation. The Seed born of the Virgin would crush the serpent's head.

Apart from Christ, the voice of God is a troubling and terrifying sound. Apart from Christ, the conscience condemns, and the alarmed and terrified conscience cannot be quieted or comforted. Without Christ, we cannot have peace with God. We know that the cost for rebellion is death. However, the message of Christ's kingdom is a proclamation of peace. He does not come to make enemies. He comes to make us His friends. We become friends of God by faith. Better yet, we become adopted sons. Even better yet, we become coheirs of God's kingdom with Christ. But He does not bring His kingdom to us at no cost to Himself. In order for us to become adopted sons by grace, our treason and transgression must be punished. The punishment for rebellion is death. The only-begotten Son of God willingly took our place and was executed for our rebellion.

God clothed Adam and Eve with animal skins to cover their nakedness and to console their timid consciences. God killed an animal in their stead, a temporary substitutionary atonement for their sins. "The wages of sin is death" (Romans 6:23), and "without the shedding of blood there is no forgiveness of sins" (Hebrews 9:22). All the animal sacrifices of the Old Testament reminded the people of God of the promise of the Christ Child, the Seed who would be born of a woman to crush the serpent. He would be born to give His body as a sacrifice and to shed His blood. He would bear their sin and the sin of all people of all time. He is the only Savior, the only answer for the troubled human conscience. He is the only true deliverance from death and the place of the dead, Sheol.

> Many have argued about getting ready for death. Many have gone into the desert to prepare themselves for dying well. I do not disparage spurning the world, but whether we shall accomplish this by withdrawing from this spurned world, I do not know. However, victory and preparation for death must be sought in Christ, not in the wilderness and in monasteries, where bellies are fattened. You must look to Christ, in whom you see death conquered. There the serpent's head is bruised (Gen. 3:15), and there you will see the whole image and the trophies of victory against our foes. We must not look at our sins and disgraceful acts, but we ought to get out of ourselves, away from our sins and our presumption, and go to Christ Himself, to the Lamb of God that bears the sins of the world (John 1:29); to Him we should rise, on Him we should look. None have correctly dealt with this manner of preparing for death, although countless treatises on the preparation for death have been written. As for you, do not consider your death as it is in you, but see it in Christ, the Victor. (16:337–38)

The power of sin over our bodies is ultimately seen in death.

The gaping jaws of death take hold of us, the grave opens wide, and Sheol swallows us whole. Only Christ can save us from death, the venom of sin. God prepared a body for Him in order to perfectly fulfill all the requirements of the Law for us. The eternal Father sent forth the eternally begotten Son in the likeness of sinful flesh to condemn sin in the flesh. On the cross, the gaping jaws of death took hold of Him, the grave opened wide to consume Him, and Sheol swallowed Him whole. However, He was not abandoned to Sheol. He swallowed up Sheol. He opened the grave. He broke the jaws of death. He put death to death by His death. He is life! He came and conquered! He is the victor! He has overcome the world! He has defeated the devil! He is living and forgiving. In Him, we have victory over death and the grave; we have conquest over sin and Satan. By faith, we take hold of Christ and trust in His promises. We have the New Testament in His blood, shed to grant us pardon and peace. We have no need for any other covenants or agreements.

When the people of Judah made covenants with death and agreements with Sheol, Isaiah pointed them to Jesus:

> Therefore thus says the Lord GOD, "Behold, I am the one who has laid as a foundation in Zion, a stone, a tested stone, a precious cornerstone, of a sure foundation: 'Whoever believes will not be in haste.' And I will make justice the line, and righteousness the plumb line; and hail will sweep away the refuge of lies, and waters will overwhelm the shelter." Then your covenant with death will be annulled, and your agreement with Sheol will not stand; when the overwhelming scourge passes through, you will be beaten down by it. (Isaiah 28:16–18)

The Lord threatened to remove their ridiculous refuge and smash their sham of a shelter. He would annul their agreement with death and overrule their covenant with Sheol. When their consciences were alarmed and terrified, the Lord wanted them to take refuge and shelter in the rock, Christ—the only one who would not be put to shame.

Paul explains this passage thus: "He will not be put to shame" (Rom. 10:11). Therefore let us inscribe this passage in golden letters, as if to say: "All other works, rites, kinds of

Only he who believes will not be in haste and will not be put to shame.

—MARTIN LUTHER

righteousness and piety are put to shame and are in a hurry. Only *he who believes will not be in haste* and will not be put to shame. Hence, apart from faith there is nothing but confusion. *To be in haste* and to put to shame mean the same thing. For to be in haste and to flee are the precise characteristics of a terrified conscience that hastily flees the rustling of a leaf (Lev. 26:36). Most aptly therefore he attributes "being in haste" to an alarmed conscience. *He will not be in haste* is for the godly, who do not flee but have Christ as their stone and mediator. It follows, then, that a Christian must not believe that we are justified by another righteousness. Let all works by which we aim to gain righteousness and all our own merits depart, because we are built upon the foundation not by doing works but by believing. Therefore let every godly man, terrified by sin, run to Christ as the Mediator and Propitiator, and let him leave all his own works behind. (16:230–31)

Being in haste and fleeing are the characteristics of a terrified conscience. Without faith in Christ, the conscience is left in confusion and haste. The bad conscience becomes terrified at the sound of God's voice, and there is no place to flee from God's presence. Only Christ fulfills the demands of the Law for us. Only in Christ, then, is there peace for the conscience.

When King Ahaz refused to ask for a sign to assure his terrified heart, Isaiah gave a sign of future peace for those who would listen:

> And he said, "Hear then, O house of David! Is it too little for you to weary men, that you weary my God also? Therefore the Lord Himself will give you a sign. Behold, the virgin shall conceive and bear a son, and shall call His name Immanuel." (Isaiah 7:13–14)

Therefore the Lord Himself will give you a sign, that is to say, "Since you refuse to ask a sign of God, He Himself will provide one of His own will." These things are said by a wrathful prophet. And he foretells two signs: The one is hidden, the other open. The latter he explains in chapter 8 in a way not much different from Hosea, chapter 1. But Isaiah includes both signs. The first one does not apply to Ahaz, because he did not live to see it, but the second does. But since he now resists the Word of God and refuses a sign, how can his faith be strengthened? Therefore the prophet speaks of a sign to come, against which they will dash, just as the sign of Jonah was given to the Jews (cf. Matt. 12:39), and those who refuse to believe will perish. Nevertheless, it is a sign of lifting up and building up and strengthening for those who believe (Matt. 12:39; 16:4). And this is the summary of this chapter until the end, because he says that this prediction is already in the process of fulfillment in these unbelievers. . . .

In Hebrew it is "has conceived," and that is the indication of a miracle; it is as if the prophet were already seeing it. Again, since he says that it is God's sign, it is necessary that that conception and birth be in a different manner than is commonly and naturally the case, for it would not be a sign if one who today is a virgin would become pregnant after a half year. Therefore she has to be both a virgin and with child. Matthew 1:21f. clearly explains this.

Immanuel. This describes what kind of person it will be. This is not a proper name. He is indeed the Son of a virgin, and yet He is "God with us," therefore God and man.

He shall eat curds and honey. This is a description of His childhood and humanity. As He is said to be born as a true human being, so He will be reared in a true human fashion. . . .

Before the Child knows, etc. That is to say, You, ungodly man, do not believe anything. But they will be there because of this unbelief, so that those enemies of yours will perish, but nonetheless you too will follow not long afterwards. But this will happen before the Boy has learned to name butter and honey. This is said for the purpose of making the prophecy dark and as an obstacle for the Jews, who to this day do not understand this passage and say that Immanuel is Hezekiah. But this sign was given for the sake of the remnant, that the kingdom of Judah should not be destroyed until Christ would come. It is, however, a hidden sign for the sake of the ungodly. (16:84–85)

God continued to point us to the sign of Immanuel, God

dwelling with us, through the rest of Isaiah's prophecies. As Isaiah wrote in the last chapter of his book,

> Thus says the LORD: "Heaven is My throne, and the earth is My footstool; what is the house that you would build for Me, and what is the place of My rest? All these things My hand has made, and so all these things came to be, declares the LORD. But this is the one to whom I will look: he who is humble and contrite in spirit and trembles at My word." (Isaiah 66:1–2)

In their high speculation about the height of God many have climbed too high. Summary: God is inside, outside, below, above the world. He sits outside of heaven and has His feet on the earth. That is, He sits on all creatures. But in these speculations you must beware of making many deductions. Stay with the manger and the incarnate Christ. Stay with that lower level speculation and nourish your faith by it. Let those who are perfect in these high thoughts occupy themselves with fighting against the opinions of the Enthusiasts and enemies. Beware of high speculations and stay with the lower ones in government, household, Scripture, and you will not go wild on the higher ones. In the human context we cannot teach anything but hand and foot, that is, the external conversation. In faith, however, you must remain with Christ incarnate in the manger. If you want to climb higher and take a look at our Lord God's work, you will fall. I often give you this advice, because I know what I am talking about. . . .

The most beautiful court and palace of God is a contrite heart and a humble spirit (cf. Ps. 51:19). Therefore we must all strive to be contrite and afflicted. . . .

Trembling hearts that are ready to fall into hell, such are the palaces of God. Thus we see by experience that prophets, who were under trial, after their affliction gloried in the power of God, as Paul says (2 Cor. 12:9), "I will all the more gladly boast of my weaknesses, that the power of Christ may rest upon me."

To whom I will look. Here we have a description of the workshop and royal palace of God, who lingers with the contrite. These are words of life and consolation. That poverty is not a physical one (although it, too, might be God's workshop), but He is speaking about that which is involved in justification, since the prophet is here speaking about justification. But outward poverty rarely helps toward justification, as we see. But he is thinking of those poor people who have theological afflictions where there is no human remedy against death, sin, and the Law. It is to such poor people that God here says He will look, such as fear God. But the ungodly do not fear God. On the contrary, they proceed with extreme smugness against God, as the papists, tyrants, and Enthusiasts do, despising faith and paying no attention to threats. Others, however, who are frightened and afflicted and squeezed together as they are confronted by the Word, think: "God is standing behind me with a club." These are the humble ones who fear God. But the hypocrites despise all of God's commandments and go their way smugly in their own traditions, as it were, trampling all of God's commandments with their feet and boots. The godly man, however, knows that he is not fulfilling the law of God. Then follows a restless conscience, a constant evil which must not be treated by any human help but only by God's help. Summary: The Christians' poverty is the despair of conscience because of sin and death, but in such a way that we may know fully that this is God's workshop and place of operation. Given these materials, God begins to work. This is our Lord God's workshop, to make something out of nothing, to provide comfort where there is no comfort. Let this be our certainty and faith and hope, that we may know we must not despair in such spiritual poverty.

Humble, contrite, trembles. These words can be distinguished and applied to death, the Law, and sin. This is one part, where the greatest merits, such as the temple, are rejected, and where poverty and unworthiness are commended, since God looks to the *humble,* the *contrite,* and the one who *trembles.* Here there is no room for merit. There is room only for the grace of God. To look and to show the face is a Hebraism. When God's countenance is calm, it means mercy and grace. This is called God's face. This face appears to those who are afraid, as if to say, "Do not be afraid. I will show you another face." Now He even goes on to reject the use of the temple itself. He casts the temple and its worship aside. (17:396–97, 398–99)

Christ as the Word made flesh is the one who sits on the throne for us. He is the eternal Word of God that Isaiah saw sitting on the throne, quieting the alarmed conscience:

> Then one of the seraphim flew to me, having in his hand a burning coal that he had taken with tongs from the altar. And he touched my mouth and said: "Behold, this has touched your lips; your guilt is taken away, and your sin atoned for." (Isaiah 6:6–7)

The conscience is terrified when it hears that everything is condemned and Christ alone is holy, and He alone enlightens every man coming into this world (John 1:9). The house was filled with smoke. In other places, such as Ex. 40:34 and 1 Kings 8:10, Scripture says that clouds filled the house and calls the cloud the glory of the Lord. And it denotes a "smoking" faith, one that knows that all our own things are defiled. Here Christ dwells, a light rising and justifying after the old man has been put to death. Confession then follows this hovering smoke, and the confession is: "Holy, holy, holy is the Lord of hosts." Then the severe judgment of God is felt, which forcibly elicits the confession. This is the first part of penitence, namely contrition, which shakes the thresholds and raises the smoke, namely, a feeling of the divine Word condemning the entire human righteousness. Then comes the seraph, that is, the preacher of the Gospel, which is the fiery coal, and promises the forgiveness of sins for Christ's sake and lifts one up to righteousness. Therefore "through the Law comes knowledge of sin" (Rom. 3:20), through the Gospel comes the knowledge and reception of grace and righteousness. The glowing coal is the Word kindled by the Holy Spirit in love, whereby those who have been put to death are revived by the cry of the seraphim. To touch the mouth is to strike the heart with the Gospel, which is sweet to the bitter heart. Then the heart is a fit vessel for honor, because it will go for the Lord, that is, it will be His instrument for teaching others, hearing and breaking through, even though with danger, the last comfort. A remnant will be saved, even though not all hear the Word and many spit it out. (16:77)

The correct response of the people of God to an alarmed conscience is to join Isaiah and confess our sins before God. Luther writes,

For my eyes have seen the King, the Lord of hosts. For that reason, he says, "I am lost." But it turned out for the salvation of the prophet that he was thus thrust down to hell, so that he might be led away and lead others away from that uncleanness of the Law to the purity of Christ, so that He alone might reign.

Then flew one to me. Here now a resurrection from the dead takes place. We see that sinners who acknowledge their sins are not abandoned. The prophet cries out that he is lost, that he is oppressed with the consciousness of a defiled mouth, and that he has felt sin and death. And on that account he obtained forgiveness. "If we confess our sins, etc." says 1 John 1:9; and 1 John 2:1 says: "If anyone does sin, we have an advocate with the Father"; so also 1 John 5:18. God hates the sin of hardening and its being defended. Let them be cleansed and let them confess their uncleanness, especially that of the mouth. For where lips and doctrine are unclean, there unclean works follow. Therefore the seraph approaches to set the prophet free from his sin. But he uses means. So, then, two things are set forth to the prophet, namely, Word and sign. The Lord often acts this way. The lips are cleansed by fire. This is the sign. The Word is: "Your guilt be taken away." Here our sacraments are established. Yet these are disdained and shamefully handled by some who say: Nothing external benefits the soul. But let them criticize as much as they want. What Isaiah experiences here is not a fairy tale, but as there are fearful and serious voices, so there is also absolution, which then is granted through the addition of the sign to the Word. Now, what that sign could do, this our Baptism can also do. (16:72–73)

Conclusion

When King Ahaz's heart shook like a tree, he rejected the simple promise of God and resisted the work of the Holy Spirit. His heart trembled before earthly kings but was proud before the heavenly King. Instead of receiving gentle waters from God to refresh his soul, he would be overwhelmed by the flood of the Assyrians. Yet, for the sake of the remnant who heeded God's promises, God gave the house of David the sign of the incarnation. Ahaz only had eyes to see the external attacks on his body and on his kingdom. But God promised through His Son a Kingdom that would endure forever.

Isaiah, on the other hand, was undone when he stood before the heavenly King. In humility, he confessed his weakness and sin. He saw the incarnate One sitting on the throne. God's response, though, was to be gentle toward Isaiah and to atone for his sin. Then Isaiah was sent to proclaim the message of atonement and comfort through God's Word made flesh, the incarnation, to the house of David. The true Son of David would reign eternally, no matter what temporary kingdoms may do.

The conscience, like a smoke detector that cannot rescue a person from a burning house, cannot rescue from death. The conscience detects sin and sounds the alarm. The conscience can only alarm and terrify. Where there is sin, there is the fire of God's wrath. Where God's fire is present, there is the danger of death. Only the firefighter can rescue and save. Jesus is the true firefighter who comes to rescue and to save. The promise of Jesus quiets and comforts the conscience. Through the proclamation of the Gospel, Jesus speaks tenderly to the heart, saying, "Fear not. Do not be afraid." Jesus is the one who extinguishes the flames of hell and rescues us from the fire of God's wrath. As the true firefighter, He not only risks His life, but He also gives up His life to save us.

SATAN ATTACKS THE CONSCIENCE LIKE A CITY

CHAPTER 5

The Gospel message of the person and work of Christ establishes our consciences before the Father. Because of Christ, we are absolved from all our sins, adopted as children of God, and accepted by Him into eternal life. Through the Gospel, the Holy Spirit continues to strengthen our faith in Christ and our love for one another. The conscience is a gift from God. But the devil likes to twist good gifts into tools for his own ends. Therefore, the ancient foe attacks the conscience and tries to choke out the Gospel from the heart of the believer. He constantly tries to rob the conscience of any certainty before God. Thus, there is a struggle in the life of the believer. The believer's conscience is like a city under siege.

Satan's Tactics to Siege the Conscience

One of Satan's tactics is to convince the world that he isn't real or isn't truly powerful. Yet, our culture thinks it understands how Satan works. The cultural portrayal of Satan that we see occurs in movies. There, Satan is depicted either to give people the thrill of imaginary terror, or he is depicted in a most silly style. Cartoons depict the father of lies as a little demon in a red jumpsuit with a pitchfork, goatee, and a pointy tail. Such a silly image is not threatening and inspires jokes. Such a figure typically is portrayed as one of two angels whispering in the ears of a person contemplating an action. The bad angel encourages bad behavior. The good angel seems to represent the conscience promoting good behavior. Usually, the red angel is far more convincing, causing the person to make a decision based on what is fun. The red angel emboldens the individual to ignore the guilt from the conscience. Notice, the cartoons and comics illustrate the activity of the conscience as the court of deliberation between the individual, one angel on the right shoulder, and one angel on the left shoulder. A ruling is required at the time of temptation to misbehave. When the good angel is more persuasive, the bad angel disappears. The decision is made to do the right thing. When the bad angel is more convincing, the good angel disappears. The choice is exercised to do the wrong thing. Yet, it is just a comical depiction of the conflict of the conscience. The attacks of Satan are relegated to the land of make-believe.

Even when movies depict Satan as a serious threat, we receive that message through a horror movie, which we still perceive as very different from real life. Horror movies portray the work of the devil in demon possession, witchcraft, murder, and darkness that stimulates nightmares. He is manifest evil scaring us with the danger of death. The devil is a hideous monster frightening us by his mere appearance. There are those who are fascinated with such an imagination of the spiritual realm. But for most who watch such films, they are just movies. The attacks of Satan are still relegated to the land of make-believe. The stories seem to be so far-fetched that moviegoers see the threats of Satan as pure fiction.

Another one of Satan's tactics is to disconnect the conscience from God's Word, falsely soothing a person's heart and causing him to set up his own image of God (idolatry). Since the Word of God instructs the conscience, Satan does whatever he can to remove it from the heart of the individual and prevent it from taking root. He chokes it out, distorts it, twists it, takes away from it, and adds to it. He assaults people in the time of tribulation and in the time of prosperity. Thus, the individual ends up thinking, "If things go well, it is because I have caused it to happen. If things go poorly, it is because God caused it to happen." As the deceiver, Satan uses the conscience to deceive people in sin. He masquerades as an angel of light (see 2 Corinthians 11:14). He is neither scary nor silly. While believers are warned about the reality of the spiritual realm, Satan blinds the eyes of the unbelievers (see 2 Corinthians 4:3–4).

Satan is the inventor of iniquity and idolatry. He sets up a shop to sell the sweetness of sin. Next door he opens a store to push pretend piety. His goal is to form a false image of God in the heart. This form takes many shapes. Idolatry encourages human effort and endeavor and delivers the devout followers with a false security. They think they please God with their actions. Behind such false beliefs and practices are false spirits. The demons deceive people into presuming everything is right between them and God. Just like he did to Eve, Satan offers his services as a life coach; he is a liar and a murderer from the beginning. He is a fallen messenger with a false message. Satan tries to steal the joy of Jesus from the heart. The devil desires to either oppress with a guilty conscience or soothe with an erring conscience. Sometimes Satan works against the conscience, and sometimes he works with it. Rather than seeing the conflict of the conscience as merely a decision-making dilemma (as our culture would frame it), Luther wants the reader to see the conscience as a spiritual battleground for the soul.

The City under Siege

> In that day this song will be sung in the land of Judah: "We have a strong city; He sets up salvation as walls and bulwarks. Open the gates, that the righteous nation that keeps faith may enter in. You keep him in perfect peace whose mind is stayed on You, because he trusts in You. Trust in the LORD forever, for the LORD GOD is an everlasting rock." (Isaiah 26:1–4)

Based on this imagery, Luther describes the Church as a strong city, the city of God.

We have a firm and powerful city. This is the praise and preaching of the church, against which the gates of hell shall not prevail (Matt. 16:18), because the city is strong in government and priesthood.

He sets up salvation as walls and bulwarks. Wall and dungeon are well guarded, not with wood and iron, but with salvation and

> victory and triumph. These are the fortifications of this new city, that is, the church, which is unconquered, whose salvation is Christ, its Fortification. (16:200)

While earthly Jerusalem would come to an end under the Babylonians, heavenly Jerusalem will stand forever. Even though we have the promise that the gates of hell shall not prevail against the Church, Satan still tries to overthrow the heavenly city. Therefore, the Church still faces problems and persecutions. Rather than fall into doubt and despair, the Church stands firm in faith and hope. Christ does not give peace like the world. He grants us peace in the conscience even though we will experience the hatred of the world.

The individual Christian is assaulted by Satan because the Church is always under attack from Satan. As Luther also says about Isaiah 26,

> The Christian is daily attacked by Satan, and therefore he must keep on trusting forever. Since the battle and struggle to keep the faith is very great, Satan is so wicked that he plots how to sap the strength of him who stands in the Word by making him tired. Satan devises this plan in order to weary those who endure in the Word. So Cyprian describes his wickedness in that he did not want some martyrs, who were most eager to die, to be killed before he had wearied them for a long time. Therefore we must keep on trusting, not for one hour, but always, from the morning watch even to the night. Because the Lord is *an everlasting rock*, that is, greater than the whole world, for that reason Satan attacks us. . . . These things combat the presumption of those who presume upon their own resources, like the superbly situated city that was brought low nevertheless. No one is so fortified and so safe that he cannot fall, and therefore we dare not trust in ourselves. But, on the contrary, even the weak must trust in the Lord. (16:201–2)

Not only is the city of the Church attacked by Satan, but each individual is assaulted too. When Luther discusses the Church, he refers to all believers from all times including the patriarchs; the prophets; the apostles; the martyrs; the Church Fathers; and the believers in his day, our day, and future days. Luther uses the example of Satan's attacks on the consciences of

Christian martyrs in the day of Cyprian, a bishop in North Africa in the third century, to show the continuity between the current Church and the saints who have gone before us. Satan is so wicked that he was not satisfied by the death of these martyrs. He wanted them to suffer as much as possible before they died. Because Satan attacks Christian consciences in all times and places like a relentless siege against a city, the only hope is trusting in the Lord of the city.

The Assyrian Siege of Jerusalem

During the time of Isaiah's prophetic ministry, Judah was attacked by the Assyrians. The Assyrians conquered all the fortified cities of Judah and laid siege to Jerusalem.

> In the fourteenth year of King Hezekiah, Sennacherib king of Assyria came up against all the fortified cities of Judah and took them. And the king of Assyria sent the Rabshakeh from Lachish to King Hezekiah at Jerusalem, with a great army. And he stood by the conduit of the upper pool on the highway to the Washer's Field. And there came out to him Eliakim the son of Hilkiah, who was over the household, and Shebna the secretary, and Joah the son of Asaph, the recorder.
>
> And the Rabshakeh said to them, "Say to Hezekiah, 'Thus says the great king, the king of Assyria: On what do you rest this trust of yours? Do you think that mere words are strategy and power for war? In whom do you now trust, that you have rebelled against me? Behold, you are trusting in Egypt, that broken reed of a staff, which will pierce the hand of any man who leans on it. Such is Pharaoh king of Egypt to all who trust in him. But if you say to me, "We trust in the LORD our God," is it not he whose high places and altars Hezekiah has removed, saying to Judah and to Jerusalem, "You shall worship before this altar"? Come now, make a wager with my master the king of Assyria: I will give you two thousand horses, if you are able on your part to set riders on them. How then can you repulse a single captain among the least of my master's servants, when you trust in Egypt for chariots and for horsemen? Moreover, is it without the LORD that I have come up against this land to destroy it? The LORD said to me, "Go up against this land and destroy it."'" (Isaiah 36:1–10)

In chapter 4, we discussed how the kingdoms of Israel and Syria threatened the kingdom of Judah, terrifying King Ahaz's conscience. He refused to be comforted by the Word of God from the prophet Isaiah. Now we have an account of King Hezekiah in the days when the kingdom of Assyria laid siege to the city of Jerusalem.

The Assault on Hezekiah's Conscience

The Rabshakeh, the official messenger of the king of Babylon, addresses Hezekiah and the people of Jerusalem. He comes to negotiate the terms of surrender. But to make matters worse, he claims to speak with not only the authority of the great king of the Assyrians, but also the authority of Yahweh. Since God alone is the one who hands peoples over to the hands of powerful kings, the Rabshakeh's words shake Hezekiah. Hezekiah questions if perhaps Yahweh is speaking through this foreign official. And yet, as Luther shows, in actuality, Satan is using the Rabshakeh to mock King Hezekiah's faith.

> There follow the blasphemies and attacks of Satan by means of which he assails faith. Let those who were captives consider this blasphemy, how Satan assails a struggling faith by means of boastful examples in order to snatch the Word of the Lord out of the heart. They are deceitful and extremely dreadful schemes, more dreadful than all wars, and appalling blasphemies.
>
> *The great king.* First he introduces the royal majesty. *Thus says the great king*, as if he were God. Here he sets the great king against the little king. The devil is good at this. I am a very small candle; the whole world is nothing but a wind. This is the conclusion Satan and reason come to on the basis of such comparisons.
>
> *On what do you rest this confidence of yours?* This is an inductive argument by which he meets all arguments that could be brought up in reply: "(1) In you there is neither counsel nor power. (2) The trust you put in the king of Egypt amounts to nothing; it is vain. (3) You trust in your God. But He cannot help you and has no desire to do so." Thus these words of the Rabshakeh are the devil's own words, whereby he attacks not the walls but the faith and heart of the king himself. The

The Christian is daily attacked by Satan, and therefore he must keep on trusting forever.

—MARTIN LUTHER

devil attacks you where you are most vulnerable. So they saw the king's faith wavering, and the devil assaults this also. . . .

Behold, you trust that broken reed. Reason might easily do this and rely on physical resources, but faith will not. Thus by a clever device, Satan, that scoundrel, here turns a most beautiful statement of the Holy Spirit against the struggling Hezekiah. It is true. We must not rely on men, as this statement shows. Every human idea is a reedy staff. This is an outstanding maxim to be written over all human reliance, because it will apply to all in line with this comparison. It has been most useful to me to this very day. The comparison is very apt. Outwardly a reed looks whole and solid, but inside it is hollow and weak. It pierces like a spear, but it is nothing, nothing at all. Thus human power is nothing but an empty show. Let us therefore not be deceived by its outward appearance. For if we should lean on it, our hand would be pierced, that is, we would be put to shame in our faith. We are disappointed in the end. The end of this is confusion and destruction. This is what it means to pierce the hand. This is the godless comparison Satan employs against faith. Now follows the third attack.

But if you say to me. Here Satan himself attacks the supreme and unique fortification, namely, to trust in the Lord, something that Isaiah the prophet has long been building up with the utmost effort. The king of Assyria is saying, "You rely on your Lord, but He cannot help you." He grants that He is their God, but he maintains that He is wrathful and does not want to help. "Imagine that your God can help (as He cannot), yet He does not want to, because you, O king, have an angry God, whose statues you have demolished. He would be on our side, not on yours." These are indeed poisonous and loathsome arrows. . . .

These are the techniques of slander. He turns this most godly work of the king into the most criminal rage against King Hezekiah, as if to say: "You have destroyed these altars, where God was worshiped by the fathers. Oho, what you have done?" Satan can advance a similar argument against us, so that all

> the best things we have done, such as the demolition of the Mass, the liberation of monks and nuns, etc., are slandered. By such means Satan assails a struggling faith. (16:308–10)

The Rabshakeh's words strike real fear in Hezekiah. After all, Judah is a small kingdom compared to the large kingdom of Assyria. The Rabshakeh is right: Hezekiah does not have the strength to stand up to Assyria, and Egypt will not help Judah. But what cuts Hezekiah even more sharply is that the Rabshakeh confidently asserts not only that the king of Assyria is Yahweh's instrument, but also that the Rabshakeh even talked to Yahweh and speaks on behalf of Yahweh. These words afflict Hezekiah's conscience. Who should he heed? Is the Rabshakeh speaking the Word of God? Should Hezekiah listen? Should he respond? The voice of the Rabshakeh sounds a lot like what Yahweh has spoken, even through the prophet Isaiah. For example, in Isaiah 8, Yahweh declares that He is bringing judgment on earthly Jerusalem through the Assyrians as His instrument. In Isaiah 31, Yahweh warns His people to not put their trust in earthly kingdoms like Egypt in the time of trouble.

The devil loves to impersonate God's voice. The devil does not want the heart to be sure it knows what is true and what is false. He uses pieces of God's Word to trap the hearer into listening to him, and then he ensures one does not hear the rest, the true voice of the Lord. Even parts of God's Word become a completely different word when it is a word not from the Holy Spirit, but from the evil spirit. How can the conscience be certain that it hears the true voice of God?

Luther explains,

> [It is as if the Rabshakeh is saying,] "I have a propitious God, you have an angry one." So Christ was assailed on the cross. "Let God deliver Him now, if He desires Him" (Matt. 27:43). This is what Satan wants. He moves against our faith, as if to say: "God can help you (something the flesh easily believes), but He does not want to." In this way Satan undermines the spirit of one who suffers wrong, as he did also to Christ on the cross. Above all, Satan bears down on the third confidence, namely trusting in the Lord's mercy. For he says: "Hezekiah is mortal, he is a sinner, he has destroyed the worship of God." Then he says: "I do not come on my own, but I have been ordered by God." He has made of Hezekiah not a petty

> sinner, murderer, or adulterer but an ungodly idolater who has transgressed the first three commandments and whom God does not favor. This was the feeling in Hezekiah's conscience as a result of the slanders of Satan, who makes us believe that all our best works are the worst. The devil makes us feel very guilty. Secondly, he frightens the king by analogy. "Yours is the guilt because you are ungodly. I am holy, and I come by God's order. Yours are the scourges because you have deserved them by your sins." By these fiery darts (Eph. 6:16), of which Peter speaks (1 Peter 4:12), Satan attacks the conscience and confidence, and he must be resisted by a very strong faith. Here the work and toil must not waver. We must say: "Whether I have committed sin or not, I shall not be condemned." Satan must not be listened to, otherwise he will put us to shame. We must not give in to him by agreeing with him, but let us say: "I do not concede this point. Even if I were in the wrong, I would not give in to you." This is what we must do when we are attacked because of the Gospel. Let us not listen to his slanders but say simply, "I believe most certainly that this is true." We must flee for refuge to the Lord's Prayer, lest Satan tempt us beyond our strength. Here, then, you see with what destructive weapons Satan attacks faith. Therefore we must cling to the Word alone. (16:310–11)

Satan spoke through the Rabshakeh. Satan tried to trick Hezekiah into thinking his reform of the liturgy, his extrication of Judah's idols, caused God's disfavor. He tried to give Hezekiah an internal cross to bear before God.

The devil boasts that God is a very present help in time of trouble but that God refuses to help. Like the ancient serpent's approach to Eve, asking the question "Did God really say that?" Satan asks us, "Why hasn't God saved you, since He promised He would?" Satan twists God's Word to create doubt in us regarding the promises of God. Luther notes that the old evil foe tempts Hezekiah to believe that true worship is, in fact, idolatry. Satan calls good evil and evil good; he turns everything upside down. As with Hezekiah, Satan is the accuser who uses our consciences to accuse us and make us feel guilty before God. Thus, Satan portrays the divine image as an unmerciful judge.

However, Satan, working through the Assyrian Rabshakeh,

did not stop there. He also tormented the people of Jerusalem's consciences.

> Then the Rabshakeh stood and called out in a loud voice in the language of Judah: "Hear the words of the great king, the king of Assyria! Thus says the king: 'Do not let Hezekiah deceive you, for he will not be able to deliver you. Do not let Hezekiah make you trust in the L ORD by saying, "The L ORD will surely deliver us. This city will not be given into the hand of the king of Assyria." Do not listen to Hezekiah. For thus says the king of Assyria: Make your peace with me and come out to me. Then each one of you will eat of his own vine, and each one of his own fig tree, and each one of you will drink the water of his own cistern, until I come and take you away to a land like your own land, a land of grain and wine, a land of bread and vineyards. Beware lest Hezekiah mislead you by saying, "The L ORD will deliver us." Has any of the gods of the nations delivered his land out of the hand of the king of Assyria? Where are the gods of Hamath and Arpad? Where are the gods of Sepharvaim? Have they delivered Samaria out of my hand? Who among all the gods of these lands have delivered their lands out of my hand, that the L ORD should deliver Jerusalem out of my hand?'"
>
> But they were silent and answered him not a word, for the king's command was, "Do not answer him." (Isaiah 36:13–21)

Through the taunting of the Rabshakeh, the sly serpent entices the people of Jerusalem to trust him to provide abundant water, wine, and wheat if they rebel against Hezekiah, their king, and switch sides to join the Assyrians. Again, notice how similar the words of the Rabshakeh are to the Word of God. Yahweh promised His people a land of fertile fields and the fruitful vineyards (see Deuteronomy 28:1–14).

To the people, faithfulness to Yahweh seems to elicit the opposite response that they would want. When Ahaz was king, fostering worldly worship, the people had peace and prosperity. Now that Hezekiah has made liturgical reforms to more closely follow God's Word, the Assyrians are breathing down Judah's neck. So, the people have conflicted consciences as well. Should they listen to Hezekiah, who changed their worship style? Or should they listen to the Rabshakeh, who promised them peace and prosperity? The people's conflicted consciences only compound the assaults on Hezekiah's conscience. He may lose the people's trust and support if they decide he is not their righteous leader but rather a sinner who provoked Yahweh to anger.

Luther comments on the Rabshakeh's address to the people in Isaiah 36:13–20 in response to the Jerusalem leaders' request in verses 11–13 that the Rabshakeh not speak to the people:

> *Then Eliakim said: Speak to your servants in Aramaic.* Here is an example of the trial of one who is near despair. He seeks some little support and counsel (as human reason is wont to do) so that the matter might be held in check. So it is in our time. When people say that a peaceful Word should be preached, the result is that the devil becomes all the more insulting, as we see here. These people have asked for quiet, and Satan shouts all the more. Learn this: One must not debate with Satan. Keep this well in mind. The more we wrestle with him in this debate, the more we despair. Do not argue with Satan. Note this, for example: The more someone thinks about the evil lust that should be laid aside, the more he falls into those thoughts, so that one follows closely upon the other and finally he will be in a frenzy. The same happens in the case of the anger that is directed against someone and that should be laid aside. And so it goes in all dangers. When we strive for the remedies, we play into Satan's hands, so that he argues with us all the more and you finally fall into despair, hang yourself, and fall down headlong. So it is always in great trials. Other thoughts keep occurring to a person, as happens in the case of the sick and the troubled. Let go of those thoughts. . . . For Satan is in the habit of disturbing the tenderest consciences in this way. . . .
>
> With mocking and most poisonous words he confounds the weak. His endeavor is altogether contrary to the Holy Spirit. The Holy Spirit reforms, terrifies, and crushes the exalted and the proud and lifts up and nurtures the lowly. The devil, on the contrary, puffs up the proud and causes them to be haughty, but he confounds and destroys the weak and the lowly. Learn to distinguish one spirit from another. Be sure to learn this. In all dangers stop arguing with Satan

altogether. Do not listen to him and think about him. If you do want to think, think about the opposite. If he argues about death, then think about life. . . .

Note that Satan is the supreme orator, who can turn the worst cause into the best one, and the purest faith into treachery and disobedience. . . . He never stops attacking us. Do not listen to him. . . .

He said earlier, "The Lord does not want to help you, because you are sinners." Now he draws a different conclusion. "Granted: He may be merciful to you; He wants to save you. But He cannot." That is indeed an attack! He proves it by citing an example.

Where are the gods of Hamath and Arpad? That is to say: "So many and such great gods were not able to protect their own people from me. How do you expect to be saved by one small god?" Thus you see Satan's oratory pictured in all its unlimited colors and shapes. The king's great army did not have as much force as that internal conflict of the consciences struck by Satan's words. That is: Fighting without, and fears and terrors within (cf. 2 Cor. 7:5).

The king's command was: Do not answer him. You may earnestly observe this advice of the king, for it is thoroughly dependable. This is true, because the more we hear him arguing, the more he reviles us. The more we answer him, the more he wins. Keep still. This is what Ps. 4:4 teaches: "Be angry, but sin not. Be silent." So here we see the king's counsel: "Do not answer him." (16:311–13)

Because Satan is a great orator, Hezekiah does not engage him in a war of words. Instead, he runs for refuge to the promised place of God's presence—the temple.

The Fortification of Hezekiah's Conscience

> As soon as King Hezekiah heard it, he tore his clothes and covered himself with sackcloth and went into the house of the LORD. And he sent Eliakim, who was over the household, and Shebna the secretary, and the senior priests,

covered with sackcloth, to the prophet Isaiah the son of Amoz. They said to him, "Thus says Hezekiah, 'This day is a day of distress, of rebuke, and of disgrace; children have come to the point of birth, and there is no strength to bring them forth. It may be that the LORD your God will hear the words of the Rabshakeh, whom his master the king of Assyria has sent to mock the living God, and will rebuke the words that the LORD your God has heard; therefore lift up your prayer for the remnant that is left.'"

When the servants of King Hezekiah came to Isaiah, Isaiah said to them, "Say to your master, 'Thus says the LORD: Do not be afraid because of the words that you have heard, with which the young men of the king of Assyria have reviled Me. Behold, I will put a spirit in him, so that he shall hear a rumor and return to his own land, and I will make him fall by the sword in his own land.'" (Isaiah 37:1–7)

Though one mouth of Satan be stopped, ten others are opened. Here, I say, the prophet depicts the heart of the holy and godly king. He saw the wavering populace and the blasphemies, and even his heart trembled, as his words show. . . .

This is where he confesses plainly that he has altogether given up and is wavering in his faith, as if he were saying: "Already the day of distress and rebuke and of blasphemy is here." He does not say "a day of deliverance and counsel." . . . These are clearly the words of a despairing king. . . .

The king is in utter despair. But note where the despairing king turns. He joins the prophet and asks him to pray for him. This is the power of despair that it does not permit a man to pray. For a despairing man cannot pray. Therefore he pleads for the intercession of others: "Pray for me." Such is Satan's attack by outside forces. Inside, in the city Satan was a sifter, who drove the people to despair, as Peter experienced at the hand of Satan, the sifter (Luke 22:31). In short: No one, not even the holiest one, can be saved from that cunning of Satan's except by God's grace alone. And God alone sees him, as He showed Peter. No one can escape his siftings. May

> God protect us from him! . . .
>
> Now there was no longer any counsel, hope, or encouragement. Then came the prophet bringing counsel, hope, life, and encouragement. . . .
>
> It is as if he [Isaiah] were saying by way of disparagement: "So far these are just empty words. Do not be afraid of Satan. But the words of Rabshakeh are poisonous and they soften up the spirit. Listen to My [God's] words. They are not empty but very powerful." (16:314–15)

Luther describes Satan's assault on Hezekiah's conscience as a siege against a city. Luther notes that Hezekiah prays during this attack. Prayer is a manifestation of faith, which is rooted in the promises of God. In the time of trouble, the heart becomes forgetful of these promises. Thus, Isaiah assures Hezekiah of the gracious promises of God. With a fortified conscience, Hezekiah can be confident that God is at work even when His work is hidden from the eyes.

Hezekiah received the letter from the hand of the messengers, and read it; and Hezekiah went up to the house of the LORD, and spread it before the LORD. And Hezekiah prayed to the LORD: "O LORD of hosts, God of Israel, enthroned above the cherubim, You are the God, You alone, of all the kingdoms of the earth; You have made heaven and earth. Incline Your ear, O LORD, and hear; open Your eyes, O LORD, and see; and hear all the words of Sennacherib, which he has sent to mock the living God. Truly, O LORD, the kings of Assyria have laid waste all the nations and their lands, and have cast their gods into the fire. For they were no gods, but the work of men's hands, wood and stone. Therefore they were destroyed. So now, O LORD our God, save us from his hand, that all the kingdoms of the earth may know that You alone are the LORD." (Isaiah 37:14–20)

> Hezekiah, somewhat refreshed by words of comfort, now dares to pray to the Lord, when earlier in his despair he did not dare to pray. Now, as one reborn, he dares not only to pray but also to refute the written blasphemies. He is strong again, though not completely restored; yet his faith is constantly

growing, as his very beautiful prayer shows. . . . Then follows the prayer which should be an example to us. . . .

Satan readily lets God be the Lord of hosts, the God of Israel, some little deity, and he permits Him to be enthroned above the cherubim, but that he should be God alone, this Satan opposes. Therefore with a strong faith Hezekiah raises up his spirit and sets his superbly confident prayer against Satan's blasphemies. This is part of the art, that we can overcome Satan, the adversary, from the opposite, as Hezekiah does here. He concedes that Satan has despoiled many lands and conquered many gods, but he does not let him conquer this God. It is as if he were saying: "In this little God he will more than meet his match." . . . Therefore the king here stands by faith, although his God might appear weak, hemmed in, sitting upon the cherubim in one city, while the god of the Assyrians appears strong and capable. Nevertheless, he is not made to stumble because of the weakness of his God, nor is he offended by his foolishness, nor put to shame by the power of the Assyrian. Therefore he says: "I call Thee alone the true God, enthroned above the cherubim." This is the sure method of faith, that for a sure reason we lay hold of our God not on the basis of our ideas, as the forms of righteousness which the sects hold are unsure and unreliable. We, however, cling to our God (though He may seem weak). We know God in the Scriptures, where He is revealed to us, and we ought to know about this God alone and withstand all adversaries. . . . The true worship is to remain with the small and weak God according to His Word and His religion and the place ordained by God. As this is foolish in the eyes of the flesh that seeks a glorious God—and we have found Him in just that foolish form of the flesh—so it is necessary for us not to be offended either by His majesty (which cannot be fathomed) or by His weakness. I have often told you to beware of investigating the Divine Majesty, because this knowledge is not for our head, but it terrifies and oppresses us. As for you, place your foot and your heart in Christ the Propitiator and do not explore loftier matters. . . . *Thou art the God, Thou alone, of all the kingdoms of the earth.* First he begins in weakness and lays hold of his God in foolishness, then he rises to higher ground in the faith that He is the only God of all the kingdoms. This is an excellent example of prayer, in which we see true faith.

Incline Thy ear, O Lord. There again he sets his faith against the blasphemy, as if to say: "The ungodly say that My God is dead, but I know that He is living." All the afflicted have these feelings. They believe that God is dead or asleep. We know by faith, however, that He is living and watchful, that He inclines His ear and opens His eyes. To Him we cry, although any delay disturbs us. This delay is a very heavy cross for the flesh, yes, for outward appearance itself, because in this delay God appears to our spirit to be altogether dead and asleep. In waiting for Him we sense the power of faith, even ours, and we may put ourselves to the test. . . .

Of a truth, O Lord, the kings of Assyria have laid waste. Here he [Hezekiah] indeed grants the major premise. It is true, he [the king of Assyria] has conquered many nations. But it does not follow that he can deliver me. You must say thus: "It is true, Satan is the prince of this world and is more powerful than the weak Christ Himself. But I deny the conclusion, because this foolish and weak God is wiser and stronger than all. He can deliver me and all the rest, because He is enthroned above the cherubim. . . .

So now, O Lord our God. The prayer is short but pregnant with spirit, strongly fortified by faith. Ardent and ready for the battle through the Word, it seeks only the glory of God, not its own advantage. (16:316–18, 319, 320)

When Luther says, "We may put ourselves to the test," he alludes to St. Paul's exhortation that Christians should examine themselves and see if they are still in the faith (see 2 Corinthians 13:5). It is while the believer waits for God to act that he learns the power of God's Word, trusting that God is faithful to His promises.

Though Satan attacked Hezekiah's conscience like an enemy army besieges a city, God spoke His promises to Hezekiah through Isaiah. Hezekiah was strengthened to trust in Yahweh by this proclamation, even in the face of Satan's deception and lies.

The Attacks on the Conscience in Luther's Day

Luther readily applied the example of Hezekiah's response to Satan's attacks to how Christians in Luther's day should respond to Satan's attacks on their consciences. Luther writes,

> *So now, O Lord our God, save us from his hand*, that is, "Hallowed be Thy name." Note, then, that God's victory consists in this, that first we conquer the enemies in our own hearts so that we may drive out the enemy, Satan, the sifter of faith. When by the power of faith in the heart we shall have conquered our enemies and are sure about God's mercy, then despair will leave us, then the comforts and counsels will very easily follow. This is the gist of this passage. For it is characteristic of faith that in our desperation it kills all our own resources and then through the external Word comforts and strengthens and renews us. Ponder this power of the external Word so that you do not despise it, as our Catabaptists dream. (16:319–20)

Catabaptist means "against Baptism." The Catabaptists taught that Baptism was a "work of men's hands." Luther perceived that Christians in his own day who rejected Baptism as the Word of God in visible form applied to the body were attacking the conscience. The Catabaptists rejected the promises of the Lord attached to this outward Means of Grace. Instead, they looked inside their hearts to find the certainty of God's grace. Luther urged Christians to cling to God's external Word—given through Baptism and the other Means of Grace—because the heart can be comforted only by an external word, the voice of God, spoken from outside of the heart. If the believer looks inward, he will hear all kinds of voices that do not belong to God. God's Word comes from outside, entering a person's heart through his eyes and ears. The conscience cannot be reset by what is within a person. It must be overridden from the outside. The Catabaptists in Luther's day only saw in Baptism water with their physical eyes. They thought external experience was weak and insignificant. But Luther frequently pointed the troubled heart to the tangible promise of the Gospel in Baptism. He maintained that the eyes of the heart are lifted up to behold the heavenly reality through the promises of God. He maintained that Baptism is God's work, not a human work.

The Devil's Invasion of Our Consciences

Regardless of time or place, the devil is a tyrant, tyrannizing people by trying to reign over their consciences. One way he tries to reign over our consciences is by instructing us to practice pretend piety based on human effort. When the conscience alarms us, then Satan lies to us. He teaches us to take self-defense classes. He speaks to those of us who are prone to self-help guides, saying, "Hide your iniquity by your own efforts. Make satisfaction for your sins. Self-chosen methods of self-justification and self-righteousness impress God. After all, God helps those who help themselves." Thus, he erects the image of a god who is a crooked judge who can be bribed. This leaves us in empty hope.

When the conscience becomes dirty and malfunctions, the ancient serpent seduces us into thinking that since our deeds are right in our sight, then they are all right with God. He reminds us that God is love. Thus, he sets our eyes on the image of a god that is not holy. This leaves us with an empty faith. The devil loves to give a false sense of spiritual security.

When Satan has twisted our consciences to excuse us and confirm that we are blameless and innocent in our thinking, speaking, and acting, the devil fuels our downward spiral to do more and more of what we say is right. He inflates our ego and increases pride in our heart. He praises our work. He whispers in our ear, "You are good. You are righteous. You are holy." Thus, he places before our eyes the image of a god who is merely a parole officer checking up on our progress in the work-release program from prison.

Once the conscience is broken, the evil foe commends us and compliments us on advancing beyond childish games of guilt. To such people, he loves to be a cartoon character that poses no threat. He whispers his lies, "You have now become free to sin. You no longer need to worry about pleasing others. Please yourself. There is no other God besides you to tell you what to do." Thus, he establishes that there is no image of God except oneself. After all, God is invisible. Since one cannot see God, He must not exist. At this point, the conscience is seared and completely turned off because when the conscience is bound to anything other than God's Word, it is idolatry.

One of the craftiest ways Satan tries to tyrannize the Christian conscience is to take God's Word and threaten the Christian with

God's Law. Luther allegorically interprets the Assyrian's siege of Jerusalem as Satan's siege of our consciences with the Law. Generally, Luther was cautious to use allegorical interpretation methods. However, Luther loves to give us examples of properly using allegories to point us to faith in Christ.

> Faith must be built up on the basis of history, and we ought to stay with it alone and not so easily slip into allegories, unless by way of metaphor we apply them to other things in accordance with the method of faith. So here Jerusalem can allegorically be called our conscience, which has been taken and laid waste by the terror of the Law and then set free out of the remnant and the sprouts, and the restored conscience is saved by the Word of the Gospel, through which we grow up into mature manhood by the knowledge of God (cf. Eph. 4:13). Such allegory must be used in accordance with the Word of the Law and the Gospel, and this is the explanation of different matters by the same Spirit. These things must not be twisted to apply to works and station in life, as our papists have done, and both Origen and Jerome in their allegories are members of the same allegorical clan. Therefore note that allegories properly pertain to the Word, as Paul used it in Galatians (Gal. 4:22ff.). I have called these things to your attention so that you may beware of a vulgar use of allegories. So here, where I refer it to the Word and to faith when I compare Jerusalem allegorically to our conscience that is terrified by the Law. . . . This is the summary of Scripture: It is the work of the Law to humble according to history, externally and internally, physically and spiritually. It is the work of the Gospel to console, externally and internally, physically and spiritually. What our predecessors have experienced according to history externally and physically, this we experience according to our history internally and spiritually. . . . Allegorically we can refer it to the conscience, killed and revived. . . . This is the comfort, that we do not despair in matters that to the flesh appear impossible to restore. (16:327–28)

The Law of God condemns us all because of sin we inherited from Adam and Eve and because of sin we have committed. We all stand guilty before God as sinners. But when God's Law through our consciences accuses us of sin, Satan loves to join

Therefore these are the greatest blessings of God: To believe that God takes hold of us and makes us alive.

—MARTIN LUTHER

in and become our accuser all the more. He agrees with the Law and our conscience. He proclaims to us loud and clear that we have sinned and are guilty before God. He convinces us so much of our sin that we start to believe God could not possibly love us. Thus, he places in our heart the image of a god who is an unmerciful judge who cannot be appeased and is not love. He wants to scare the heaven out of us. This leaves us in despair. In this spiritual battle, the goal of the Christian faith is to let God be God and give God the glory. Thus, we are called to cling to the voice of God and not listen to Satan, who is the father of lies. God's voice tells us that though we are sinners, we can never pay for our sin by our guilt. God does not give us an internal cross to bear. Rather, we have freedom through what He has done to pay for our guilt. Christ came to set the captives free, giving sight to the blind, hearing to the deaf, freedom to the heart, and joy to the conscience. The Lord's voice never promises us the lack of external trouble. In fact, the external crosses that God gives us are for the mortification of our flesh, which is for our benefit. But He does promise us peace in our consciences now and external peace for eternity, no matter what trouble may come in this life.

> Every trial has this misery that it scares man into thinking that this is sin. When sickness and misfortunes come, Satan, too, soon comes and troubles the conscience, and for that reason a Christian must fight with his conscience and with his body. Here Satan shakes us with various conscience scruples and attacks us as if he were fighting against Cerberus, the Lernaean Hydra, and other monsters. Soon Satan draws the conclusion in our consciences: "God is not at all well disposed toward you because He did not help you." Thus any affliction has a tail, namely, that we think God is unmerciful. Such a conscience thoroughly frightens man, so that we imagine death has a thousand teeth, while it has none; and the greater our weakness, the more Satan harasses us with despair, when our conscience ought to be surrounded with the more joy. Let all trials have their heartache. Therefore these are the greatest blessings of God: To believe that God takes hold of us and makes us alive. (16:343)

Sometimes Satan enters the conscience like he's taking over a city. Thus, we end up fighting against our own conscience.

Here Luther uses the images of Greek mythology. Cerberus was the multiheaded hound of Hades who prevented the dead from leaving the underworld. Hydra was the multiheaded sea serpent stationed at the entrance to the underworld. His breath was poisonous. If you cut off one of his heads, it would regenerate and duplicate. Thus, in a similar way, Satan comes against us with multiple heads and poisonous breath. In this life, the believer is assailed by the storms of the conscience and the evil Leviathan who has more multiplying heads than a Hydra. One head pops up stating that God *can* help us but does not *want* to help us. Next, a head pops up telling us that we are doing good works and not sinning. Then, a head pops up and tempts us to sin. Subsequently, a head pops up and accuses us of sinning, which brings God's displeasure. Another head pops up declaring that God is not disposed toward us. Later, a head pops up boasting that God is not merciful. The more we attempt to cut off the head, the more heads appear. This sea serpent is relentless. He does not want us to hold faith and a good conscience. He desires that we make shipwreck of our faith. Like a boa constrictor, he squeezes out the breath and breathes despair and doubt into the heart.

Isaiah writes regarding God's protection of His people,

> I, the LORD, am its keeper; every moment I water it. Lest anyone punish it, I keep it night and day; I have no wrath. Would that I had thorns and briers to battle! I would march against them, I would burn them up together. (Isaiah 27:3–4)

Luther uses this passage to describe God's response to the Christian's conflict of conscience during trials.

This is strengthening for the fearful church. He says: "I cannot be enraged. I appear to be enraged, but it is not true." We feel it as wrath, but it is not wrath, just as parents are not wrathful when they chastise their children. Let this be a gloss regarding all the tribulations of Christians, which should be inscribed for the godly in all persecutions: *I have no wrath.* Note this.

Who will give me thorns and briers! This is said in opposition to our evil and carnal thoughts and the designs of the devil, which turn one so kind into one enraged and harsh as a thorn and brier. For Satan and the flesh act thus that when the kindly Lord thrusts us into dangers, they argue impatiently: "The Lord has forgotten me, He is angry with me, He has thorns, etc."

I would set out to battle against them. It is as if He were saying: "My Christian is indeed in difficulties, but I will go to war and battle for him and defend him. Therefore he must not believe that I have thorns and briers, but much more that I am a waterer and defender and that 'a bruised reed I will not break, and a dimly burning wick I will not quench'" (Is. 42:3). Therefore with these words He here reproves those who make Him out to be hard as a thorn, and He comforts His own, so that they might take refuge with Him in all tribulations, knowing that there is no wrath in Him.

I would burn them up together. These are still the words of God, who is chiding our notion which conceives of God as wrathful and as a severe and incendiary destroyer. When He chastens us out of His goodness, then our reason argues that God is drawing us into the lowest hell. The godly and the church have this temptation in tribulations, a temptation which He reproves. They should not harbor such thoughts but rather believe that in these divine trials they are protected and never destroyed, because He Himself is their guardian and bishop. Thus the afflicted Paul prayed the Lord thrice, but God did not remove the affliction, saying: "My grace is sufficient for you, etc." (2 Cor. 12:9). Let this teach the weak and faint brothers to be consoled, because they may be persuaded by Satan that God is angry when they experience tribulations. (16:212–13)

In responding to Isaiah's words,

> Has He struck them as He struck those who struck them? Or have they been slain as their slayers were slain? (Isaiah 27:7),

Luther writes,

[It is as if God said,] "I will not smite My church the way someone is smitten by enemies. I will not allow it to be thus smitten, but I chasten and chastise it. I do not smite with the blow of a smiter, I do not kill in the manner of killing, but in the manner of making alive." "The Lord brings down to Sheol and raises up" (1 Sam. 2:6). Let every Christian know, therefore, that his tribulation is not evil but good, imposed by a good God. It is not as reason and Satan argue: "You are poor, cast off, and thoroughly afflicted. God is hard and unmerciful, He has forgotten you, He is your enemy and adversary." Such afflicted consciences can be abundantly consoled by this chapter [Isaiah 27]. For from it we can draw plentiful arguments for a letter of comfort: (1) Trust, child. (2) I, the Lord, am your keeper. (3) I will instantly water day and night. (4) I have no wrath. (5) Who thinks that I am thorn and brier and exceedingly hard? (6) I am so powerful. No one will hold back My strength. (7) I will have such a peace that My vineyard will take root and flourish. I smite and chasten you not with the smiting of the smiter, but in the manner of a keeper and a father. (16:214)

When the conscience is anchored to the Word of God, the waves and winds of this life cannot sink the heart. Christ comes to breathe the life-giving Spirit back into our hearts, assuring us to take refuge in Him. He alone can crush the head of the serpent. Christ takes hold of us and makes us alive, and no one can take us out of His hand. He is God for us and God with us. He shelters us on top of the water of the floods. He leads us on dry land through the sea. He pulls us out of the depths of the ocean. He guides us to the gentle waters and restores our souls. Where water drowns and swallows up in death, Christ resuscitates and raises up in life.

The Church Prepares Believers for Battle

Through the Church, the Word is heard. Through the Word, the Spirit is given. Thus, we become children of God through the work of the Holy Spirit in the Word. Satan is an evil spirit who attacks the Church and distorts the clear voice of God in the external Word. He robs God of His glory, and then he turns around and robs us of the comfort from God's mercy. If we become lazy, we neglect the Word of God. If we become conceited, we reject the Word of the Lord. The only way we can stand firm under the assaults of the devil is to cling to the promises of God by faith.

All your children shall be taught by the LORD, and great shall be the peace of your children. In righteousness you shall be established; you shall be far from oppression, for you shall not fear; and from terror, for it shall not come near you. If anyone stirs up strife, it is not from Me; whoever stirs up strife with you shall fall because of you. Behold, I have created the smith who blows the fire of coals and produces a weapon for its purpose. I have also created the ravager to destroy; no weapon that is fashioned against you shall succeed, and you shall refute every tongue that rises against you in judgment. This is the heritage of the servants of the LORD and their vindication from Me, declares the LORD. (Isaiah 54:13–17)

He says *your sons*, the sons of mother church. The church feeds and supports its own by means of the spoken Word. Since the church is on earth, there is need of the Word. The spoken Word is needed to produce and to keep children. *Taught by the Lord*, by the Spirit of God. Both must be there. Mother church bears her children through the Word. . . . For you see that everywhere in Scripture the Word and its teachers are commended. The children of the church have to hear by means of the Word and come to faith through the work of God. The Word is from the mother, the Spirit from the Father. The voice gathers us into the church, and the Spirit unites us with God. Thus a son of the church hears the Word and is a disciple of God. No reason, I say, can produce this meditation of faith, but only God grants it. Teaching produces the new man and rejects all thoughts clinging to things that are evident, to one's own merits and works. This is what happened to me when I was self-righteous, a monk. The thoughts of faith, however, are above all thoughts of reason. Government and business pass judgment on the basis of things that appear. The Christian faith judges concerning things that are not evident and are not seen, even in contrary matters, so that it may believe in Him whom it does not see. And yet it must cling to this Helper whom it does not see as a helper. This kind of thinking is taught by the Lord. . . . Anyone who believes has this consolation, that he is a son of the church and one taught by God, since our reason and our powers cannot achieve this. . . .

Here you see whence peace comes; it is born of faith. No work-righteous man, no Enthusiast, can have peace. Always their opinion is doubtful, they are not sure about God's grace, and they are wearied with endless works. The godly man, however, since he has the Word, is certain and at peace, and he says, "If God is for me, if I am His son, who will harm me? What harm will death or Satan do to me? None." He who has the most certain Word also has a very sure faith; he will have a serene heart.

And you shall prosper in righteousness. . . . Of this Paul says that every man who believes is also equipped for every good work (cf. 2 Tim. 3:17). The ungodly indeed is not equipped for a good work. The godly man has no peace; he has trouble, but he is a vessel prepared and an established outward figure for ruling and living. This is what [righteousness] means, an external righteousness flowing out of faith. It means to conduct oneself with a good conscience in the presence of God, and outwardly, in the presence of the world, to be ready for prayer, for control of one's wife, children, and family. The Word will cause us a lot of grief, but there will be a fruitful and abundant peace, which will turn all disagreeable things into agreeable ones for him. He can build himself up in all things, and the bad things will turn out good for him. . . .

You shall be far from slander and injury. Not that there will be no slander; that is impossible. Yea, all things will be on your back, but they will not harm you. Slander will not come near. Though it will come upon the flesh, it will not enter the conscience. Since patience is the victor over all evils, this slander in your flesh will not harm you in your conscience and the realm of the spirit. All your life they will leave good works alone. . . .

You shall be far from anxiety. There will be nothing to frighten you. The fears and terrors of the ungodly ought not trouble you

> but edify you, and they will not draw near to you. As for you, remain firm and do good works, because you have the church for a mother and God for a Father. (17:243–44, 245–46)

Satan does not want us to have and to hold on to God's Word. The devil wants to deform our consciences and print a false image of God on our hearts. He does not want us to see and know God for who God has revealed Himself to be: the baby born in Bethlehem and the man crucified on the cross. He tricks us into forming our own gods. The deceiver deceives us into thinking that spirituality is about what we feel. Feelings come and go. They are temporary, but the Word of the Lord endures forever. With the Word, the Christian can fight against his own experiences in both his body and conscience. By faith alone in the promises of Christ, we let God be God. We are taught to be still and wait patiently for His deliverance and salvation.

CHAPTER 6

THE NEW CREATION

When sin and death entered creation through the work of Satan, God made a promise that He would restore creation through the mystery of the incarnation. The Seed of the Virgin would crush the serpent's head (see Genesis 3:15; Isaiah 7:14; 9:1–7). In Christ, God would make all things new. The apostle Paul declares, "Therefore, if anyone is in Christ, he is a new creation. The old has passed away; behold, the new has come" (2 Corinthians 5:17). All the things of the old creation will come to an end: sin, sickness, sorrow, suffering, and sadness. Yet, the new things cannot come without the incarnation. God must enter into His creation, assuming the human nature, to defeat death and the devil for us. For Luther, everything in the new creation revolves around the incarnation. The new preaching of Christ crucified creates a new Zion. The person and work of Christ, the mediator of the New Testament, brings about a new heaven and a new earth.

The End of Old Zion

Although God comforted Hezekiah and His people by saving them from the assault of the Assyrians around 701 BC, the leaders of Jerusalem continued to mock the message of

God's messengers, provoking God's wrath. Thus, He handed them over to the king of Babylon in 587 BC (see 2 Chronicles 36:15–21). Isaiah prophesied about how the earthly kingdom of Jerusalem would come to an end, just like any other physical kingdom. The threats of judgment came down like a hammer, smashing every human endeavor. The Lord was at war with His people. He worked through the new world power, the Babylonians, to painfully humiliate and defeat His people. The throne of David was overthrown. The temporary temple was toppled to the ground. The promise of the perpetual Davidic monarchy and the longevity of the Levitical sacrifices came to an end. The image of God pressed down hard upon their hearts. Their consciences cried out, "Guilty as charged! Guilty as charged!" Satan amplified the accusation, pushing them to doubt and despair. Their sin scattered them and separated them from Yahweh. The city of Jerusalem was no different from the cities of Sodom and Gomorrah. It was a wasteland, and the leaders were led in captivity to a foreign land, leaving the people in a dry land.

The destruction of Jerusalem, by all appearances, looked like the end of Yahweh's covenant with His people. It seemed the Babylonians had triumphed. God's promises appeared to be null and void (see Isaiah 40:27). His own temple was destroyed, while the Babylonian Empire seemed to extend to the ends of the earth. As a result, the idolatry of the Babylonians seemed more enticing than ever. The prosperity of Babylon seemed to show that Yahweh was blessing their style of worship.

In the people's minds, the glory of the Babylonians overshadowed the glory of Yahweh. The people were left unclean and unholy. There was no more shedding of blood with the Word of God to atone for their sins at the temple in Jerusalem.

The New Preaching Brings About a New Creation

But God did not leave His people wondering why Jerusalem was destroyed. Nor did He let them think the Babylonians were more powerful than He. Through Isaiah, God revealed that He was the one working through the Babylonians. And yet in His mercy, He also promised that His word of judgment would not be His final word. Instead, He would speak a renewing word that would create anew all that had been destroyed.

As Luther notes, there is a switch that takes place between Isaiah 39 and 40. Isaiah 1–39 is for the people before the Babylonian captivity. Isaiah 40–66 is for the people after they have been sent into exile in Babylon.

We rightly divide Isaiah into two books. We have heard the first one, in which the prophet has functioned as a historical prophet and leader of the army, because so far he has prophesied concerning Christ and concerning the defeat of the king of Assyria. Then he has both comforted and reproved the people.

In the following book the prophet treats two matters: Prophecies concerning Christ the King and then concerning Cyrus, the king of Persia, and concerning the Babylonian captivity. This second book is nothing but prophecy, first external, concerning King Cyrus, and then spiritual, concerning Christ. And here the prophet is the most joyful of all, fairly dancing with promises. The next four chapters prophesy the most joyful things concerning Christ and the church in our time. (17:3)

A voice cries: "In the wilderness prepare the way of the LORD; make straight in the desert a highway for our God. Every valley shall be lifted up, and every mountain and hill be made low; the uneven ground shall become level, and the rough places a plain. And the glory of the LORD shall be revealed, and all flesh shall see it together, for the mouth of the LORD has spoken." (Isaiah 40:3–5)

By this prophecy Isaiah promises a new kind of teaching beyond that which had been in vogue heretofore. For in this way the evangelists begin. *The voice of one crying.* It is as if he were saying: "The preaching of the Law was a muttering, incomplete and unpleasant to all ears, and produced nothing but hypocrites. But here comes a *voice*, a clear and complete and universal proclamation which purely and joyously and most loudly declares that the warfare is ended and that sins are forgiven." This is received from a "voice," that is, through the public preaching of the Word. It must be heard and received from a speaking voice. Away with our schismatics, who spurn

> the Word while they sit in corners waiting for the Spirit's revelation, but apart from the voice of the Word! (17:7–8)

Luther constantly teaches the importance of the external Word in opposition to the inward experiences and imagination of the corrupted heart. The external Word is a preached Word heard from the mouth of Isaiah, John the Baptizer, Jesus, the apostles, the evangelists, and the successors to the apostolic office in our day—the preaching office. Thus, Luther refers to the Church as the mouth-house of God where the living voice of God is heard through preaching—preaching that brings the new creation.

The New King

God humbles the exalted and exalts the humble (see Isaiah 2:11). He wounds and He heals (see Deuteronomy 32:39). After the demolition of the old Zion, Yahweh was ready to begin the rebuilding project. When the old kingdom was gone, then the people could look for a new King.

> In that day the branch of the LORD shall be beautiful and glorious, and the fruit of the land shall be the pride and honor of the survivors of Israel. (Isaiah 4:2)

> The *Branch* is Christ. Yet there is nothing that He seems to do less than grow. The world would rather say that Christ and His Christians are a dried up tree trunk. But they are not regarded as such before God. . . .
>
> The kingdom of the Jews was glorious in a physical way, but the kingdom of Christ is now glorious in the spirit. He says, however, that Christ should be extolled with great majesty. . . .
>
> He calls Christ One who comes from the fruit of the land because He was born great from the earth, and it is His greatness that He can prevail over all His enemies and protect all His own; and this is a description of Christ as He defends us. Such a One, he says, Christ will be, but for those who will be from among those who have been snatched out of Jerusalem, as he also says. And here he sets forth the fruit of their riches which He will distribute, because Christ will

be such a One not only for Himself but will distribute His benefits to the rest. Thus because of Him and through Him they will be called saints, that is, people set aside for divine purposes, people in whom God dwells and who belong to the employment and service of God. (16:51)

The title *Branch* refers to the promised messianic King; we also hear in Jeremiah 23:5–6 that the Messiah will be a righteous Branch for David, raised up to reign as king. He will be called "The LORD is our Righteousness" (Jeremiah 23:6; see also Zechariah 3:8; 6:12). Similar imagery is reflected in Isaiah 11 when the coming Davidic King is called a "shoot from the stump of Jesse" and "a branch from his roots" (v. 1). The image of a branch and a shoot are used because they represent new life and new creation in agriculture. The kingdom of the Branch will sprout out and extend to the ends of the earth and into eternity (see Isaiah 42:9; 43:19; 44:4; 45:8; 55:10; 58:8; 61:11).

> There shall come forth a shoot from the stump of Jesse, and a branch from his roots shall bear fruit. (Isaiah 11:1)

A Branch shall grow out of his roots. Better: a "Shoot," . . . will bear fruit from his root. This is what he called Christ, and such is the beginning of the rising spiritual kingdom. It is obviously different from that of an earthly kingdom, where an assembly of people is provided with a king. In this case the King is born first, and then He gathers a people for Himself. At first there will be a single Sprout risen out of the root, from the old and hopeless trunk, which is nevertheless watered with a divine strength. *The stump of Jesse* is the family of David. To him the promise was made in Ps. 132:11: "One of the sons of your body." To this promise the prophet refers here, and he points to the time in which the spiritual kingdom is to have its beginning, namely, when the stump of David will be regarded as lost, so that nothing is less hoped for than that a shoot should sprout up from the root. (16:117–18)

When Isaiah sets our eyes on the new King, he uses a whole list of images that are not typically associated with a king. This is a new Kingdom bringing new things. The new King's kingdom is spiritual, through which the Holy Spirit is active in the hearts of believers. The Holy Spirit brings righteousness and justice, cleansing those who believe in Christ and making them holy.

> And he who is left in Zion and remains in Jerusalem will be called holy, everyone who has been recorded for life in Jerusalem, when the Lord shall have washed away the filth of the daughters of Zion and cleansed the bloodstains of Jerusalem from its midst by a spirit of judgment and by a spirit of burning. (Isaiah 4:3–4)

When the Lord shall have washed away, etc. This is also a part of the riches distributed through Christ. He who has begun to believe in Christ departs from evil. For to the faithful is given the Holy Spirit, who cannot be inactive when He is in your hearts. For first He cleanses the flesh from sin in order that the eyes, the hands, the tongue, and the other members may be clean; and indeed He cleanses more every day. Then He fights with death and the devil in order that He may drive them away too. For the most part they stay with us to serve as an exercise for us and as tempters. Otherwise we would not know how much filth there is in us. Likewise that Christ may have something to do in us. And in this way the Holy Spirit is the consuming fire, etc. For this reason we are attacked by many in order that He may always have something to boil away. . . .

And cleansed the bloodstains of Jerusalem, that is, the guilt and the old Adam. But at heart we are all thieves, fornicators, murderers, and envious persons. All these are evidences of the filth that must be washed away through the Spirit. (16:51–52)

Next, Isaiah uses imagery from Israel's first exodus to describe the new exodus that will take place with the new King (see Luke 9:31; the Greek word for "departure" is ἔξοδος [*exodos*]).

> Then the LORD will create over the whole site of Mount Zion and over her assemblies a cloud by day, and smoke and the shining of a flaming fire by night; for over all the glory there will be a canopy. There will be a booth for shade by day from the heat, and for a refuge and a shelter from the storm and rain. (Isaiah 4:5–6)

The Christian has no other cover than Christ.

—MARTIN LUTHER

First he describes the riches of Christ's kingdom, then the mortification resulting from the fruits of Christ's kingdom. Now comfort in the cross follows.

Then the Lord will create. He comforts in the way the Holy Spirit usually does. It is as if He were saying: "You will be sheep for the slaughter." This is what we see today. There are no people so wretched as the Christians. They are deprived of honor, riches, life, etc., and they are afflicted with so many evils that they would all fall away from Christ if they did not receive help from God in Christ. What Christ said (John 13:16) must be fulfilled: "A servant is not greater than his master." And Paul says (Rom. 8:17): "Provided we suffer with Him in order that we may also be glorified with Him." And this fight is very much against the flesh, because it is weak. The flesh has eyes only for present things; it considers good only what turns out advantageously and concludes that God is favorable only in prosperity. From adversity it concludes that God is hostile. And yet the very opposite is true here, so that it may be strengthened in such experiences. This comfort is here written by the prophet. (16:52–53)

> Christ is the new king who will be present with His people in the new exodus just like He was present with them in the old exodus in, with, and under the pillar of cloud by day and the pillar of fire by night.
>
> Luther also understands Isaiah's imagery to mean Christ will be the protection for God's people night and day. He goes on to say more about how Christ is the only true and sure covering and protection for God's people.

The Christian has no other cover than Christ; he does not rely on the arm of flesh, for there is no salvation in man, nor on good works, for they are not good in the presence of God. The Christian should teach and act in such a way that he may dare to stand in the presence of God. But the faithful are supported by the Word alone. The heat [in Isaiah 4:6] is an internal attack, when the conscience is smitten by the wrath of God, an attack which it also feels when the wrath of God is experienced. It is called the lash of God, and that because it is a punishment that God thus inflicts in a fatherly spirit.

Yet because our nature feels it with extreme anguish, it is called wrath, even though God is not angry but loves whom He chastises. Satan is added to this anguish, and despair is increased. As a result there is distress within and without, which is the heat, and it is called spiritual. God, however, chastises so that the power of the Word may be shown to us and Satan may see that the Word is invincible and so that thus the power of the Holy Spirit may be glorified. He who has regard for the crowd or tries to gain the good will of princes is deceived, because there is no help in man. Such people cause destruction. Thus God said to Ahaz that he should not fear the king of Syria and promised that He would be his protector, but Ahaz did not believe it (cf. Is. 7:3ff.). Faintheartedness is not made strong with hands but by the Word of God, which alone heartens and causes to stand. If you trust in men, you will have help neither from them nor from God, who forsakes those who forsake Him. For the Word of God is the exceedingly strong tower of Zion and the pavilion of God offering protection in prosperity and adversity.

Rain. These are the external pressures. In all things Christ is our Defense. (16:54)

Both from the internal attacks of our conscience and the external attacks of the world, Christ is our defense. He covers us and protects us. Luther goes on to say,

To be sure, it is true that one who has never felt his sin can contemplate God, or better, weave his phantasies about God; he can for a while reach out for the godhead he has invented for himself. But one who feels his sin and becomes fainthearted from fear of God will soon withdraw his foot from his speculations and turn to Christ, and he will be better off. He will have coolness in the shade, protection in the pavilion, banishment of Satan and of evil thoughts, also strength against all the gates of hell (Matt. 16:18), etc. The names applied to Christ in this text should, however, be carefully studied, so that we may know what has been given to us in Christ and that in Him there is victory and light. (16:56)

The New Zion

> Go on up to a high mountain, O Zion, herald of good news; lift up your voice with strength, O Jerusalem, herald of good news; lift it up, fear not; say to the cities of Judah, "Behold your God!" Behold, the Lord GOD comes with might, and His arm rules for Him; behold, His reward is with Him, and His recompense before Him. He will tend His flock like a shepherd; He will gather the lambs in His arms; He will carry them in His bosom, and gently lead those that are with young. (Isaiah 40:9–11)

> [Isaiah] prophesied that Jerusalem would be destroyed, but now, on the contrary, that it would be made a strong dwelling. These two conflict, and therefore Zion should here be taken for the church, which is the new Zion. Wherever the Word of God is preached, there is Zion. (16:53)

> Having driven out the glory of the flesh, the prophet establishes the judge on Mount Zion who shall rule over us. Having torn down the contrary worship of God, he undertakes to build the new worship of the Gospel and the New Testament, which teaches, consoles, and builds up. (17:13)

Luther says the new Zion, the re-created Zion, is the Church. In the new Zion, the true, life-giving worship of God takes place. The true worship of God through the Gospel proclaims, "Behold your God!" concerning the incarnate God, that is, the glory of God becoming flesh for us. "Though He was in the form of God," He emptied Himself and took "the form of a servant, being born in the likeness of men" (Philippians 2:5–11). Although He was rich, He became poor for our sake so that we by His poverty might become rich in Him (see 2 Corinthians 8:9).

In the new Zion, there is no need to be afraid. In Christ, God's re-creative Word works in the heart and opens human ears to hear the voice of God once again. Christ is the Good Shepherd who lays down His life for His sheep. His sheep know His voice. Luther notes how charming it is to hear that Christ carries the weak little lambs in His arms. He receives all who hear His Word. The Lord loves to freely give His grace and shine His face upon us through His works that He does for us. He brings truth and grace. He is incarnate truth, and from Him we receive grace upon grace. Behold, the true Man who knew no sin but was made sin for us so that "we might become the righteousness of God" (2 Corinthians 5:21).

The New Name

> For Zion's sake I will not keep silent, and for Jerusalem's sake I will not be quiet, until her righteousness goes forth as brightness, and her salvation as a burning torch. The nations shall see your righteousness, and all the kings your glory, and you shall be called by a new name that the mouth of the LORD will give. You shall be a crown of beauty in the hand of the LORD, and a royal diadem in the hand of your God. You shall no more be termed Forsaken, and your land shall no more be termed Desolate, but you shall be called My Delight Is in Her, and your land Married; for the LORD delights in you, and your land shall be married. For as a young man marries a young woman, so shall your sons marry you, and as the bridegroom rejoices over the bride, so shall your God rejoice over you. (Isaiah 62:1–5)

And you shall be called by a new name. These are pure promises. "From now on you shall have a different name." Which is that name? Before this they were called Zion, Jerusalem, the people of Israel, the seed of Abraham, whose are the covenant, the fathers, and the promise. These were their physical names which have been done away in the New Testament. You are not a Christian because you have Moses, the Law, the promises, and Christ in a physical sense. But this is our name: He who has come to faith in Christ on the basis of the Word. This is the new name, derived from Christ and the Son of God, and it is not carnal but spiritual. The Christian is proud of this name even in the most severe persecutions. He is properly called Christian because he simply depends on Christ without all merits, his own righteousness, and without all works. It is not because of these that he is called Christian. But here his heart and his boasting rest in Christ's righteousness, salvation, and redemption. . . .

> Note, however, that according to substance and appearance the church is a harlot, illegitimate and forsaken. But in the Word the church is seen as a bride, Hephzibah ["My Delight Is in Her"], and beloved son. In faith the heart must be convinced that it is Christ's Beulah ["a land that has a master"], Hephzibah, and bride, and in the midst of tribulations such a person rejoices and is glad. For he knows that Christ's righteousness is his own. This produces cheerful hearts and consciences and good theologians, who are then in the best position to teach and console others. (17:345, 346–47)

A new name comes from the incarnation. Jesus is called "My servant" by the Father (Isaiah 42:1) and believers in Him are also called "My servants" (65:13–14). Jesus is called the witness (see 55:4), and those who are in Christ are to be His witnesses (see 44:8). The One who is called the Branch, Immanuel, Wonderful Counselor, Mighty God, Prince of Peace, and Everlasting Father comes to make all things new. So, He gives us a new name. Jerusalem was the unfaithful city, but now in Christ she is called the faithful city (see 1:21, 26). She was forsaken and desolate; now in Christ she is called "My Delight Is in Her" and God rejoices in Her (see 54:1–7; 60:15; 62:4–5). Isaiah also announces the new name of the forgiven people of God as "The Holy People," "The Redeemed of the LORD," "Sought Out," and "A City Not Forsaken" (62:12). We are named Christians. It means we depend on Christ for all things. So, we do not live by sight. We do not draw near to God based on our own strength or righteousness, because that would be trusting in the things we see with our eyes. Rather, we live by faith, trusting in Christ's promises. He opens the eyes of our hearts and enlightens us (see Ephesians 1:18). We have seeing ears because we behold God with us, Immanuel, when we hear God's Word. We have hearing eyes that know His voice connected to tangible means. The Sacraments are the visible Word of God. We look at water, bread, and wine. We approach the Father with "hearts sprinkled clean from an evil conscience and our bodies washed with pure water" (Hebrews 10:22). We listen to Jesus baptizing us with the Holy Spirit, giving us His body to eat, and pouring out His blood to drink. With faith, we come into the Father's presence as the result of Christ's strength and His righteousness, trusting in the things we see with our ears and hear with our eyes.

The people of the new name will be a blessed people, but this will not be apparent. Nevertheless, they will have their being forever in the faithful God, because it is such a name of blessing that people may bless themselves with it and swear by it. As surely as I am a Christian, we who swear by this name speak a word of blessing. A second stumbling block for Christians is a matter not only of faith but also of the Word. They throw up to us that Christ is completely human, hence He is not God. With this word he secretly attacks the stumbling block of the Jews who take offense at the incarnation of Christ. To them he replies that Christ will be God in whom the oath will be and who will be the *faithful God*. Thus in a hidden way he replies to the Turks and Jews and all unbelievers who take offense at Christ, the man. Reason quickly turns the eyes away from that man to some God, as Philip said (John 14:8), "Lord, show us the Father." He did not wish to give up Christ the man. For that reason Christ says, "Philip, he who has seen Me," as if to say, "Where are you looking? Because I am *God Amen*, that is, 'the faithful and enduring,' and you must look for God in Me alone." Let each Christian beware of seeking in matters of conscience to behold the Divine Majesty. Stay with Christ. "He who has seen Me has seen the Father" (John 14:9). "I am the Way and the Truth, and the Life" (John 14:6). "I want everyone faithfully warned to beware of speculation." (17:386)

Notice that in this life, the world hates Christians as it hated Christ (see John 15:18–19). The Church is persecuted. Thus, it does not seem like Christians are blessed; rather, it appears as if Christians are cursed by God. Yet, Christians are called to walk by faith and not by sight (see 2 Corinthians 5:7). In this way, the people of the new name are to have hearing eyes, that is, eyes that are enlightened by the Word of the Lord. They are to have seeing ears, that is, ears that behold the vision of God from the voice of God.

The people of the new name walk in a new way. Their senses are changed. In fact, both Jesus (see John 14:6; Hebrews 9:8; 10:20) and the Church (see Acts 9:1–2; 19:9, 23; 24:14, 22) are called the Way. For Luther, this new way of thinking is rooted in the way we see and hear God in the incarnation.

If we try to glimpse into the invisible spiritual realm, then we will not find God acting at all in the visible physical realm. If we try to observe God apart from the incarnation, the water, bread, and wine, then we will overlook God in the baby born of Mary, the man standing in the water of the Jordan River, or the body hanging on the cross with blood pouring from His wounds. If we try to see the Father apart from Jesus, then we see a false image of God who did not send His Son for the life of the world. Without Christ, the true image of the invisible God, we can only behold an image of God that is formed out of the imagination of our hearts. Thus, the Lord tells us to lift up our hearts and see the things that cannot be seen. The Lord teaches us to lift up our hearts and hear the external Word that cannot be heard from the inner voice.

The New Kingdom

> You shall leave your name to My chosen for a curse, and the Lord GOD will put you to death, but His servants He will call by another name, so that he who blesses himself in the land shall bless himself by the God of truth, and he who takes an oath in the land shall swear by the God of truth; because the former troubles are forgotten and are hidden from My eyes. For behold, I create new heavens and a new earth, and the former things shall not be remembered or come into mind. But be glad and rejoice forever in that which I create; for behold, I create Jerusalem to be a joy, and her people to be a gladness. (Isaiah 65:15–18)

Because the former troubles are forgotten. The prophet begins to deal with the transfer of the kingdom which was achieved not only from people to people, but from substance to substance. The kingdom of the Jews was physical, established with government and ceremonies. This indeed was changed. The kingdom of the church, however, is only spiritual. Hence there is a difference between a kingdom of faith and an external kingdom, not according to the matter but according to appearance. Faith has to do with hope and expectation. For that reason the prophets write as if the kingdom of Christ were standing and flourishing, and even though it does not appear, it is visible to hope and faith. We are truly in the kingdom of Christ, yet, as it were, in a mystery. Paul often follows this line. God has "raised us up with Him, and made us sit with Him in the heavenly places in Christ Jesus" (Eph. 2:6). This kingdom began the moment He was raised from the dead. From that time on we have the treasure, and whatever interval of time remains must be thought of as a dream and a tiny moment. Therefore this kingdom is hidden, and yet it flourishes; there is death, sin, and unrighteousness, and yet life, righteousness, and faith are hidden. This is our art on which we rely. This is the source from which as from the head the separate parts of the Christian religion arise, so that we may know ourselves safe from the deceit of all. If Christ's kingdom is truly with us, we shall be justified, whether we are sinners or righteous, and this life is like a poor skin which must be stripped off. The papists divide Christ's kingdom into a kingdom of penitence and a kingdom of the righteous. But this is unintelligible. We are all under the rule of Christ, and meanwhile we live under the government in our outward life, which is like a poor skin. For that reason this kingdom is here described. It is as if he were saying: "There will be a new kingdom of blessing, salvation, and life over against curse and damnation, against the Law, sin, and wrath. All of these have been removed so that in this kingdom the former things are forgotten."

And are hid from our eyes. The emphasis lies on *our*. As to the thing itself, the evils are still present in the eyes of the world, but in our eyes, in the promises, they are not there. Even if the Law and conscience still remain, when we believe in God, the Law and conscience are forgotten through this faith, even if they are still there. This, then, is a description of the kingdom of God. It is a condition of blessedness. And if blessing is there, curse, sin, and the Law depart. Even though we should feel sin, death, and the Law, the kingdom of Christ is there nevertheless, but the treasure is hidden in this outward life. Externally the Christian life is a sack and a skin, and the internal treasure must not be evaluated on that basis. Our outward life is like a wretched sack which has beautiful gold in it. Thus our life is hazardous because of sin, the Law, and death, but that life is nothing but the reign of Christ. It is being in Christ and believing in Him, and in it there is nothing but fearing and trusting. Why is this? Because:

For behold, I create new heavens and a new earth. "I will bring it about and do it." He is not speaking only of the spiritual heaven, but He makes all things new, spiritual and physical, although I do not see a new heaven and a new body in us, but only the one born of our parents. Yet we believe it. We must turn the sack inside out, and then they will appear. (17:386–88)

The New Image

In chapters 40, 41, 43, and 44, Isaiah mocks the false images of God made from the imaginations of the peoples' hearts. Then in chapter 42, the prophet sets the true image of the invisible God before our eyes. Isaiah writes,

> Behold My servant, whom I uphold, My chosen, in whom My soul delights; I have put My Spirit upon Him; He will bring forth justice to the nations. (Isaiah 42:1)

In the new creation, we see this Servant, God's Son, because He is the only true image of the invisible God. The person of the Father draws all eyes and ears to the person of the Son, being anointed by the Holy Spirit. We see this in the Baptism of Jesus. In the waters of the Jordan River, the only-begotten Son of God stands on earth. Both the Father and the Spirit focus our attention on the Son. At the Baptism of our Lord, we hear the voice crying out in the wilderness from Isaiah 40 and the voice of the Father in Isaiah 42, saying, "This is My beloved Son, with whom I am well pleased" (Matthew 3:17). While John the Baptizer is the voice preparing the way for the Lord on earth, God the Father speaks from heaven and the Holy Spirit descends from heaven in the form of a dove (see John 1:23, 32–34).

Now he [the prophet] draws near to the Leader Himself, Christ, concerning whom he earlier began, "Comfort, comfort" (Is. 40:1). This is an outstanding statement. He speaks of the Head, who is nevertheless a man, and he unites

Here our ears must be glued to His mouth. Look only at His mouth and Word, and you will not be led astray.

—MARTIN LUTHER

a man with divine glory and calls Him Servant. From various idolatries and sects he calls us to this one Christ, who is the unique sign that heals us.

Behold. These are words of demonstration, as if he were pointing to something worth seeing. He is calling us away from errors and therefore showing us someone else. This also applies to our Enthusiasts, who dream that they are masters and stand in their own opinions, trusting in the heavenly Spirit. Here, however, the prophet points us to the Incarnate One and says that in this Head alone, in the unity of faith, we who were formerly scattered must be brought together. To one who asks, "Where can I gather all the scattered people?" he replies by pointing us to the means, *Behold My Servant*. Here He gives Him the doctor's degree. "If you want to know and be wise, look to this Christ, the Doctor and the One in charge and up and doing. Him I have put in charge. Keep your eye on Him, observe what He does, says, and teaches, because He is My Servant." This was not written for Christ's sake but for ours, so that we may be sure about His work and teaching and may have certainty about the emptiness of our idolatry. Nobody understands these things unless he believes. You must believe that Christ is a servant. It is as Paul says (1 Cor. 2:2): "I decided to know nothing among you except Jesus Christ and Him crucified." . . .

"If you want to avoid error, if you want to find Me, please Me, then hear Him, receive His Word, teaching, and Spirit, for He is My treasure." Here our ears must be glued to His mouth. Look only at His mouth and Word, and you will not be led astray, though meanwhile Satan rages, by force through the tyrants and by cunning through the Enthusiasts. Pay no attention to the various offenses of the armies of the demon and of the Enthusiasts. "I promise you that I shall be found in Him. You will not be offended if you receive Him." (17:60, 61)

The Enthusiasts did not cling to Christ, the only true image of God, because they valued the inspiration of the Spirit in the imagination of their hearts and their extrabiblical visions. They despised the preaching office and the external Word, the very sin Luther warns against in his explanation of the Third Commandment in the Small Catechism. Because they did not look to Christ's mouth and His Word, through which He is set before the eyes, they began to know Christ as something other than the Crucified One. They became theologians of glory. But without the true image of Christ as the Crucified One, there is no Gospel. The message of comfort to crushed consciences only comes to the heart when the true image of God replaces any other possible idol.

Isaiah describes that true image of God—Christ—by saying,

> He will not cry aloud or lift up His voice, or make it heard in the street; a bruised reed He will not break, and a faintly burning wick He will not quench; He will faithfully bring forth justice. He will not grow faint or be discouraged till He has established justice in the earth; and the coastlands wait for His law. (Isaiah 42:2–4)

> This is a golden text which most beautifully sets Christ before us. It should be expounded at great length. It begins with metaphors. With these words he indirectly attacks the ungodliness and plague of the self-righteous, who went about with extreme severity and approved of no one. The gray hoods, the monks, were the very best, although they, too, were without faith. St. Paul has this in mind when he says (Rom. 14:1): "As for the man who is weak in faith, welcome him." It takes real skill, for the teacher of the church should not confuse but build up the bruised and timid conscience. This is what Paul is saying: Have patience with all, because there are many such consciences tormented by Satan. This text sets forth Christ as the true Physician, Guide, and Pastor, who is able to provide healing for them. This is a hymn of praise to Christ, who is commended to us. All self-righteous, on the contrary, go by with closed eyes and let a disturbed conscience lie, saying, "Thus it is written; thus it is spoken." Clinging to this Scripture passage, they break the bruised reed. (17:64–65)

God deals gently with us; the Father sends the Son as our advocate and comforter, and the Father and the Son send the Holy Spirit as another advocate and comforter (see John 14:16). The former things have come to pass, and He makes all things new. He renews us. He declares new things to us. And we learn to believe new things, think new thoughts, speak new words, and walk in new ways. The Holy Spirit is at work in the heart of the believer re-creating, restoring, and renewing.

The New Offspring

> Until the Spirit is poured upon us from on high, and the wilderness becomes a fruitful field, and the fruitful field is deemed a forest. Then justice will dwell in the wilderness, and righteousness abide in the fruitful field. And the effect of righteousness will be peace, and the result of righteousness, quietness and trust forever. My people will abide in a peaceful habitation, in secure dwellings, and in quiet resting places. (Isaiah 32:15–18)

These are the fruits of faith, of justification, and of grace. For such trust in the flesh does not exist, but it is by faith alone and by the grace of God. The accent is on the words *My people*. "My, My people," because this is a new people renewed by the Spirit, a people set free from the demanding Law, from biting sin, and from gloating death. These foes are vanquished, and therefore we have great confidence. (16:280–81)

Christ gives peace with God, not peace with the world. Thus, Jesus says, "Let not your hearts be troubled, neither let them be afraid" (John 14:27). In this world, the people of God will be troubled. The Church should not fear, because Christ has overcome the world (see John 16:33) and promised the gift of the Holy Spirit (see John 15:26).

> Thus says the LORD who made you, who formed you from the womb and will help you: Fear not, O Jacob My servant, Jeshurun whom I have chosen. For I will pour water on the thirsty land, and streams on the dry ground; I will pour My Spirit upon your offspring, and My blessing on your descendants. (Isaiah 44:2–3)

Our church, though lowly, is not perishing but is bound to have descendants and offspring. Even in time of affliction the church begets the church in blessing. Hence we must not lose heart, since we have the life-giving Spirit. (17:104)

Through the words of the Gospel, the Spirit of adoption testifies to the baptized that we are adopted sons of the Kingdom, absolved sinners for the sake of Christ, and accepted into eternal life (see Romans 8:12–17). And not only does He adopt us and forgive us, but also in Christ, we are formed into the image of the true Man. Instead of us forming God into our fallen image, God forms us into His image and likeness (see Romans 8:26–30).

Christ is a tested stone, that is, distressed and afflicted, or He is a testing stone, that is, a stone by whose shape all other stones are tested, so that we may be conformed to the image of the Son of God (Rom. 8:29). As Christ was polished, hewn, and squared by the promise, by death and the cross, so we, in His image, should become well polished by such suffering and such a cross. (16:229–30)

The renewal of God's image comes through a new birth, but the labor pains must come first. In a similar way, Luther connects the suffering of the Servant (the Bridegroom) in Isaiah 53 with the rejoicing of the Bride (the Church) in Isaiah 54.

"Sing, O barren one, who did not bear; break forth into singing and cry aloud, you who have not been in labor! For the children of the desolate one will be more than the children of her who is married," says the LORD. (Isaiah 54:1)

The prophet, having described the King [Christ] and His work, proceeds in this chapter to describe the kingdom of Christ and now endeavors to describe His fruit and seed that will long prosper. As he has described the Head, so he now describes the church. It remains in the same form; as Christ was in contempt and in lowly form and on the cross, so every Christian will be like the image of the Son of God. Thus he here ascribes the same form to the church that he ascribes to the Head in the preceding. As I have said, after having pictured the Head of that kingdom, Christ, as dying in His own appearance before the world abominably and most shamefully, so that the Jews were highly offended, he now introduces the form of His body, the church. Paul cites this passage in his letter to the Galatians (4:27), where he makes a distinction between church and synagogue, and that passage must be understood as speaking of the repeal of the old law and the reception of the new law and people. This is the difference between the old and new law and people. The new people and sons are free inwardly in their conscience, but outwardly they are oppressed by misfortunes and the cross. On the contrary, the people of the old law were inwardly bound, while outwardly they shone and were resplendent. The godly and the new people, however, externally suffer shamefully. Isaac is persecuted by Ishmael. Hence there is a very great difference between these people. He consoles His church by conceding indeed that it is forsaken and laid waste, outwardly, that is, but that inwardly it will be spiritual, strong, and most holy. Once we understand the status of the Head, this text is easy, but with our experience we find it difficult to arrive at its meaning. (17:233)

When we trust that God promises to work together for the good in all things for those who are in Christ (see Romans 8:28), then we can "rejoice in our sufferings" (Romans 5:3). Christ suffered for us and He continues to be with us in our suffering.

The New Song and Sacrifice of Praise

In Christ, we learn to sing a new song. It is a different song than the ones we sing in our culture. We resonate with the new heavens and the new earth. In Christ, we are given a joyful conscience that is manifest in mouths filled with His praise.

Behold, I am doing a new thing; now it springs forth, do you not perceive it? I will make a way in the wilderness and rivers in the desert. The wild beasts will honor Me, the jackals and the ostriches, for I give water in the wilderness, rivers in the desert, to give drink to My chosen people, the people whom I formed for Myself that they might declare My praise. (Isaiah 43:19–21)

> *The people whom I formed for Myself.* "I have given them the whole New Testament with its own form of worship, and I have abolished the Old Testament, so that the people might declare My name. This people was formed and created by Me. The people of the old law formed and fashioned themselves. They are their own people. But this is My people, formed by Me, together with their office, kingdom, and priesthood." *That they might declare My praise*, that is, to teach and to preach and to praise God, at the same time rejecting everything else. These are the sacrifices and whole burnt offerings that reject all our own offerings before God. To declare the praises of Christ is the priesthood and kingdom of the Christians. In the act of praising we become priests and kings. . . . This is the greatest sacrifice, not our own offerings. (17:97–98)

> "Behold, the former things have come to pass, and new things I now declare; before they spring forth I tell you of them." Sing to the LORD a new song, His praise from the end of the earth, you who go down to the sea, and all that fills it, the coastlands and their inhabitants. Let the desert and its cities lift up their voice, the villages that Kedar inhabits; let the habitants of Sela sing for joy, let them shout from the top of the mountains. Let them give glory to the LORD, and declare His praise in the coastlands. (Isaiah 42:9–12)

The new song is a song about the New Testament, the new heavens, and the new earth. Through the Gospel, the Holy Spirit is poured out on us to begin to do new things, think new thoughts, and sing a new song. Jesus is the propitiation for the sins of the whole world (see 1 John 2:2). Isaiah tells us that He will sprinkle the nations with His blood (see Isaiah 52:15). The root of Jesse will stand as a signal to people of all ethnic backgrounds (see 11:10). The apostolic message will go forth from Jerusalem to the ends of the earth (see 2:2; 49:1; 51:5; 55:4–5; 60:3–9; 65:1). Isaiah ends his book on the promise of the conversion of the Gentiles in the new heavens and new earth (see 66:18–23). This song will be sung to the nations, and they, too, will join in the singing (see 24:14–16).

Luther, as a successor to the apostles in the preaching office, states,

[We] preach about a new Head, Priest, and King, who will not be confined to a specific place.

From the end of the earth. Not only in the temple. The point at issue here is the worship of the New Testament. It is nothing else than song, praise, and thanksgiving. This is a unique song. God does not care for our sacrifices and works. He is satisfied with the sacrifice of praise. Bring God the sacrifices of righteousness and praise and of Ps. 110:3: "Your people with willing offerings in beauty." These words indirectly do away with the old worship. To sing, therefore, is to praise, to give thanks, to preach, to do kindly deeds, to extol, to magnify. The preachers of Christ sing, and their hearers respond with thanksgiving. This is the song and evangelical worship. I, therefore, am a priest when I deal with the Gospel. A worldly priest is characterized by an offering of works. . . .

Our religion is to preach, to praise, and exalt God. It is not concerned only with ceremonies, as the papists think. We have the highest worship in that we do not make it highly ceremonial but use ceremonies only in the service of promoting Christ. We are not bound to ceremonies for specific times, persons, or vestments, and besides, we pass judgment on their use. This old song we sing not to the Lord but to ourselves. Therefore there is nothing else for us to do but to receive everything as a gift. If you want to do something else for God, then praise Him and give thanks to Him. (17:72, 73)

The New Liturgy: Luther's Reform of the Mass

Since the days of the Early Church, the word *Eucharist* has been associated with the Lord's Supper. It comes from the Greek word εὐχαριστία (*eucharistia*), which means "thanksgiving." When Jesus instituted His Supper, He took the bread and gave thanks (from the Greek verb εὐχαριστέω [*eucharisteō*]). In like manner, He took the cup and gave thanks. By Luther's day, the term *Eucharist* meant the Lord's Supper. However, the people were taught that the priest offered up the Eucharist, the body and blood of Jesus, to the Father as a sacrifice. Luther wanted to make a clear distinction between what was offered to God, a sacrificial act, and what was offered to the people, a sacramental act. The Lord's Supper is a sacrament and not a sacrifice. While the Lord's Supper could be called the Eucharist, the true eucharistic sacrifice is a sacrifice of thanksgiving, prayer, and praise.

> You will say in that day: "I will give thanks to You, O LORD, for though You were angry with me, Your anger turned away, that You might comfort me. Behold, God is my salvation; I will trust, and will not be afraid; for the LORD GOD is my strength and my song, and He has become my salvation." (Isaiah 12:1–2)

Here the prophet depicts the true and lawful worship and sacrifice of the New Testament and sets up, as it were, a certain hidden antithesis over against the Old Testament and its sacrifices, which were many and varied. But in the New Testament there was a single sacrifice of praise and thanksgiving. Thus the Lord's Supper is called Eucharist, that we may gather around it and give thanks to God. However, the best thanksgiving is that public confession before the world, where Christians who confess walk in danger. The prophet foresaw this future preaching and confession of the Gospel, which did not take place in the Old Testament. In the voice of the Gospel God is glorified and preached in Christ. *You will say*, namely, in the church: *I will confess*. This is what will take place in preaching. Nor shall anything else be heard in the church but the voice of praise and proclamation of God's blessings which we have received. This song is in conflict with all human wisdom and righteousness, which are our works and in which we seek our own glory rather than give thanks to God. Hence, to be pleasing to God is simply to acknowledge that we are the recipients of His blessings, not the donors. A Christian confesses that he was condemned and lost and that he has received from Christ everything that belongs to salvation and righteousness; all his own merits he considers worth nothing. This is the fullest and most perfect sacrifice, and it embraces everything in the Old Testament. There animals and cattle were slaughtered; here our own wisdom and righteousness, our endeavors and works. (16:128)

When Luther reformed the Mass, as the Divine Service was known in his day, he wanted to clarify for the people that the priest does not sacrifice the Lord's body and blood to God. Instead, it is our own wisdom and works that are sacrificed to God. In fact, Luther preferred to use the term *priest* for anyone who was baptized; all believers are part of the new priesthood in Christ's kingdom. Thus, commenting on Isaiah 61:4, Luther says,

> This is the sum of the prophets, to attribute to the Christian these two sacrifices: to praise God and to convert sinners, instead of all the endless ceremonies of the Law. (17:336)

At the same time, Luther wanted to make a clear distinction between the priesthood of all the baptized and a man in the preaching office, commonly called a priest. Commenting on Isaiah 60:7, Luther states,

> This is the sacrifice, when we are offered as a sweet-smelling sacrifice through the ministry of the Word and of the apostles. The sacrificers are the preachers themselves, who offer and sacrifice us to God. This is the sacrifice of the Gospel.
>
> *And I will glorify My glorious house*, that is, "I will glorify My house more fully than Solomon's house was glorified, because at that place all will offer their sacrifices to God in the new church—all who by faith bring an acceptable offering." Thus whoever will kill his attitudes, his wisdom, his righteousness, and whatever will be grand in the world, will subject all this to the Gospel and to Christ. *I will glorify.* In the New Testament there is no other sacrifice than the ministry of the church, those who by teaching the Word spiritually "kill" the animals, that is, people who submit to the Gospel. Then there is the second sacrifice, that each one privately present himself as a sacrifice to God by cleansing his desires and by mortifying himself. These are the noblest sacrifices of the New Testament, prefigured in the Old Testament by outward and physical ones. All of these have, however, been abolished, and the new ones have taken their place. (17:315)

Here Luther makes a distinction between the preacher in the public office as a "sacrifice" who publicly offers the people to God through the preaching of Christ and the individual members of the baptized priesthood who privately offer themselves to God through daily dying to sin.

> And they shall bring all your brothers from all the nations as an offering to the LORD, on horses and in chariots and in litters and on mules and on dromedaries, to My holy mountain Jerusalem, says the LORD, just as the Israelites bring their grain offering in a clean vessel to the house of the LORD. And some of them also I will take for priests and for Levites, says the LORD. For as the new heavens and the new earth that I make shall remain before Me, says the LORD, so shall your offspring and your name remain. (Isaiah 66:20–22)

Luther comments,

> The nations being offered is nothing else than that the nations are gathered through faith. All the nations who believe are offered to Christ. Paul speaks of this offering in Rom. 15:16. Every preacher is a sacrificing priest. . . .
>
> [God] promises a new kind of sacrifices, new men, who are offered through the Gospel, that is, in a clean vessel. . . .
>
> Here He is speaking about a new order of priests. . . .
>
> In the Mosaic system the Levites were the servants of the priests. So today all teachers are priests. Hence the priesthood has been shifted from a single tribe of the Jews to all nations. We are all priests. It is the priest's task to bring sacrifices to God. This he does through prayer, mediation, and worship. Let no one, however, assume the exercise of this function without a call. This sacrifice must be not only acceptable but also lasting, just as the new heavens are lasting. . . . Thus Christ and all who believe in Him will be priests forever. Here that new priesthood begins, and it will last forever. (17:414, 415)

The "sacrificing priest" is the preacher who has been called to exercise the "function" of the pastoral office.

In the Apology of the Augsburg Confession, Philip Melanchthon, a fellow faculty member at the University of Wittenberg, codified Luther's teaching on the eucharistic sacrifice. Melanchthon made a distinction between two different types of sacrifices: the propitiatory sacrifice and the eucharistic sacrifice (see Ap XXIV 19–26). The propitiatory sacrifice is the atoning sacrifice of Christ on the cross (see 1 John 2:2; 4:10). This sacrifice reconciles us to God and merits the forgiveness of sins. The eucharistic sacrifices are spiritual sacrifices of praise and thanksgiving by those who have received the propitiatory sacrifice. Such eucharistic sacrifices of praise and thanksgiving do not merit the forgiveness of sins. Instead, they proceed from a cleansed heart and from a conscience that is at peace with God through faith alone.

During the time of Luther, the people of God were left with troubled consciences by the Latin Mass. First, Latin was not the common language spoken among the people. Therefore, they did not know what was being proclaimed through the Mass. Second, because of their sins, the people did not feel worthy to partake of the Holy Supper of Christ's body and blood. Third, the preachers were not preaching Christ crucified as the atonement for the people's sins and the gift of salvation. Instead, they told the people to live holy lives, imitating the saints, if they wanted to receive salvation. Fourth, the Mass promoted the saints as mediators for the people. The people feared the image of Jesus the judge. The image of Jesus as the Redeemer was replaced by the image of Mary the merciful mother. Mary and other saints became new mediators between sinful humanity and the wrath of Jesus.

When Luther reshaped the Mass, he removed the rituals that robbed Jesus of His proper glory and honor. He cut out the petitions to Mary and the saints for help in obtaining reconciliation with God. He cleared away all that obscured the image of Jesus the Lamb of God who takes away the sin of the world. Luther wanted to emphasize the comfort that comes from the incarnation in the body and blood of Christ given to the people of God in the Lord's Supper. Therefore, Luther more explicitly tied Isaiah's vision of God in the temple in Isaiah 6 to the Christian's vision of Jesus in the Lord's Supper. Luther wrote the hymn "Isaiah, Mighty Seer in Days of Old" as a modification of the traditional Sanctus ("Holy, Holy, Holy"), using more of the words and images of Isaiah 6. In Luther's Mass (Setting Five in

LSB), after the pastor sings the voice of Jesus at the altar, "This is My body, which is given for you. . . . This is My blood, which is shed for you," the congregation then sings Luther's hymn,

> Isaiah, mighty seer in days of old,
> The Lord of all in spirit did behold
> High on a lofty throne, in splendor bright,
> With robes that filled the temple courts with light.
> Above the throne were flaming seraphim;
> Six wings had they, these messengers of Him.
> With two they veiled their faces as was right,
> With two they humbly hid their feet from sight,
> And with the other two aloft they soared;
> One to the other called and praised the Lord:
> > "Holy is God, the Lord of Sabaoth!
> > Holy is God, the Lord of Sabaoth!
> > Holy is God, the Lord of Sabaoth!
> > His glory fills the heavens and the earth!"
> The beams and lintels trembled at the cry,
> And clouds of smoke enwrapped the throne on high.
> (*LSB* 960)

Using this hymn in the liturgy showed a strong connection between the hot burning coal that touches Isaiah's lips and the bread and wine that touch the lips of the communicant. The Lord's Supper is no ordinary meal. In, with, and under the bread and wine, our mouths receive the atoning body and blood of Jesus. While the eyes see bread and wine, the ears see the body and the blood. While the ears hear the voice of the pastor, the eyes hear the voice of Jesus. Faith comes through hearing, and seeing is believing.

As Isaiah wrote,

> In the year that King Uzziah died I saw the Lord sitting upon a throne, high and lifted up; and the train of His robe filled the temple. Above Him stood the seraphim. Each had six wings: with two he covered his face, and with two he covered his feet, and with two he flew. And one called to another and said: "Holy, holy, holy is the LORD of hosts; the whole earth is full of His glory!" (Isaiah 6:1–3)

Luther's allegorical interpretation of this passage reads,

The Lord sitting in glory is Christ at the right hand of the Father. The temple is His church or heaven. The fact that He appears in visible form indicates that He is man, for everywhere the appearance of God denotes the humanity of Christ. Now He rules in the church through His humanity, but finally as the glorious God. The seraphim are the apostles and preachers of the Word. Winged angels everywhere signify the ministry of the Word. The two wings are the two Testaments, or the testimonies of the Law and the Prophets. The flying denotes the course of the ministry. "The Lord gives the command; great is the host of those who bore the tidings" (Ps. 68:11). There are many indeed, but all of them with one accord preach the same Christ. Veiling the face and feet means that the life of the godly is hidden in Christ. The feet signify conduct. Faith is not seen and its conduct is not grasped by the ungodly; in fact, it may seem strange and stupid to them. John 3:8 says: "You hear the sound of it, but you do not know whence it comes or whither it goes." Christians certainly live without glory in the world. The seraphim stood ready to serve the Lord. Their cry is a declaration of preaching. "Holy, holy, holy." "No one has ascended into heaven but He who descended from heaven, etc." (John 3:13). And chapter 16: "He will convince the world of sin and of righteousness and of judgment" (John 16:8). Those who boast of their own holiness do not cry, "Holy is the Lord God," but as desecrators of God's name they make their boast in man. The "Sanctus" in the Mass is a song for the boys. But the preacher is the public singer of it. As long as we live, there is never enough singing. When Peter sang this song in Acts 2:37, "they were cut to the heart and said to Peter and the rest of the apostles, 'Brethren, what shall we do?'" There will never be a lack of fruit and faith for the true preaching of Christ and for His purified holiness. Just as here, too, the lintels of the temple, that is, the house itself, were shaken by their voice, so also those who are in the church are moved by the Gospel and do not belong to the number of the blinded. Paul says, the Gospel "is bearing fruit and growing" "in the

> whole world" (Col. 1:6). It makes an impression because it is high and exalted. (16:76–77)

In the Divine Service, Isaiah 6 is seen and heard. The choir sings the words "Holy, holy, holy" in the Mass, but the public preacher, the sacrificing priest, sings those words when he preaches that Christ alone is holy and that He comes in His body and blood to make His people holy. Before Luther's reform of the Mass, the presiding priest silently spoke the Words of Institution during the consecration of the Lord's Supper. In Luther's reform, the presiding priest takes the role of the seraphim and chants the words of Jesus loudly and clearly for all to hear. Likewise, he places the holy body and blood of Jesus in the mouths of the people to cleanse them.

The Lutheran Liturgy

In *Lutheran Service Book*, Luther's reforms of the Mass are embraced in a variety of ways. For example, as stated above, in Divine Service, Setting Five, Luther's "Isaiah, Mighty Seer in Days of Old" is sung in place of the traditional Sanctus.

In Divine Service, Setting Four, before the Words of Institution, the people of God offer up the eucharistic sacrifice by singing with thanksgiving and praise. The pastor sings, "Let us give thanks to the Lord our God," and the congregation responds, "It is right to give Him thanks and praise." Then the pastor prays, "It is truly good, right, and salutary that we should at all times and in all places give thanks to You" (*LSB*, p. 208). After singing "Holy, holy, holy Lord God of Sabaoth adored," the pastor prays the Prayer of Thanksgiving, in which he says, "We give You thanks for the redemption You have prepared for us through Jesus Christ" (*LSB*, p. 209). After giving thanks, then the pastor speaks the Words of Institution of the Lord's Supper.

In Divine Service, Setting Three, the pastor chants the Words of Institution, as Luther suggested. After the Distribution of the Lord's Supper, the pastor chants, "O give thanks unto the Lord, for He is good" to emphasize the true eucharistic sacrifice of thanksgiving (*LSB*, p. 200). Then the pastor offers up the Post-Communion Collect, saying, "We give thanks to You, almighty God, that You have refreshed us through this salutary gift"—the Lord's Supper, which we have received (*LSB*, p. 201).

In Divine Service, Setting One, the correct eucharistic sacrifice is highlighted by the Offertory from Psalm 116. The congregation sings, "What shall I render to the Lord for all His benefits to me? I will offer the sacrifice of thanksgiving and will call on the name of the Lord. I will take the cup of salvation" (*LSB*, pp. 159–60). After the Distribution of the Lord's Supper, the congregation sings the Post-Communion Canticle, "Thank the Lord and sing His praise; tell ev'ryone what He has done. Let all who seek the Lord rejoice and proudly bear His name. He recalls His promises and leads His people forth in joy with shouts of thanksgiving. Alleluia, alleluia" (*LSB*, p. 164).

Through the Lutheran liturgy, our consciences are properly instructed as we, with the prophet Isaiah, see the vision of the Lord sitting on the throne. First, in the Confession and Absolution, we acknowledge that everyone must give an account before God of what we have done in the body. We are taught to be conscious of sin, wrath, and judgment. Throughout our daily lives, our consciences cry out, "Guilty as charged! Guilty as charged!" Thus, when we confess our sins, we recognize that God is the only judge, and His judgment is true. We acknowledge that practice does not make perfect. Rather, we draw near to God's presence, seeking His grace for the sake of Christ. Like Isaiah, we confess our sins in thought, word, and deed. We acknowledge that we cannot free ourselves from our own sinful condition. Like Isaiah, God's response is to show us the image of the Lamb who was slain, who atones for our sins.

Next, in the Service of the Word, we learn to believe that Jesus alone is the Holy One who makes us His holy people. We desire that His kingdom would come to us through His Word where Christ reigns in our consciences. Throughout the service, we hear the words of pardon and peace spoken to our hearts. "Comfort! Comfort!" says your God. Later, in the sermon, we hear the Savior confirming His comfort, because the goal of the sermon is to preach Christ crucified for the hearer (see 1 Corinthians 1:21–24).

Then, in the Service of the Sacrament, we learn to believe in the mystery of the incarnation. We sing the Sanctus ("Holy, Holy, Holy"), which combines the words of Isaiah 6:3 with Matthew 21:9. Notice that seeing Christ on the heavenly throne with Isaiah is spliced together with seeing Him as the Son of David riding into Jerusalem on Palm Sunday. This is because heaven and earth are joined together in Him. His name is Jesus because He comes to save us from our sin (see Matthew 1:21). He comes in weak and lowly means: body, blood, bread, wine, water, ink, and the voice of the pastor. He does not come to judge the world. The same God who is so holy that Isaiah was terrified in His presence comes on a donkey to save us so that we may have eternal life. He comes to give us a joyful conscience, rejoicing in His salvation. In the Lord's Supper, we behold the salvation of Yahweh through means.

For Luther, the worst idolatry of the Medieval Church was the idea of offering up the Lord's Supper as a sacrifice being offered to God instead of a sacrament being offered to the people. On the other extreme, he decried those who denied the possibility that Christ's body and blood could be present in bread and wine:

> Even the miracles of Christ were such as were grasped by the senses. Isaiah saw the Lord sitting, yet not except in the vision. Nevertheless, they are called Lord and seraphim, who were seen and yet cannot be seen. Someone voices the slander that the body of Christ is not in the bread because it cannot be seen and that it cannot be anything else except what is seen. Against those people stands this passage, where the prophet saw what cannot be seen. He saw a form, and yet he says he saw the Lord Himself. One thing is shown, another is hidden. He who eats the bread eats also the body of Christ. Christ's way of speaking, "This is My body," is of the same kind as the Father's, "This is My beloved Son." (Matt. 3:17). Thus in the dove the Holy Spirit was seen. (16:71)

With our physical eyes we see bread and wine, but with the eyes of our heart we see the true body and true blood of Jesus given to us. We lift up our hearts unto the Lord and give Him thanks. We are gathered with angels and archangels and all the company of heaven, which could not be contained in the largest sports stadium on earth. It is at the Lord's Supper that we rejoice in the voice of God revealing to us the mystery of the incarnation. He is Immanuel—God with us. Thus, we sing the Agnus Dei ("Lamb of God"), which contains the words of John the Baptizer, echoing the words of Isaiah 40 and 53.

When we gather as the people of God in His presence, He comes to bless us and give us peace. He pardons us from all guilt and then sends us back out into the world with a pure conscience assured that the Father is pleased with us for the sake of the Son. In the Divine Service, we learn to see this vision of God with our ears. With Isaiah, our eyes "hear" the biblical canticles of the Sanctus, Agnus Dei, and the Nunc Dimittis taking place in the sacred space. It is only through the proclamation of God's Word that God's glory and His true image—Jesus—are revealed and our consciences are formed. In the Divine Service that Luther presented as a reformation of the Mass, we see the new liturgy of God's new creation—the new liturgy that places the image of Christ upon our hearts. Only through the preaching of the Gospel can there be true peace with God in the conscience. In the words of Thomas Kingo, we sing,

> On my heart imprint Your image,
> > Blessed Jesus, King of grace,
> That life's riches, cares, and pleasures
> > Never may Your work erase;
> Let the clear inscription be:
> Jesus, crucified for me,
> > Is my life, my hope's foundation,
> > And my glory and salvation! (*LSB* 422)

Conclusion

Through the mystery of the incarnation, God brings forth the restoration of creation. In Christ, God does a new thing. Jesus is the new king who brings a new Zion through new preaching. Christ is the new true image of God, and in Him, we are formed into His image and likeness. In Christ, we are a new creation through the blood of the New Testament. He creates new people with new names through a new liturgy. He makes our hearts and consciences new and places a new song on our lips. Consequently, we rejoice and praise Him with new sacrifices of praise and thanksgiving.

The goal of the Divine Service is to give God the glory due His name and to receive comfort for our restless hearts through Christ's name. In the Lutheran liturgy, we gather before God's face of grace to receive the gifts of the forgiveness of sins, life, and salvation. In the Divine Service, we assemble to hear the voice of the Lord and see the Word of God. So the Holy Spirit gives us ears to see and eyes to hear. We see His Word in the waters of Baptism as we hear His voice saying, "I baptize you in the name of the Father and of the Son and of the Holy Spirit."

We see His Word in the justifying Words of Absolution as we hear His voice saying, "I forgive you all your sins in the name of the Father and of the Son and of the Holy Spirit." We see His Word in the bread and wine as we hear His voice saying, "Take, eat; this is My body, which is given for you. . . . Drink of it, all of you; this cup is the new testament in My blood, which is shed for you for the forgiveness of sins." Through the lowly means of a man in the pastoral office, water in the font, and bread and wine on the altar, we receive Jesus, the incarnate Word. In Christ, we are a new creation. Through the incarnation, He is making all things new—a new heaven and a new earth.

CHAPTER 7

ISAIAH AT THE FOUNDATION OF THE REFORMATION

Through Martin Luther's life experiences, personal reflections, biblical studies, theological lectures, public sermons, and printed writings, the Reformation spread from the small town in Wittenberg, Germany, throughout Europe. For Luther and his students, the central doctrine of the Church is justification through faith alone (*Sola fide*). This teaching was obscured in the Middle Ages. In this sense, we could rightly call them the Dark Ages. Luther brought the light of the Gospel back into the Church. The purpose of the Reformation was twofold: (1) to restore the proper glory to Christ and (2) to bring comfort to the terrified conscience. In the Book of Isaiah, Luther saw the foundation of this "new" teaching.

Thundersnow in the Jemez Mountains

One Christmas, a friend invited me to go cut down a Christmas tree. I took my kids, and we went up into the Jemez Mountains in New Mexico. We were walking in a winter wonderland. There was snow everywhere on the ground. It was picture-perfect. After a pleasant stroll through the forest, we finally found a tree and started heading back toward the vehicle. However, we became disorientated and could not locate our parking spot. Everywhere we looked, it was white. In every direction, we beheld tall ponderosa pine trees. My friend suggested that my children and I wait by the road and stay put. He would continue looking for his vehicle. By this time, snow began to fall, and it seemed we were in a gently shaken snow globe—the snow was all around us. Then it happened. It was as if the glass of the snow globe cracked. I heard the sound of thundersnow. That's right—thundersnow. We were caught in the middle of a snow and thunder and lightning storm. A flash lit up the white sky and then came the "BOOM!" If you have never been caught in a thunderstorm in the mountains, let me assure you, it is loud. It echoes! It seemed like the thunder kept coming closer and closer. I began to literally fear for my life and for the lives of my children. I very quickly became acutely conscious of my own mortality. I persistently petitioned the Lord to keep us from dying. At one moment, we had been in harmony with nature. The next moment, the music had stopped, and there was nothing but a cacophony.

We live in a fallen creation that is falling apart. The glass of the snow globe of our world is not just cracked, it is shattered. In fact, we are the ones who shattered it. And we cannot fix it. When mankind fell, we caused creation to fall with us, and now we are stuck in it.

Our conscience is a gift because it bears witness to the reality of our situation. It brings the awareness of sin, death, and the judgment of God. Each one of us experiences events that amplify the alarm of the conscience. Sometimes even experiencing the chaos of the fallen creation, like my experience in the Jemez Mountains, is an alarm to our conscience, reminding us of our sin that contributes to a world that has fallen apart. Sometimes these occasions become life-changing.

Thunderstorm at Stotternheim

Martin Luther had such a life-changing encounter. In 1505, Luther completed a master's degree and began to study to be a lawyer. He had no intention of ever becoming a monk, let alone a priest or a professor of biblical studies. His father, Hans, was a copper miner in Mansfeld, Germany. Hans had high hopes for his son's academic training. But on July 2, 1505, an unexpected event took place. Luther was traveling back to Erfurt on foot from Mansfeld. Just outside of his destination, he was trapped in a terrifying thunderstorm at Stotternheim.

He became aware of his own impeding death; his conscience alarmed him concerning his sin and God's judgment. Fearing for his life, he cried out to St. Anne, the patron saint for miners. He vowed to her that he would become a monk if his life was spared. On July 17, he fulfilled his promise and entered the Black Monastery in Erfurt in order to become a monk. He looked for peace for his conscience through the vows of chastity, poverty, and obedience to the Augustinian Order. However, the more he tried to ease his conscience, the more he was tormented and tortured. He could never do enough to avert the coming judgment of God. Luther states,

> The more our conscience asserts itself, the more we are in doubt. Who knows whether this will please God? Hence, because we do not know, we are in doubt as to what we must do. We have toiled to the point of madness. (17:261)

Luther Lectures on the Epistle of Romans

In 1507, Brother Luther was ordained as a priest in the Catholic Church. In 1512, Father Luther earned his doctorate in theology and became a professor of biblical theology at the University of Wittenberg. In the spring of 1515, Dr. Luther began lecturing on St. Paul's Epistle to the Romans. The apostle Paul writes, "Therefore, since we have been justified by faith, we have peace with God through our Lord Jesus Christ" (Romans 5:1). With these words, St. Paul connects faith in Christ to peace with God the Father.

> *Since we are justified*, through God's imputation, *therefore by faith*, not by works, *we have peace*, in conscience and spirit, *with God*, although not yet with men and the flesh and the world and the devil, indeed, we have the more trouble, *through our Lord Jesus Christ*, as through our Mediator and not through ourselves, even though we are already justified by faith. *Through whom*, as our Mediator, *we have obtained access*, to God by loving and knowing and delighting in Him, *by faith*, because there will be no salvation through Christ without faith, *to this grace*, of peace, remission of sins, and justification, *in which we stand*, through the firm confession of faith, *and we rejoice*, not in a present thing before men but *in our hope of sharing the glory*, the exaltation, that is, the glorification in the future life *of the sons*

of God, those who are of God. (25:6, italics in original)

While lecturing on the Epistle to the Romans, Luther began to realize a distinction between the Law of God, which confronts the conscience and induces guilt because of sin, and the Gospel of God, which frees the conscience and brings true peace through faith in Christ. With the Law, the individual correctly sees God as the judge. With the Gospel, the individual correctly sees the incarnate God, Jesus, as the mediator, the propitiation for our sins, our advocate with the Father, and the true image of God. With the Gospel, the individual sees that Jesus bears our sin and only God can justify us.

After two years of lecturing on Paul's Epistle to the Romans, Luther could not stomach the selling of plenary indulgences, especially the aggressive exploitation of indulgences by Johann Tetzel. On October 31, 1517, Martin Luther posted the Ninety-Five Theses, challenging the selling of plenary indulgences. Tetzel was offering a different image of God. Out of pastoral care, Luther wanted the baptized with terrified consciences to hear the true Gospel, rather than to believe the lie that their consciences could have peace by purchasing a piece of paper. Luther knew they were buying a false peace that would be stripped away on the Last Day. Their consciences were being bound to something other than God's Word, and they were selling themselves into idolatry. Luther was appalled that Jesus was being robbed of the glory and honor that properly belongs to Him alone.

Although Luther's Ninety-Five Theses did not spark the response among leaders of the Church that Luther had hoped for, his thinking about God's Word and our relationship to God through Christ had been so altered by the true Gospel, he could not give up the liberating treasure that he saw being buried by the Medieval Church. The Reformation was all about re-forming the conscience with the Word of God, because Luther realized that only the Law can teach us what is right in God's sight. However, the Law cannot justify. Only the preaching of the Gospel makes us right with God, because it points to Jesus, the Savior, who gives true peace to the conscience as He takes away all sin, fulfills the Law in our stead, and gives us His own righteousness. God justifies through faith alone apart from the works of the Law. The Gospel projects the image of Christ as our mediator who stands for us before the judge.

Luther Lectures on the Book of Isaiah

Luther continued this distinction of Law and Gospel and applied it to his lectures on Isaiah starting in 1527. He referenced the Book of Romans in forty-one of the sixty-six chapters in his commentary on Isaiah. Furthermore, he directly referred to Romans 5:1 (discussed above) while commenting on Isaiah chapters 12, 26, 29, and 32. Commenting on Isaiah 12:1, Luther ponitificated,

Because Thou wast angry with me. The church gives thanks not for wrath that is present, but for wrath that has been taken away; for when the yoke of sin and death has been removed, then it will help to remember the evils. Paul says in Rom. 1:18 and 4:15 that "the Law brings wrath," and from this wrath the Gospel frees when it is believed.

Thou didst comfort me, that is, Thou didst restore to me the voice of rejoicing. Luke 7:48: "Your sins are forgiven." John 1:29: "Behold, the Lamb of God, who takes away the sin of the world." Rom. 5:1ff.: For without the forgiveness of sins there is no peace, but the opposite. He is therefore speaking of public, not private, consolation through the Gospel.

Behold, God is my Salvation. This is a description of the peace that comes after the forgiveness of sins has been received. Thus the heart stands firm, and this is proclaimed. Now I have someone on whom I may rely and in whom I may trust, to whom I may look, namely, God, who no longer is angry and punishes but saves from every danger and evil. Christians are surrounded by countless evils and varieties of death; many are their enemies and detractors, but God provides wings so that they may fly away. Christ is with them and preserves them and does not destroy them.

I will trust. This is the peace and safety of the conscience when it knows God as reconciled and Christ as Savior and Protector. But if it is still afraid of something, this is a temptation of the devil or a residue of the old man. (16:128–29)

While discussing Isaiah 29:22, Luther states,

This is the greatest comfort of the godly. It is as if he were saying: "Until now, while the ungodly teachers were in

> control, there was nothing but confusion, sadness, and constant fear. But now that Christ the Shepherd and the Gospel have been revealed and the ungodly have been rooted out, we stand justified and have peace with God in our hearts through Him, as Paul exquisitely depicts that glory and joy in Rom. 5:1." (16:250)

As he realized from the Book of Romans, Luther continued to teach that in this life, sin constantly plagues the individual. The Law brings the knowledge of sin and increases the trespass. Where the trespass increases, the guilt becomes overbearing (see Romans 3:20; 5:20). Sin enslaves, the Law imprisons, but the preaching of the Gospel sets the conscience free. When we are justified through faith alone in the person and work of Christ alone, we have peace with God.

Isaiah writes,

> And the effect of righteousness will be peace, and the result of righteousness, quietness and trust forever. (Isaiah 32:17)

Restoring the Way of Peace

Luther was accused of introducing a new teaching to the Church. He did not sing the same song of his contemporaries. His song sounded similar to that of a goose, namely, Jan Hus, who was burned at the stake in 1415 for being a heretic. Those who challenged the authority of the pope were deemed heretics. Luther challenged the authority of the pope. Thus, he was officially condemned and excommunicated from the Church in 1521. Luther maintained that the only "new" teachings brought into the Church came from the theologians in the Middle Ages. Luther anchored his authority in the written Scriptures. In fact, he saw prophets like Isaiah engaged in the same conflict with the authorities of their days.

> The way of peace they do not know, and there is no justice in their paths; they have made their roads crooked; no one who treads on them knows peace. (Isaiah 59:8)

> Hence the doctrine concerning the forgiveness of sins must

It is the proper office of this king to preach the Gospel, to proclaim good news.

— MARTIN LUTHER

> be diligently treated. Where this is lost, the church perishes, and minds become fainthearted and full of doubt and torture themselves with endless works. . . .
>
> They do not know by what process the afflicted conscience is given peace. Even if they hear it, they cannot judge sincerely. They do not know which way leads to peace. Christ is the way of peace, in Him alone one must believe and simply commit oneself to His mercy, as all of Scripture invites us to do. "Cast your burden on the Lord" (Ps. 55:22). Take the risk in the name of our God. Thus the psalmist says, "He will sustain you." This is very difficult for our nature, to move beyond the knowledge of nature and to cling to God alone. If we have not had this way of peace, we will not be safe. This happened under the papacy, where we sought the support and the prayers of the saints. Christ was bypassed like an angry judge. In this way we were estranged from God, and we ran to the uncertain intercessions of the saints. This is what it means to have desolation and not to know the way of peace. (17:299–300)

The theologians in Luther's day busied themselves with their own speculations about God's hidden majesty. Thus, they overlooked the peace to be found in the mystery of the incarnation. Jesus is the Prince of Peace who comes to bring peace with God.

Christ, the Preacher of Peace

Luther emphasizes that the faith that justifies and brings peace comes from hearing the preached Word. In Luther's reading of Isaiah, he notes that Jesus Himself was sent to preach peace. After Jesus was baptized in the Jordan River and anointed with the Holy Spirit, He began to preach. In Luke 4, He went to the synagogue in Nazareth, His hometown. He took the Isaiah scroll and read from the following passage:

> The Spirit of the Lord GOD is upon Me, because the LORD has anointed Me to bring good news to the poor; He has sent Me to bind up the brokenhearted, to proclaim liberty to the captives, and the opening of the prison to those who are bound; to proclaim the year of the LORD's favor, and the

> day of vengeance of our God; to comfort all who mourn; to grant to those who mourn in Zion—to give them a beautiful headdress instead of ashes, the oil of gladness instead of mourning, the garment of praise instead of a faint spirit; that they may be called oaks of righteousness, the planting of the LORD, that He may be glorified. (Isaiah 61:1–3)

This text is most clearly understood from Luke 4, where Christ Himself uses this text as a most clear witness to His own person (Luke 4:18). Let us diligently consider this text so that we may hold to Christ as defined and properly depicted. Just as we can so define a matter that we can separate it from all foreign tasks, so Christ is here most properly defined, as well as His tasks and His function. Satan cannot bear this idea of Christ, and he constantly attacks it. Under the papists Christ was turned into a stern judge. This is a devilish idea by which men, servants of Satan, have been persuaded. Therefore we must always strive to know Christ well. For this knowledge is the head of Scripture. . . .

First He says that He was anointed, indicating that He was made King and Priest. He is the Messiah. . . .

He has sent *Me to bring good tidings to the afflicted*. Here Christ is defined as Servant, Messenger, Apostle, to whom the office of the Word has been committed. This is in force against the Jews, who were looking for an imposing Christ. *To the afflicted*. In the Scriptures the afflicted are the poor and the distressed. So Matt. 11:5 reads: "The poor have good news preached to them." . . . Here Christ is sent and called to preach to the afflicted and the wretched. This is very clear in opposition to the Jews, who are hoping for a Christ who will reign and rule over a worldly empire, when in reality it is the proper office of this King to preach the Gospel, to proclaim good news. Now, the pope wants to be the vicar of Christ, not of the Christ described here, but of a glorious Christ. But Christ did not leave any vicars of His except those who are true to His primary office, that of preaching. The pope, however, wants to be enthroned in majesty, to have all things in his power, and to change things to suit himself,

> meanwhile neglecting Christ's true office. All of our bishops are doing this. They are not true vicars of Christ, namely, the preaching, crucified, suffering, serving Christ. Here the prophet is describing Christ and His office. (17:329, 330)

Notice how Luther draws our attention to both the person and work of Christ. He is anointed and sent. One who is sent is sent with a message. Thus, Christ is the messenger who brings the message of Good News to the afflicted and distressed. Luther continues his train of thought:

Christ is the person sent by God and filled with the Holy Spirit to be the Preacher and Evangelist to the poor, that is, the afflicted. This was not done for Christ's sake but for our sake. Thus Paul boasts about his calling in a most ostentatious way, not for his own sake but for the purpose of strengthening us who are weak and of terrifying the ungodly. It is only this preaching and function of Christ that makes the poor and afflicted very strong in the will of God, so that they may know that all things turn out for them according to the will of God. Note this especially, that we must be content with the God of majesty when we consider His hidden but grand and terrifying offices. When we fall into this labyrinth, we become involved in speculations about divinity, and we want to become investigators of His majesty at our peril.

As for you, be content with the God incarnate. Then you will remain in peace and safety, and you will know God. Cast off speculations about divine glory, as the pope and Mohammed speculate. You stay with Christ crucified, whom Paul and others preach. But those who immerse themselves in their own speculations about the divine, for example, why God spares so many Turks and condemns so many, they are plunged into confusion with their speculations. So it happened to Erasmus and the pope that they say there is no God and despise God. Others fall into despair because of such speculation. But since Christ and His office are here set forth, we must be content with that description.

It is because of His humanity and His incarnation that Christ becomes sweet to us, and through Him God becomes sweet to us. Let us therefore begin to ascend step by step from Christ's crying in His swaddling clothes up to His Passion. Then we shall easily know God. I am saying this so that you do not begin to contemplate God from the top, but start with the weak elements. We should busy ourselves completely with treating, knowing, and considering this man. Then you will know that He is the Way, the Truth, and the Life (John 14:6). So He set forth His weakness that we may approach Him with confidence. (17:330–31)

Again, Luther emphasizes the importance of the incarnation. Jesus is Immanuel, that is, God with us. He becomes poor and afflicted to dwell with us in our existence. We should not speculate about the hiddenness of God in His majesty. This will lead to idolatry and terror. Instead, we are to seek God where He promises to be present. This will lead to comfort and peace, which comes from the message of the Messenger. Luther goes on to contemplate the purpose of this message.

To bind up the brokenhearted. "It is My office to heal, or to bind up, as the physicians do." He describes these three tasks. 1 Cor. 15:56 depicts three wounds, the Law, sin, and death. The prophet here describes the office of Christ as the cure for these wounds. Paul is speaking of the Law, whereby God's wrath is experienced and perceived, and he convinces us that we have no strength in which to excel. Then, in conformity with this, sin follows, whereby the Law troubles us. Then follows eternal death. These are the three chief things with which Christ, our Bishop, struggles. "The sting of death is sin, and the power of sin is the Law" (1 Cor. 15:56). Here no man can help. I take Christ's three tasks as applying to these three things. To heal *the brokenhearted*, this is the first. Those who are crushed by the Law I bind up and heal, so that they may not despair. Second, *the captives*, those who are captive under sin. For sins have snatched us like thieves. Then third, *opening to those who are bound*. The judge pronounces sentence, which is death. Against these three evils the knowledge of Christ is in force, if we would know Christ to be the man who can free us from these evils. Therefore let us know that Christ is not a judge or a teacher of the Law, but He does the opposite: He heals, He consoles, He frees us from these evils. In the second place: *To proclaim liberty to the captives.* The prophet is referring to the year of release (Deut. 15:1ff.). We are held captive under debts and are bankrupt, but Christ sets us free from them. These are two victories, over sin and over death. In the third place, *the opening of the prison to those who are bound*, namely, under the Law, for we are bound by the Law, since we are sinners. From these bonds Christ delivers us so that we may not be condemned by the Law. (17:331–32)

With these words, Luther draws our attention to the imagery of healing a broken heart through preaching peace. A wounded conscience cannot be made healthy with more Law. Christ comes to provide care and cure for the soul. Although the Law accuses, it cannot condemn those who are in Christ. Luther continues by stating,

Note that Christ is a preacher to the poor and is sent to free us and help us, and this happens by the Word alone. "Through the Word I heal them so that they may know that they are free from sin, death, and the Law." . . . The deliverance from these afflictions, I say, is ours through Christ, but in this respect there is a deficiency, that we cannot believe these words. We think heaven is filled with our sins, with the Law and death. Therefore these words must be carefully weighed. In them we should see life, salvation, and deliverance. This will not come to pass in this life. By faith we shall only see that the matter has been begun, not that it is completed. For here he sets forth bonds, captivity, and the anguish of death. We experience them in this life, and yet in the Word of Christ we should triumph over these things that are against us. While the Law is done away as far as the spirit is concerned, so that it does not accuse and trouble us, it is, I say, not done away as if the Law were no longer there. It is abolished in that it does not sting us, and the Christian can say, "Although I feel the Law and sin, in opposition to them I have Christ, the Preacher who heals and consoles me." Christ is greater than Law, sin, and death, for it is His special office not to be conquered by them but to conquer them and help others to be free of them. Therefore you have Christ defined as the

> Preacher of peace. The *poor* are the afflicted and well-nigh despairing. Thus the human heart can learn where to find refuge, with Christ the Mediator alone. Neither papist nor ungodly man understands these words, and therefore they seek other mediators. (17:332–33)

Luther wanted to emphasize that Jesus is not an angry judge. Rather, He is our one mediator between God and us. He did not come to condemn us, but He came to preach Good News to the heart, liberating it.

As Luther made a distinction between the Law and the Gospel in his lectures on Romans, he saw this same distinction in the Book of Isaiah. Luther states,

> Therefore we sinners and imprisoned should accustom ourselves to this saying, *the agreeable year*, because the terrible law does not apply to those who are Christ's, but rather the promise concerning sins does. Hence it is a great art rightly to divide the Word, to proclaim a hard message to the hard and a soft and gentle one to the afflicted. The despondent set terrible things before themselves, and then Satan comes and terrifies them. Those who are experiencing such affliction are to be consoled. The presumptuous, on the contrary, are forever flattering themselves and ascribing all manner of good and pleasant things to themselves, in such a way that they are always being hardened. They are to be terrified. As the psalm says (Ps. 36:1f.), "There is no fear of God before his eyes. For he flatters himself in his own eyes." He turns the threats away from himself and applies the promises to himself. The conscience of the afflicted acts in the opposite way. Hence in the midst of good we must not forget the evil, and in the midst of evil we must not forget the good. We must always apply the one to the other, and then we will not become either presumptuous or despondent. Thus this passage concerning the *agreeable year* is of great help to the afflicted, but it serves the purpose of wounding the presumptuous. All consolations are addressed to the godly, because the Word of Christ consists in this, that in His time, when He will have come into the world, there will be nothing but the *agreeable year*, no terror, no law, no judge. (17:333–34)

Again, for Luther, the godly are the justified believers. The wicked, that is, the ungodly, have no peace (see Isaiah 48:22; 57:21).

Preaching Comfort and Peace

In the first half of the Book of Isaiah (chapters 1–39), the kings and the priests are warned about leading the people astray. The Lord threatens them with fire and the sword. Yet, the first half closes with God delivering His people from the hand of the Assyrians. In the second half of the Book of Isaiah (chapters 40–66), Jerusalem is handed over to the Babylonians. God is the one who brings Babylon against Jerusalem. Fighting against Nebuchadnezzar is fighting against the Lord. The people of God fight against Him and lose the rebellion. The sentence for treason is death. With these words, the prophet Isaiah speaks to the people of God who have found themselves in captivity under the Babylonians. Isaiah writes to those who are crushed. Their consciences are troubled, causing them to doubt and despair, leading them to ponder if they have been forsaken by God. Are they still God's people? Is God still angry? Isaiah writes,

> Comfort, comfort My people, says your God. Speak tenderly to Jerusalem, and cry to her that her warfare is ended, that her iniquity is pardoned, that she has received from the LORD's hand double for all her sins. (Isaiah 40:1–2)

The people whom Isaiah addresses here have wounded consciences. The Gospel proclaims Christ's kingdom as a kingdom of comfort and peace. The words of the Kingdom declare, "Comfort, comfort My people, says your God." Luther draws our attention to the little pronouns *My* and *your*.

> *My* has the accent, as if to say, "I have a people which I will not forsake." . . .
>
> A troubled conscience does not think it has God but considers God to be a devil, a judge, a prosecutor, and an enemy. This word *your* contradicts that opinion, as if to say, "Don't be afraid, because God is not your enemy. Rather, He is on your side, He is gracious to you." (17:3, 4)

Luther says the pronouns *My* and *your* make all the difference in the world. The words of comfort proclaim, "You are Mine! I am yours!" God tells Isaiah to speak comfort to "My people." Believers who doubt that they are part of God's people are to rest assured that God calls them His people. Rather than listening to the loud voice of the terrified conscience, which yells, "You are not part of God's people, and He is not your God," the crushed believer is assured by the comforting voice of God declaring, "You are My people, and I am your God."

> But they are God's people not according to the flesh but rather as people who are of a crushed and humble conscience and of a troubled heart and who call upon God in the day of trouble. Others who trust in their own merits, resources, riches, etc., are not the people of God. They do not need comfort, they are not in sadness and tribulation, because their vessel is full and can hold no consolation. Summary: God's people are those who need comfort because they have been wounded and terrified by the Law and they are an empty vessel capable of receiving comfort. Only those who are afflicted have comfort and are capable of it, because comfort means nothing unless there is a malady. (17:3)

In this life, sin continues to cling and bring down the believer. The conscience alarms the believer of the consequences of his or her own iniquity. For the heavy-laden heart that is overcome by the weight of transgressions, the only solution is to have the weight lifted by hearing God's Word and being filled by the peace of Christ. Endless labor of self-righteousness produces nothing but the anguish of the conscience. Only in Christ is the Law repealed and sin forgiven.

The tortured conscience hears the Law and only thinks of God as the judge. Yet, the Holy Spirit comes to bring comfort to the conscience based on the promises of God fulfilled in Christ. With the promise of God's grace, the conscience is assured of who God is and what God desires to do for His people. What kind of God is He? He is a God who dwells with His people, bearing their sins and being their Savior.

> *Speak tenderly to Jerusalem.* The Hebrew . . . denotes speaking in public, not in a subdued voice. *To speak tenderly,* or "to the heart," is a Hebraism which means to flatter, to cajole, as in

Gen. 34:3: "He spoke tenderly to her." So here, the heart, groaning and sighing, is comforted by the Spirit, for the Spirit speaks to the heart as He wills. Do you want a gracious God? He answers: "You have a gracious God." Do you want to be comforted? He answers: "You are comforted." Here, then, you observe God's people, afflicted and sad. To them the Gospel is spoken, to their heart and feeling. For Gospel preachers are commanded to say joyful things, more than the heart can grasp, as Paul says (Rom. 8:26), "with sighs too deep for words." So these groans are comforted with consolations too deep for words. Let the preacher say, then: "I not only preach Christ to you as the One who forgives, but I also give you His righteousness, so that, clothed with Him, you may have all that is His. The comfort is therefore far more excellent than all groanings. Do you want to be holy? I will make you holy, yes, most holy through Christ." (17:4)

God speaks to the downtrodden heart and lifts it up with true peace. The heart is troubled because of the impending judgment against sin. The only remedy is to preach Christ who forgives sins. When the conscience detects evil actions, the believer is left naked, ashamed, and guilty. When the comfort of Jesus quiets the conscience, the believer is comforted and filled with joy beyond expression. Christ's righteousness cleanses and clothes the believer. Christ's righteousness is imputed to us through faith, which means Christ's righteousness becomes our own. The Gospel message announces that the Lord gives a double measure from His hand, iniquity is pardoned, and the warfare is ended.

Here the prophet explains what the words of comfort are and what his treasure is: "Our warfare is ended, and double gifts are given in its stead." Let these words avail against the advocates of free will. *Warfare.* In the Sacred Scriptures every striving, attempt, and religious exercise represents this warfare of the Law. May the Spirit change it into the warfare of Christ! For to conduct warfare under the Law is to strive and to toil under the Law. Certainly those who are zealous in offering works of the Law have this warfare, like the self-righteous, just as the Jews conducted warfare under the Law with an evil zeal (Rom. 10:2). Warfare is the anxious and

Your warfare is finished and ended through Christ, the Redeemer.

—MARTIN LUTHER

> agitated concern to render satisfaction to God. For under the Law we are as it were under a custodian (Gal. 3:24). To love and to strive is to conduct warfare, and they are zealous in these works of loving and striving. When these works are finished, it is said that "your warfare is ended." Thus those who are zealous of works here conduct warfare under the Law. For them another warfare is set forth by the Spirit and the Word, namely, Christ as the Mediator and the One who renders satisfaction, as the apostles teach. Every man must necessarily first be disturbed by the scepter of the Law, of death, and of hell and must experience a confounding of his conscience. Such people truly conduct warfare under the Law. To them properly belongs the comfort of the Gospel which says, "Do not fight any longer. Your warfare is finished and ended through Christ, the Redeemer." (17:4–5)

When we are born into this world, we are born in sin. Our sin separates us from God, and we do not want His kingdom to come because we see it as an assault on our autonomous, though rebellious, realm. The threat of death and hell confound the conscience to act. Luther describes warfare in the sense, then, of one fighting against the accusations of the Law by laboring and toiling in attempt to make satisfaction for sins. For Luther, this struggle and strife is no different from an attempt to make God merciful as if He were not merciful. To see God as wrathful unless we appease Him, making Him well-disposed toward us, is idolatry. Just as we cannot merit God's favor by our works, we also cannot earn God's forgiveness.

However, the only-begotten Son assumes our human nature to restore us and reconcile us. He comes to bring peace between the Creator and fallen creation. In Christ, there is a peace agreement. Christ is the end of the warfare under the Law. In Christ, we are no longer enemies but friends with God. In Christ, there is more than just a temporary cease-fire or even a formal armistice; we have peace with God. When we behold Christ as the true visible image of God, we see the one mediator between God and humanity. We see God as He truly is. He is merciful and abounding in steadfast love. He brings peace and pardon. In Christ, your warfare is ended, and your iniquities are pardoned. Through His struggle and strife, He has made satisfaction for our sins. Christ alone has merited God's favor and forgiveness for us. By God's grace alone, we receive the free gift of salvation.

Your iniquity is forgiven. This is the second thing. This is the reply to those who strive in warfare and say: "I would gladly get rid of this warfare and my works, but how shall I be freed from my sins? What help will there be for me?" The prophet answers, *Your iniquity is forgiven*, that is, forgiven by grace and mercy. You are set free from sins, not by working and struggling but by forgiveness. Scripture teaches deliverance from sins by forgiveness and divine pardon, gratis and apart from works of the Law. This is contrary to the self-righteous, who teach that forgiveness of sins lies in works and strivings. For all seek remission of sins in their own powers, merits, and devotions as they busy themselves with the object of the Law. They want to be delivered by means of cowls, pilgrimages, etc. You shameless hypocrite, you want to revive those things which the Gospel looks back on. The Gospel says, "Believe God, trust in God. For your faith receives pardon for sins." This is a grand text. Satan has often scolded me for believing the Christian faith to be contained in such few words, "The warfare is ended and iniquity is forgiven." Meanwhile he wanted to have me turn to the objects of the Law and tried to lead me back to this finished warfare. Against his stratagems, therefore, you must firmly say this: "I'm not concerned one whit about this warfare. It is ended. I will gladly bear it as a custodian of the flesh, but as a spiritual custodian of the conscience I will under no circumstances admit either the Law or the fathers, or Ambrose, or Jerome." Say rather to your adversary, "Have you not read Isaiah, *the warfare is ended?* Don't hang me up with the works of the fathers and the commandments of the Law." It is a great thing to cling firmly to these words. We indeed can believe these words, but it requires strength to rely on them and to shed blood for them. Let us not take it lightly. Whether sin or righteousness come, say, "I have my righteousness, Christ." This is a difficult passage and one of prime importance. May you diligently learn it, something that none of the schismatics have done so far. I cannot sufficiently urge this passage upon you, because it

> is so necessary, lest it again fall into forgetfulness. Therefore this text says *the warfare is ended*. Stop trusting in works, but seek righteousness in the kingdom of Christ and of mercy, where sins are forgiven gratis. All other works, however, are works that may be sincerely done without peril to conscience. Act in this way that the Law remains as a civil taskmaster, only do not let it touch your conscience. Learn, then, to rely on this text against all things, against sin, righteousnesses, and merits. (17:5–6)

Again, God's people, with wounded consciences, had been entrusted with the Law of God. When the conscience encounters the Law, there is a flight-or-fight mentality. We either run for cover in our own self-made bomb shelters or we run headfirst into battle. The Law of God was not given to the people of God so that they could become self-sufficient. It was not intended to be a self-help guide for the accomplishment of self-righteousness before God, as if God's people would no longer need grace, mercy, and the forgiveness of sins. The proper place for the Law is as a custodian of the flesh. Luther calls it a civil taskmaster, not a spiritual custodian of the conscience. The Law keeps our corrupted sinful nature in check. It is a curb and a guide. But Luther says to "not let it touch your conscience" because it was never meant to reign and rule over the conscience. If the Law takes control of the conscience, then the conscience can only condemn.

On the other hand, the Gospel cleanses the conscience and sets it at peace. The warfare is ended! No longer is there a need to learn war. As hearts are converted, swords are turned into plowshares and spears are made into pruning hooks (see Isaiah 2:4). God is merciful. Sins are forgiven freely for Christ's sake. Faith receives the pardon as a gift from God. In fact, the promises of God give double comfort.

> *She has received from the Lord's hand double.* Here he describes the power of the comfort, double gifts. Sin no longer weighs us down, the source is removed, and the tree has been chopped down. We can easily master the branches, now that sin has been overcome by Him who is the Fount. . . . *She has received double for all her sins.* All merits and righteousnesses are rejected. The word is, "she has received double." *For all her sins.* This is a great gain.

We have heard the words of comfort and of faith whereby the apostles are commanded to console the afflicted, namely, forgiveness of sins and repeal of all laws. But hitherto this passage has been treated not only in an ungodly manner but also in a perverted one. Rare were the teachers who did not make terrors out of promises and consolations out of the Law, who did not turn Christ into Moses, because human nature always attempts to achieve things by itself and has no desire for Christ. Yet in Christ there is complete repeal of laws and forgiveness of all sins. This is the chief affirmation of Christian philosophy. At this article of faith the Greeks are offended and the Jews are scandalized. Here all reason is offended. I say this: All the most excellent writers did not devote even two lines to the treatment of this passage, excepting only Augustine and his followers. Dr. Jerome explains the *she has received double* as saying that the Jews were punished twice, once by the Babylonians and then by the Romans. But this contributes nothing. For the wisdom of the flesh argues thus: "I have received punishment for my sins." All laws agree with this. But we see praise of grace here, that for all our sins we receive double gifts contrary to all human reason and counsel. *For all her sins*, that is, "because of." *For* in place of *because of* is a Hebraism. Grace is wonderful. Not only is a single gift given for sins, but doubled and outstanding gifts are given. Summary: By the pure mercy of God doubled gifts are given for all sins. We have learned this by experience. By our endless works and labors and in endless ways we have resisted this grace and achieved nothing but anguish of conscience. Here, however, you see it said by the wisdom of the Spirit that we attain to all these things by the grace of God alone, not as a result of our merits, but for our sins. (17:6–7)

In Luther's comment, we can see how he gave the Gospel preeminence in his reading of Isaiah. Luther followed the interpretation of the Early Church Fathers, unless the Gospel was obscured. When he disagreed with Jerome, he made it known. Jesus is not another Moses. Christ does not tell humanity to listen to Moses; rather, Moses tells Israel to heed Christ. As the prophets redirected the wayward sheep to Moses, Moses moved their memory to the promises of the coming Prophet like him; Christ is the one to be heard (see Deuteronomy 18:15). Luther states,

> Christ Himself speaks in the New Testament. Moses has been repealed. The Word of God is set forth with full clarity, and through it Christ will be proclaimed. (17:10)

Jesus says, "Do not think that I will accuse you to the Father. There is one who accuses you: Moses, on whom you have set your hope. For if you believed Moses, you would believe Me; for he wrote of Me. But if you do not believe his writings, how will you believe My words?" (John 5:45–47). The Son of God is sent to overcome sin and destroy death. He fulfills the Law of God so that it no longer can condemn. He alone is holy and righteous in God's sight. And His holiness and righteousness become ours by faith. He is the fount and source of our life, salvation, pardon, and peace. Only the Lord can atone for sin. Only Christ can give pardon and peace. He overcomes sin and gives double grace.

Consequently, sin no longer weighs down the believer in Christ. The only way heavy-laden hearts can be lifted is if the Lord's hand lifts them. Comfort does not come from inward feelings. God's voice is not the inner voice of the conscience. We do not receive double comfort from the heart. No, we receive double comfort from the hand of God. True comfort comes externally through the Word of the Lord because it brings faith; and faith clings to the person and work of Christ in whom is true peace.

The Man without Peace

Perhaps the most important text in Isaiah from Luther's perspective was the description and promise of Christ in Isaiah 53. One image of Christ in this passage is that of a man rejected by men.

> Who has believed what he has heard from us? And to whom has the arm of the LORD been revealed? For He grew up before Him like a young plant, and like a root out of dry ground; He had no form or majesty that we should look at Him, and no beauty that we should desire Him. He was despised and rejected by men, a man of sorrows and acquainted with grief; and as one from whom men hide

their faces He was despised, and we esteemed Him not.

Surely He has borne our griefs and carried our sorrows; yet we esteemed Him stricken, smitten by God, and afflicted. (Isaiah 53:1–4)

In this vision of Jesus, everything is turned upside down. We know He is the Son of God. Yet, here He is weak and helpless. He is stricken, smitten, and afflicted. His glory is robbed. Isaiah describes Jesus as a man rejected by men. Isaiah sees a man of sorrows who is acquainted with grief. Psalm 32:10 says, "Many are the sorrows of the wicked." Deuteronomy 28:15–68 warns that grief is a curse caused by breaking the covenant of God. So it seems Jesus is pronounced guilty of breaking God's Law and guilty of wickedness. He is handed over to be judged by God, and He is condemned. He is left in despair and darkness. Moses writes, "A . . . man [who is hung on a tree] is cursed by God" (Deuteronomy 21:23). And again he states, "Each one shall be put to death for his own sin" (24:16). The image in Isaiah 53 is of the sinner of sinners, cursed and forsaken by God. He is hung on a tree, tossed into the open grave, and swallowed up by Sheol.

> We thought that He was suffering because of His own sin, as it were. In the eyes of the world and of the flesh Christ does not suffer for us, since He seemed to have deserved it Himself. . . . The Law is that everybody dies for his own sins. Natural reason, and divine as well, argues that everybody must bear his own sin. Yet He is struck down contrary to all law and custom. Hence reason infers that He was smitten by God for His own sake. Therefore the prophet leads us so earnestly beyond all righteousness and our rational capacity and confronts us with the suffering of Christ to impress upon us that all that Christ has is mine. This is the preaching of the whole Gospel, to show us that Christ suffered for our sake contrary to law, right, and custom. (17:221–22)

The picture of Jesus in Isaiah 53 is the opposite of everything we'd expect. By nature, we reject God. Jesus became a man rejected by God for us, so that we would not be rejected by God. He is the man of sorrows, because He carries all our sorrows. He is acquainted with grief, because He bears all our grief. Our iniquity is laid upon Him, and He is crushed for our iniquities. He is pierced for our transgressions. Transgression is rebellion against the King. We are the rebels. He is the King. Yet, He takes our punishment and even makes intercession for us, the transgressors. He becomes the Suffering Servant who is wounded for us. Our wounded consciences are healed by His wounds. He is chastised, and we receive peace. He is afflicted, and we are comforted.

Christ did not suffer for His own sins. He committed no sin. Thus, He was not smitten by God for His own sake but for our sake. In the mystery of the incarnation, He became like us in every manner but without sin. Our sin was imputed to Him, that is, our wickedness was counted against Him. He was counted guilty and was put to death so that we could be counted innocent and could have life. He was cursed and killed for us, so that we would become blessed in Him and raised with Him.

> This states the purpose of Christ's suffering. It was not for Himself and His own sins, but for our sins and griefs. He bore what we should have suffered. Here you see the fountain from which St. Paul draws countless streams of the suffering and merits of Christ, and he condemns all religions, merits, and endeavors in the whole world through which men seek salvation. Note the countless sects who to this day are toiling to obtain salvation. But here the prophet says, "He for us." It is difficult for the flesh to repudiate all its resources, to turn away from self, and to be carried over to Christ. It is for us who have merited nothing not to have regard for our merits but simply to cling to the Word between heaven and earth, even though we do not feel it. Unless we have been instructed by God, we will not understand this. Therefore I delight in this text as if it were a text of the New Testament. This new teaching which demolishes the righteousness of the Law clearly appeared absurd to the Jews. For that reason the apostles needed Scripture, *Surely He has borne our griefs*. His suffering was nothing else than our sin. These words, OUR, US, FOR US, must be written in letters of gold. He who does not believe this is not a Christian. (17:221)

Just as Luther sees great things in the little pronouns *My* and *your*, he also sees the Gospel in the little prepositional phrase *for us.* Jesus did not suffer for Himself. Jesus was handed over to death for us, for your sins and for mine. This Gospel is the true treasure of the Church. It should be distributed freely. Christ alone earns and merits favor with God the Father—not with money, but by His precious blood and innocent suffering and death. He took our debt, and we get His freedom. All that we have has become Christ's and all that Christ has has become ours; it is a promise that can only be received by faith. This Gospel promise is written in letters of gold on our hearts through God's voice speaking His Word to us.

> This passage forms the basis for the church's faith that Christ's kingdom is not of this world. Now follows what He would accomplish by His suffering, whether He suffered for His own sake or for the sake of others. And this is the second part of our understanding and justification, to know that Christ suffered and was cursed and killed, but FOR US. It is not enough to know the matter, the suffering, but it is necessary to know its function. The pope retained the matter but denied the function. The Anabaptists deny both. (17:220–21)

Christ's kingdom is not like earthly kingdoms, which come by power and might. Christ's kingdom comes through suffering and death. Temporal kingdoms make enemies out of friends and execute traitors to the throne. Christ's kingdom makes friends out of enemies and exonerates those convicted of treason. Christ even intercedes for the transgressors of His kingdom. Christ's kingdom is a spiritual kingdom.

When Luther teaches about justification, he uses the Hebrew manner of speaking, in which "to justify" means to be absolved from guilt, pardoned, and acquitted. Luther's opponents used Jerome's Latin translation of the Bible. The Latin understanding of justification means to make righteous. Therefore, the emphasis is placed on the actions of the individual to make oneself righteous by good works. In contradistinction, the Hebrew understanding of justification places the emphasis on God's action. Thus, our justification through Christ is a declared righteousness and a pronouncement of innocence by God. On the cross, Christ is pronounced guilty of all of our sins, iniquities, trespasses, transgressions, and wickedness. His righteousness, blessedness, holiness, and innocence are reckoned as ours by faith. Furthermore, this righteousness is not merely an abstract concept; instead, by faith, Christ's righteousness becomes ours. Christ is our righteousness. For Luther, the crucifixion is not just a historical fact that is believed to be true; it also has a function. The Gospel gives what it says, and faith receives what it believes. When the conscience judges the believer as guilty, the Gospel overturns the ruling, announcing the believer as innocent for the sake of Christ. Christ is judged guilty so that in Him, we would be innocent.

> By oppression and judgment He was taken away; and as for His generation, who considered that He was cut off out of the land of the living, stricken for the transgression of My people? And they made His grave with the wicked and with a rich man in His death, although He had done no violence, and there was no deceit in His mouth. (Isaiah 53:8–9)

> *Although He had done no violence, and there was no deceit in His mouth.* The most innocent Christ was judged by the Jews to be the most guilty, He who was most innocent and guiltless in His teaching and His life. They had not a word to say to Him. Although He was innocent, yet the Lord willed it that He should take upon Himself to be the most criminal of men. Therefore he compares Him with all other men, and they, even though most holy, are guilty. This one Christ alone is the exception; He alone is righteous and holy. For that reason death could not hold Him. (17:228)

Christ alone is innocent before the Father. Yet, He was judged guilty of all the sins of the world. Only in Christ can the guilty conscience become innocent before God. When the conscience is troubled by its own sin, the words of justification bring comfort, assuring the believer that Jesus has made complete satisfaction for all sin. The message of the cross speaks to the troubled heart, saying, "Behold the man, Jesus! Behold, the Suffering Servant! Jesus was cursed and killed for you." His righteousness and holiness become ours by faith, which has the power to unite the soul with Jesus. Death could not hold Him. Therefore, death cannot hold us.

If we preserve this article, "Jesus Christ is the Savior", all other articles concerning the Holy Spirit and of the church and of Scripture are safe.

—MARTIN LUTHER

The Chastisement That Brought Us Peace

Another image of Christ that Luther thought was highly important in Isaiah 53 is Christ as the Lamb of God.

> But He was pierced for our transgressions; He was crushed for our iniquities; upon Him was the chastisement that brought us peace, and with His wounds we are healed. All we like sheep have gone astray; we have turned—every one—to His own way; and the LORD has laid on Him the iniquity of us all.
>
> He was oppressed, and He was afflicted, yet He opened not His mouth; like a lamb that is led to the slaughter, and like a sheep that before its shearers is silent, so He opened not His mouth. (Isaiah 53:5–7)

He was wounded. . . . From this you must infer how far apart are the teachings of Paul and the pope. Paul clings to Christ alone as the sin bearer. By means of this one word, "Lamb of God" (John 1:29), John the Baptist understands this Levitical sacrifice, that He suffered for the sins of all. It follows, then, that the Law and merits do not justify. Away with the Antichrist pope with his traditions, since Christ has borne all these things! I marvel that this text was so greatly obscured in the church. They note the concern of Scripture that faith without works is dead, and we say the same thing. In public argument, however, we say that works are indeed necessary, but not as justifying elements. Thus anyone may privately come to the conclusion, "It is all the same whether I have sinned or whether I have done well." This is hard for the conscience to believe, that it is the same and in fact something angelic and divine. Therefore this text draws the following conclusion: "Christ alone bears our sins. Our works are not Christ. Therefore there is no righteousness of works." Surely none of the papists can escape this fact when he sees Scripture as a whole, that Christ has accomplished all things for justification and therefore we have not done it. Appeal to works, rewards, and merits and make much of them in the realm of outward recompense. Only do not make them responsible for justification and the forgiveness of sins. We can preach and uphold this passage in public, but we can only believe it with difficulty in private. If we preserve this article, "Jesus Christ is the Savior," all other articles concerning the Holy Spirit and of the church and of Scripture are safe. Thus Satan attacks no article so much as this one. He alone is a Christian who believes that Christ labors for us and that He is the Lamb of God slain for our sins. While this article stands, all the monasteries of righteousness, etc., are struck down by lightning. In the light of this text read all the epistles of Paul with regard to redemption, salvation, and liberation, because they are all drawn from this fountain. A blind papacy read and chanted these and similar words as in a dream, and no one really considered them. If they had, they would have cast off all righteousness from themselves. Hence it is not enough to know and accept the fact. One must also accept the function and the power of the fact. If we have this, we stand unconquered on the royal road, and the Holy Spirit is present in the face of all sects and deceptions. When this doctrine is safe, we firmly stand up to all people, but where this article is lost, we proceed from one error to the next, as we observe in the babbling Enthusiasts and in Erasmus. Our nature is opposed to the function and power of Christ's Passion. As far as the fact itself is concerned, both the pope and the Turk believe it and proclaim it, but they do not accept its function. As for you, lift up this article and extol it above every law and righteousness and let it be to you a measureless sea over against a little spark. The sea is Christ who has suffered. Your works and your righteousness are the little spark. Therefore beware, as you place your sins on your conscience, that you do not panic, but freely place them on Christ, as this text says, "He has borne our iniquities." We must clearly transfer our sins from ourselves to Christ. If you want to regard your sin as resting on you, such a thought in your heart is not of God but of Satan himself, contrary to Scripture, which by God's will places your sin on Christ. Hence you must say: "I see my sin in Christ, therefore my sin is not mine but another's. I see it in Christ." It is a great thing to say confidently: "My sin is not mine." However, it is a supreme conflict with a

> most powerful beast, which here becomes most powerful: "I behold sins heaped on Christ." (17:222–23)

By faith, the soul is joined to Christ in a union like the bond of marriage. The conscience of the believer is to be bound to Jesus, who justifies. Being justified, the conscience is given peace. The Law, sin, death, the devil, and even our own conscience cannot judge us as guilty when Christ has pardoned us. Christ silences the conscience. As Luther states, "If Christ bears my iniquities, then I do not bear them." As the sacrificial Lamb, He was silent before His accusers. Now as the High Priest, He intercedes for us because of our accusers. The Law, sin, death, and the devil had no authority to accuse Him. Therefore, in Christ, the Law, sin, death, and the devil have no authority to accuse us, and there is no condemnation. Christ grants us a liberated conscience.

It is difficult for the conscience to comprehend that neither good works nor evil works can make a person righteous or unrighteous in God's sight. The conscience is an instrument that measures and gages the work of an individual. It then evaluates the person as either innocent or guilty. Furthermore, the conscience cannot testify to the works of another person, namely, Jesus. When faith in Christ makes works of satisfaction unnecessary, the conscience finds it difficult to believe. However, Christ alone fulfills all the works of the Law for us, and He is the sin-bearer who takes away our evil works. Faith sees the sins to which the conscience testifies heaped on Jesus.

> Blessed therefore are those who as uncorrupted young people arrived at this understanding, that they can say: "I only knew Jesus Christ as the bearer of my sins." The name of Christ, then, is most agreeable. *The chastisement, or punishment, of our peace,* that is, His chastisement is the remedy that brings peace to our conscience. Before Christ there is nothing but disorder. But He was chastised for the sake of our peace. Note the wonderful exchange: One man sins, another pays the penalty; one deserves peace, the other has it. The one who should have peace has chastisement, while the one who should have chastisement has peace. . . .
>
> *And with His stripes we are healed.* See how delightfully the prophet sets Christ before us. It is a remarkable plaster. His stripes

are our healing. The stripes should be ours and the healing in Christ. Hence this is what we must say to the Christian: "If you want to be healed, do not look at your own wounds, but fix your gaze on Christ." (17:224–25)

The Word of grace portrays the Lamb of God as the one mediator who comes to restore peace between the Creator and His fallen creation. Peace with God gives peace to our conscience. Again, Luther emphasizes the wonderful exchange. Because of our sin, we should be chastised, and Christ should remain in peace. However, Jesus trades places with us. He is chastised by the Father, so that we may have peace.

Seeking Peace in Christ Alone

> Yet it was the will of the LORD to crush Him; He has put Him to grief; when His soul makes an offering for guilt, He shall see His offspring; He shall prolong His days; the will of the LORD shall prosper in His hand. Out of the anguish of His soul He shall see and be satisfied; by His knowledge shall the righteous one, My servant, make many to be accounted righteous, and He shall bear their iniquities. Therefore I will divide Him a portion with the many, and He shall divide the spoil with the strong, because He poured out His soul to death and was numbered with the transgressors; yet He bore the sin of many, and makes intercession for the transgressors. (Isaiah 53:10–12)

And He shall bear their iniquities. . . . Who is Christ? He answers: "Christ is not a judge and tormentor and tyrant, as reason apart from the Word fashions Him, but He is the bearer of our iniquities." Yet He will become judge and tyrant to those who refused to believe in Him. It is, however, the office of Christ to bear our sins. Hence we must conclude from this text: "If Christ bears my iniquities, then I do not bear them." All teachings which say that our sins must be borne by us are ungodly. Thus from such a text countless thunderbolts have come forward against an ungodly self-righteousness. So Paul by this article of justification struck down every kind of self-righteousness. Therefore we must diligently observe this article. I see that there are many snorers treating this article. They are the ones who consider these words the way a man does who looks at his face in a mirror (as James says, 1:23f.). The moment they come upon another object or business, they are overwhelmed, and they forget the grace of God. For that reason you must most diligently consider this article and not allow yourself to be led astray by other teachings, occupations, or persecutions. (17:230–31)

As we wait for the Last Day, there will be many different voices crying out in the wilderness, including the voice of burdened consciences. For this reason, the conscience must be continuously calmed with the Gospel message, which creates and sustains faith in Christ as the only Lamb of God who bears the burden of all sin. If Christ bears our iniquity, then we do not bear it. The article of justification is the article on which the Church stands or falls. It is the article by which all glory is given to Christ, which He deserves. It is the article by which the only true possible comfort is given to consciences.

Luther helps us realize that the image of Christ as a judge is not rejected altogether. Christ will come to judge the living and the dead on the Last Day. He will be the judge to those who do not trust in Him but rather trust in their own self-righteousness, and unless they believe in Him, they will die in their sin. However, now is the day of salvation. The one who hears and trusts the voice of Jesus has an advocate with the Father. The one who believes that the Lamb of God bears his sins has the forgiveness of sins now and on the Last Day.

First He depicts the suffering, second, the kind of suffering, third, the power of the suffering, and fourth, His patience. Thus He compassionately prayed for transgressors and crucifiers and shed tears for them and did not deal with them with threats. Who can place the Christ thus depicted in love into his heart, as He is here described? Oh, we would be blessed people if we could believe this most noble text, which must be magnified. I would wish it to be honored in the church, so that we might accustom ourselves to an alert study of this text, to bring us to see Christ as none other than the One who bears and shoulders the burden of our sins. This figure is a solace to the afflicted, but to snoring readers these are nothing but idle words. (17:232)

Isaiah 53 puts Christ before our eyes as the one who bore all of our burdens just as He bore His own cross to the place of His gory death. The Gospel is good news to the afflicted, bringing joy in the midst of suffering. The burden of guilt is placed on Him who bears the sin of the world.

This is the supreme and chief article of faith, that our sins, placed on Christ, are not ours; again, that the peace is not Christ's but ours. Once this foundation is established, all will be well with the superstructure. If we do not bump against this rock, other teachings will not harm us. This article alone Satan cannot but attack by means of tyrants and sects. The whole world can put up with every sectarian teaching and even support it in peace. But it cannot bear this faith and the rejection of all works and merits. Because self-glory is brought to naught and the world likes to hear its own glory, it is not willing to reject its own. Summary: The head of self-righteousness must be lopped off. I grant that the works of the godly are good and right, but they do not justify. This Satan cannot bear, and because of this we are persecuted and we suffer to the present day, since we have taught all things in peace, tranquility, patience, and purity, more than he, certainly. By this text we have cast down every foreign righteousness and hypocrisy. Therefore write this text on the foundation in golden letters or in your own blood. That is why he says *all we*, and no one is excepted.

Each one of us all, because Christ has nothing from us but death and labor (cf. chapter 43) and we have righteousness and life from Him.

And the Lord has laid. This confirms our conscience that Christ did not take our sins by His own will but by the will of the Father who had mercy on us. *On Him*, not on us, contrary to every law and order, where whoever sins is punished. Here, however, we have the punishment of our sins on Christ Himself. (17:225–26)

The old evil foe robs Christ of His glory and steals comfort from the conscience. Thus, with a heart for pastoral care for those who have fallen into despair and for those who have been deceived by the devil, Luther teaches the comforting truth of the Gospel. When we see Jesus, we see the mercy of the Father. Thus, Luther states that it was the will of the Father to provide the way of pardon, because the Father gave up His own Son to be crucified for us.

> Something further must be noted, lest those who do not feel this despair. There Satan can turn the antidote into poison and the hope into despair. For when a Christian hears these supreme consolations and then sees how weak he is with regard to his faith in them, he soon thinks that they do not apply to him. In this way Satan can turn consolation into distress. But as for you, however weak you are, know that you are a Christian, whether you believe perfectly or imperfectly, even while weakness and a feeling of death and sin remain with you. To such a person we must say: "Brother, your situation is not desperate, but pray together with the apostles for the perfection of your faith." Paul also struggled with this problem and was deeply disturbed. A Christian is not yet perfect, but he is a Christian who has, that is, who begins to have, the righteousness of God. I say this for the sake of the weak, so that they will not despair when they feel the bite of sin within themselves. They should not yet be masters and doctors but disciples of Christ, people who learn Christ, not perfect teachers. Let it suffice for us to remain with that Word as learners. Therefore, however perfect and absolute the teaching of Christ is that affirms that all our sins belong to Christ, it is not perfect in our life. It is enough for us to have begun and to be in the state of reaching after what is before us. Hence a Christian man must be especially vexed in his conscience and heart by Satan, and yet he must remain in the Word and not seek peace anywhere else than in Christ. (17:224)

In this life, sin will remain in the baptized, but it shall not reign in them. In this life, faith in Christ will be weak and will need to always be strengthened by God's Word. For only in God's Word do we behold Christ as the Crucified One set before us and only through God's Word do we receive faith to trust Him, contrary to our conscience and to Satan's attacks. The preaching of the

Gospel delivers the forgiveness of sins. The forgiveness of sins is the word of justification before God. When the burden of sins is lifted off the conscience, then the sheep can rejoice in the voice of God. They need to hear His voice repeatedly. Christ knows His sheep and His sheep know Him.

Conclusion

As a doctor of biblical studies, Luther taught the Word of God, which revealed the works of God. He learned through God's Word in Romans who God truly is and what He did in Christ for us. Luther then read the Book of Isaiah with the same realization about God's mercy and Christ's righteousness given to us. In Isaiah 40, 53, and 61, Luther found some of the texts that he thought were most important from Isaiah and for the Gospel in the Old Testament. In turn, he instructed pastors to use the images from these passages to paint the picture of Jesus before the eyes of the baptized. The re-forming of the conscience was at the heart of the Reformation. In Luther's day, Jesus was primarily depicted as the judge of the living and the dead. The image of Jesus as the Lamb was neglected even though the Agnus Dei ("Lamb of God") was regularly sung in the liturgy. Out of pastoral care, Luther trained his students to see Jesus as the one who preaches peace; as the one who proclaims comfort because He takes away our iniquity; as the one who cares for us by becoming a man and taking on all our afflictions and pains; as the Lamb of God who is slain to take away the sin of the world; and as the one who was crucified according to God's will, so that we might be raised to new life with Him. Faith is not merely the belief in the historical fact of the crucifixion of Jesus; instead, it is trust in the function and power of that fact. When we give Jesus the glory for His work done in our stead, then the peace of Christ brings comfort to our conscience, just as it did for Martin Luther when he rediscovered the pure Gospel for sinners.

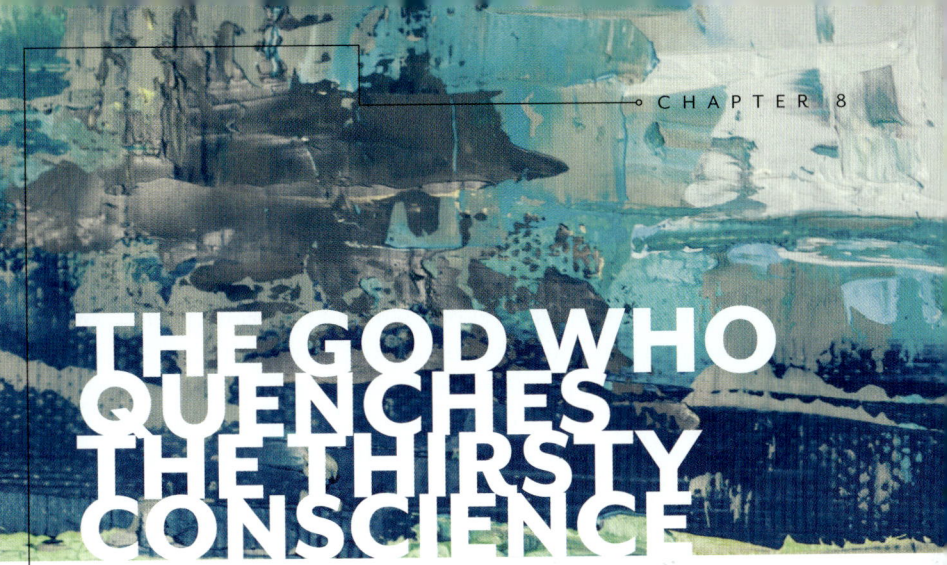

CHAPTER 8

THE GOD WHO QUENCHES THE THIRSTY CONSCIENCE

Throughout the Book of Isaiah, the prophet utilizes physical imagery to teach spiritual reality. God wants us to see and to know the same thing as Isaiah, that is, the promises of God fulfilled in Jesus. In this chapter, we will see how God uses the physical imagery of thirst to describe the refreshment and nourishment that can only be found in Him.

God's Answer to Our Thirst

> When the poor and needy seek water, and there is none, and their tongue is parched with thirst, I the LORD will answer them; I the God of Israel will not forsake them. I will open rivers on the bare heights, and fountains in the midst of the valleys. I will make the wilderness a pool of water, and the dry land springs of water. I will put in the wilderness the cedar, the acacia, the myrtle, and the olive. I will set in the desert the cypress, the plane and the pine together, that they may see and know, may consider and understand together, that the hand of the LORD has done this, the Holy One of Israel has created it. (Isaiah 41:17–20)

Furthermore, as the body and soul need to be refilled to live, the conscience needs to be filled to function properly. Just like the body, the conscience craves nourishment when it is drained and strained. Excessive work makes the body, soul, and conscience exceedingly weary and thirsty. In addition, the external circumstances exaggerate the stress and distress.

> We have described three attacks. The first is that of the flesh, against which God consoles us with His righteousness; the second is that of the world, against which He promises that we shall be conquerors and threshers; the third is that of Satan. He wearies us in our private life, he attacks individuals with various dangers, with hatred, envy, and lust. So it was with Job and Jeremiah, who in their trials wished they had not been born (Job 3:3; Jer. 20:14). This is the worst and most difficult trial, of which Christ said concerning Judas (Matt. 26:24): "It would have been better for that man if he had not been born." These are peculiarly the temptations employed by Satan. He completely wearies us needy and poor little men who are parched with thirst. St. Paul aptly speaks of "sighs too deep for words" (Rom. 8:26). "Alas and woe, I cannot endure any more. There is nothing left but groaning." Here we shall understand the text allegorically, on account of the word water. There is an analogy with those who are in such a situation, a man alone in the desert wasteland, with no tree and no shade, thirsting for water. From this analogy they make applications to the torments of afflicted consciences which are forever in trouble in sandy and arid places. But Christians are not alone. . . .
>
> Here follows the feeling of desperation, briefly and bluntly expressed. It is not so difficult to be thirsty and seek water. But the words are *there is none*. It sounds dreadful to seek and not to find. In all our temptations we hope that the end will come at length. However, in this trial there appears to be no end, but it goes on forever before my very eyes: *there is none*. . . .
>
> A bad conscience and Satan not only dry up the heart but also bruise the body and the bones in such a way that the tongue is parched. (17:47–48)

Luther identifies three different types of attacks on the believer in this life. The promise of Christ's righteousness is given to counter the attack of the sinful flesh. The promise that

Christ has overcome the world, and we are conquerors in Him, is given to counter the assaults of the world. Luther applies the promise of Isaiah 41 against the third attack of Satan. The evil foe relentlessly wearies the believer with various dangers, trials, and temptations. Thus, Luther uses the imagery of a waterless wasteland to describe the conscience in two ways. First, Luther says when the conscience is afflicted, it is like a man in a desert seeking water, but there is none to be found. Second, the conscience becomes like a dry field in which it seems there are no resources for refreshment or relief. However, the promise of God is a life-giving water that gives life where there is death.

I will open rivers on the bare heights. Both the victories and the ends of this conflict are the opposite of what we expect, because he is speaking of thirst and dryness. The promise is made allegorically. The more thirst and dryness there was, the more abundance and moisture there will be.

In the midst of the valleys. He is speaking of flat land. In Hebrew flat land is the name for places situated in the plain, producing nothing, with no pasture or arable land, not places where there are farms and fields. Therefore he says here, "in the midst of the fields," where there is nothing but sand and thirst and heat, in such places there shall be fountains and rivers. This is what it means to do everything out of desperation. Where formerly we would have said, "Nothing can possibly grow in a place like this," there everything should now grow most abundantly. Our consciences are truly "fields" like that, where we see nothing but God's wrath and no grace. Yet in spite of everything we shall win. With God's weapons the fiery darts of the evil one (Eph. 6:16) will not strike you, as Paul shows. Remember, then, that Christ is the victor for you against the world, against heretic, flesh, and all demons. This alone must be your boast, that Christ is king and that His glory and righteousness must be promoted, while we simply take off our shoes and cling to His Word.

I will make the wilderness a pool of water. Where he locates nothing but the most hopeless and trackless desert, there shall be rains and rivers. Likewise, when our situation is utterly desperate, we must not despair, because the greater the trial, the greater a blessing will follow. Where formerly there was not one drop of water, I will give rains and fountains gushing forever. Therefore, the more we are afflicted, the more we have hope, not in ourselves but in God. . . .

The discussion is about the extremely wretched thirst of the heart. This is the despair of conscience, a despair that brings forth blasphemies against God, as the experienced well know. Here He offers consolation for these trials, because He wants to take them away when despair is at its height. It is as if He were saying: "I will surely recall them, not only by supplying an abundance of water, but I will also gently lead them in shady places along the rivers which are most agreeably sweet. I will not give them seasonal rains and huts that will collapse, but I will give them a permanent water supply and eternal houses of trees full of branches; that is, as before they were engulfed in endless trials, so now they shall be refreshed in lasting strength." After that lasting affliction, "he seeks water, and there is none," there will follow a time of unending consolation, as these allegories indicate. (17:48, 49)

Our afflicted consciences cannot see anything but God's wrath without a drop of water. Yet, precisely where and when we feel the most parched by affliction, God's Gospel proclamation in Isaiah 41 promises an unending supply of refreshing water.

Adam and Eve brought the drought we experience by partaking of the forbidden tree. Sin brings death and a desert. Wickedness produces a wasteland. Our bodies, souls, and consciences become waterless and lifeless.

Jesus says, "But whoever drinks of the water that I will give him will never be thirsty again. The water that I will give him will become in him a spring of water welling up to eternal life" (John 4:14). He pours out the Holy Spirit and waters the thirsty conscience, causing rivers of living waters to flow out of the heart. With Jesus hanging from the tree, we see the reversal of the fall into sin. He emptied Himself and became poor and needy. He became tired and exhausted for us. He suffered the affliction of the conscience for us. He fasted, so that we could feast. He became weak, so that we could become strong. He was rejected, so that we could become reconciled. As the sins of the world were piled on Him, His heart began to dry up and

His tongue became parched. From the cross, He cried out, "I thirst" (John 19:28). Then, from His pierced side, the sanctifying blood and purifying water burst forth. Here we see the river opened, the fountain flowing, and the pool being filled. From Him there is an abundance of life.

The Invitation to the Thirsty

Not only does Jesus open the rivers on the cross, but He also continues to be the source of the abundant water supply. He invites the thirsty to drink. Jesus says, "If anyone thirsts, let him come to Me and drink. Whoever believes in Me, as the Scripture has said, 'Out of his heart will flow rivers of living water'" (John 7:37–38).

The voice of Jesus is heard through the words of Isaiah:

> Come, everyone who thirsts, come to the waters; and he who has no money, come, buy and eat! Come, buy wine and milk without money and without price. Why do you spend your money for that which is not bread, and your labor for that which does not satisfy? Listen diligently to Me, and eat what is good, and delight yourselves in rich food. Incline your ear, and come to Me; hear, that your soul may live. (Isaiah 55:1–3)

Without water, we are left with nothing but dry ground. Isaiah persistently invites us to listen and hear from God because through His Word, God gives us all that we need, all that we thirst for. God knows our need, and He beckons all to come and receive what He gives freely. The free gift of the remission of sins restores, refuels, and refreshes the conscience.

> The church is the assembly that clings to the Word, an assembly that is in need, in hunger and thirst. Therefore it attracts those who seek and love the Word and deals with them, lest they be slothful or give up. It is as if he were saying: "Embrace this holy teaching which is applied and offered to you free of charge." Since it is a free gift, it is not to be acquired by one's own payment, something that only the godly souls understand. The ungodly world wants to be deceived. It does not receive things offered free of charge but spurns them as worthless. . . . All things that are free are accounted

> worthless. Thus the Gospel, offered to the world free of charge, is not accepted. Only the simple and unlettered pay attention to it, receive it, and embrace it zealously, something that we scarcely achieve by supreme vigils, frequent readings, and sermons. . . .
>
> . . . You have a free gift. It is not as if someone could complain that he could not achieve it because of the high price. Indeed, teachings apart from the Word are useless; they cannot in the least strengthen minds or pacify or establish the conscience with certainty. (17:249–50)

The Church is needy, and God offers what is truly needed, free of charge. However, in this life, there is a tendency to want the things that come with a price. The Israelites chose to fast from the life-giving Word of God, to seek after something else, and to labor after that which does not satisfy. They sought to appease their appetites with pagan worship practices and false deeds. Yet, these endless pursuits left the conscience parched. The more the people drank, the thirstier they became.

We can all relate to the endless pursuits of the things that do not satisfy. When I was a child, I pursued baseball. I loved it, lived it, played it, and watched it. Yet, the more I tried to be like my sports idols, the further away my goal seemed. No matter how hard I toiled at it, I never became a star. My position became either right bench or left out. I learned firsthand that practice does not make perfect. The transition from playing baseball to only watching it was an obvious move for me. When my team wins, I win. In 2017, my beloved Houston Astros finally won the World Series. But that's not enough. I'm not satisfied with only one world championship. Now I want to see a repeat or even a three-peat.

We dwell in a land where physical fitness is more important than spiritual fitness, and stadiums are bigger than cathedrals. We have been taught to focus on the satisfaction of wins instead of the forgiveness of sins. Sports may be "recreational" for the mind and the body, but they cannot re-create the body and the soul. Appetites for winning can only be fulfilled in Jesus. He alone won the only victory that matters. He defeated death.

Our passion and thirst for that which satisfies should lead us to the One who eternally satisfies. Jesus freely and richly gives us what we need, and even more, through hearing His good and delightful Word. He sent Isaiah to Israel to satisfy the people with what they needed by speaking His Word. He continues to send pastors to feed and to satisfy our souls with the Gospel.

Isaiah says,

> For as the rain and the snow come down from heaven and do not return there but water the earth, making it bring forth and sprout, giving seed to the sower and bread to the eater, so shall My word be that goes out from My mouth; it shall not return to Me empty, but it shall accomplish that which I purpose, and shall succeed in the thing for which I sent it. (Isaiah 55:10–11)

Here you hear that He is speaking of ways and thoughts [cf. Isaiah 55:9] which have to do with the Word. He is not speaking of sublime thoughts. This paragraph is spoken in part for the confutation of the stubborn, in part for the consolation of the weak. For consolation, because the Word seems so weak and foolish that there appears to be no strength in it. How can it be believed that all the power, victory, and triumph of God are in the word of a feeble human mouth? And so He comes to meet this scandal of the weak and the stubborn. For all the enemies say, "Do you really think that everything depends on the Word? We must act, work, and think." Here the text confounds their thoughts. He does not say, "Our works and our thoughts do this," but, "My Word." It is therefore a consolation for the purpose of lifting up the weak, lest they be offended at the lowliness of God, who has every victory in His Word. At the same time He provides an illustration: *As they come down*. Rain and snow are not useless, but they *water* the earth, *giving seed to the sower*. The rain can achieve everything for the earth. "So also My Word accomplishes everything." The effect is the same. For neither one is understood. Reason says, "The strength belongs not to the rain and snow but to the earth." But when we experience the absence of rain, we see what the earth produces. So He takes away the glory of the earth and shows that it is not the earth that does it but that it is accomplished by the rain. So our building and promotion

"[God says:] My Word accomplishes everything."

—MARTIN LUTHER

> of the church is not the result of our works but of the Word of God which we preach. He rails against the Enthusiasts, who despise the Word. Here you see that everything is produced by the Word. (17:257–58)

Notice how Luther directs his attention both to the stubborn and the weak. Both focus on their own actions instead of God acting through His Word—which seems lowly and powerless. Therefore, God employs the image of little raindrops and tiny snowflakes coming down from heaven. The earth does not produce life; rather, the water from above gives life to the earth. In like manner, the individual does not produce spiritual life and vitality; instead, the external Word of God gives life to the soul.

Springs of Water

> Thus says the LORD: "In a time of favor I have answered you; in a day of salvation I have helped you; I will keep you and give you as a covenant to the people, to establish the land, to apportion the desolate heritages, saying to the prisoners, 'Come out,' to those who are in darkness, 'Appear.' They shall feed along the ways; on all bare heights shall be their pasture; they shall not hunger or thirst, neither scorching wind nor sun shall strike them, for He who has pity on them will lead them, and by springs of water will guide them." (Isaiah 49:8–10)

In this passage from Isaiah, we hear the person of God the Father speaking to the person of God the Son. The Father sends the Son to be a covenant to the people. He is the light of the world who liberates the prisoners out of darkness. He liberates them from falsehood and establishes them in truth.

Even a healthy conscience can become bad. Sin makes the conscience bad. Whether it is an unhealthy conscience recognizing pretend sin in the eyes of humanity or a healthy conscience acknowledging real sin in the sight of God, the bad conscience thirsts for a good word from God. The Law of God resets the conscience, but the Gospel of Christ reassures the conscience. When the kingdom of Christ rules and reigns in the heart through the good news of the forgiveness of sins and freedom from slavery to sin, then and only then will the conscience neither hunger nor thirst. The conscience is properly nourished and satisfied when it has a shared seeing and knowing with God through His Word. Thus, Jesus says, "Whoever believes in Me shall never thirst" (John 6:35).

Luther interprets Isaiah 49:8–10 as describing the task of the Church to gather the scattered people through the Gospel proclamation and invite them to drink from the fountain of life. Luther states,

> Christ is our covenant between God and man. So every minister is established as the covenant for you, and you may firmly believe him. Thus, whoever hears or spurns him, is doing it to Christ. So the minister of the Word is the covenant by means of which God and the people are reconciled. This office of Christ has been transferred to the church. Let no one think that Christ is dead. Rather, the ministers function in His office. . . . We do not call it church unless it preaches the Word and commandments of God. . . .
>
> It is the church's function through the Gospel to gather the scattered people to the sound faith. Let each one see to it that the one called to this office carry out its function. Now he sets forth how this office is to be discharged.
>
> *Saying to those who are bound in their hearts.* Here you see that our entire function lies in helping people, not by human strength but by the Word of God, that we may speak to those who are bound. Since Satan does not cease scattering, casting down, prostrating, there will always be an office to set free the bound and the captives. Here he binds us to this task not only by command but also by promise. *I have given you as a covenant to the people.* The bound and imprisoned are weak in the law of Moses, they are bound by Moses, hoping to be saved by their own righteousness. They are in a remarkable way held captive by the Law, and they are constantly in anxiety and toiling by their works. Whatever kind they are, freedom is offered to all of these captives through the Word. What does it say? All are saved by free grace without merits. This deliverance comes to them through the Word, not in itself but when you come. So today we see that we have been set free from Moses, the papacy, monasticism, and evil traditions. This is the bond

that the Gospel must break. . . .

He helps not only the bound but also the ignorant, he enlightens the blind, he teaches us the way of peace. Away with the sectaries who, when they hear the Word concerning Christian liberty, distort it into license for the flesh, so that they are willing to serve neither God nor men. In our teaching we must distinguish how we are free through the Gospel, noting what the Gospel teaches us, namely, that all who sweat with their merits are in darkness but that we are led by the light of the Gospel to the right way.

They shall feed along the ways, on all bare heights. These things result from your ministry, so that pastures are found everywhere. There will be no scarcity and want of pasture. We find these thoughts expressed also in John 10:26ff.: He who believes in Me "will be saved and will go in and out and find pasture." Wherever he turns he will find pasture. Before our deliverance we thought there was pasture nowhere but in the sects, as if the pasture were bound to orders. Here, however, the Word sets forth pasture for every life situation, and for all circumstances and people. The woman, the servant, the girl can hear the Word of God at home, on the hills, and in the woods. This did not happen in the Law, which had the pasture divided up among certain people and places. Here, however, he says that the Gospel will go out and come in, that is, wherever it is, there will be pasture. The papists had bound the pasture to barren and predetermined places, works, and persons. The Gospel bursts all these bonds so far as the conscience is concerned. (17:178, 179–80)

As we said in the Introduction, Luther gave his lectures on Isaiah at the University of Wittenberg as he trained future pastors. Thus, he is teaching his students about their ministry and the proper administration of their office as he comments here on Isaiah 49:8–10. He says their primary role is to teach the knowledge of salvation. They are to be shepherds who feed the flock of God under the head shepherd, Jesus, causing pastures to abound everywhere the Word of God is heard. After commenting about the importance of the preaching office, Luther directly addresses his students, saying,

They shall not hunger. As you discharge your office, there will be pasture everywhere, because "they shall never hunger nor thirst," they shall feed and be taught what is necessary to know. To eat and drink refers to teaching and exhorting. The food is teaching, and the drink is exhortation which gives life to the food. So every teacher must strive in his office to be diligent and alert, lest he lose the Word and lose it through boredom. If we preserve it, the Word will make us pure and will feed us and constantly expose and destroy errors, setting the captives free and giving light to the blind. . . . Therefore, be earnestly concerned about the pure Word. . . .

This pasture will be so ample that they will be free from the heat of the sun. I take this smiting of the sun to refer to conscience, as if to say, "They will be richly instructed by the Word so that they will be free from all terrors, anxieties, and stings of conscience." This sun of the law of Moses and of consciences shall not smite them. There are many metaphors that involve the sun. The Sun of righteousness denotes Christ, where the sun in a spiritual sense denotes any law that afflicts consciences through sin, wrath, and sting. All these will be removed by the abundance of evangelical teaching. (17:180)

> The pastor who faithfully carries out the ministry of the Church preaches Christ as our righteousness. Christ, our sun of righteousness who has healing in His wings to heal the conscience (see Malachi 4:2), protects us from the scorching heat of the sun of the Law, which dries up the conscience.

Therefore, he who abides in the Word remains under this Shepherd and in His realm of food and drink and is not smitten by the sun.

To springs of water He will guide them. He will guide, through the ministry of the Word. *To springs of water,* to the gifts and mysteries of the Spirit. Here in addition you see those who are in want of such a kingdom, the church, which hungers and thirsts and suffers the sun and everywhere feels the prod of the flesh. It is under an ungodly tyrant, in a dry place, is troubled by the continuous battle between law and liberty, so that we are forced to bear the torment of conscience. This Shepherd comes to the aid of

> this church. He provides for them this time of favor. Beware of preaching this to one who is bored and satiated. It will do him no good. Rather, preach it to the fainthearted, the captives, to those who hunger and thirst, and to those who are terrified by the heat. A Christian experiences such emotions daily, so that beyond gross sins he also feels the great heaps of sins, blasphemy of God, wrath of God, and impatience, as we observe in the saints. Such people it will benefit that we teach them these things. Know, then, that a Christian is always struck by such feelings. Always, therefore, he will hunger and thirst for His Word. He cannot tire of it. (17:181)

Luther draws a stark contrast between people who are comfortable in their own thoughts, words, and deeds and people who are comforted by God's thoughts, words, and deeds. When people are already comfortable, they have no desire for comfort in God's Word. When they are already full, they have no need to be filled. Only those who know how parched they are without God can truly rejoice in what He gives. However, when people are empty, they have no strength. All ability has dried up. All resources have been used up. They cannot run. They cannot walk. Such people have been brought down to the ground, humiliated and humbled. The people of God feel hungry and thirsty and fainthearted. They are those who are dependent on God for mercy, grace, and love. God's people are the humbled, the crushed, the afflicted who need comfort. But those who hunger and thirst for God's Word will not be disappointed, because He will never fail to give all that He has promised through His Word.

Behold, the God of the Thirsty

In this life, we live in eschatological expectation, that is, we trust the promise that we have eternal life now, but it is not yet made fully manifest. Thus, our consciences become thirsty, and at the same time, they thirst no more in Christ. Thus, in the New Testament Scriptures, John sees the same things that Isaiah saw. He sees the saints coming out of the great tribulation, washed in the blood of the Lamb. John writes, "Therefore they are before the throne of God, and serve Him day and night in His temple; and He who sits on the throne will shelter them with His presence. They shall hunger no more, neither thirst anymore;

the sun shall not strike them, nor any scorching heat. For the Lamb in the midst of the throne will be their shepherd, and He will guide them to springs of living water, and God will wipe away every tear from their eyes" (Revelation 7:15–17). While the Church Triumphant is no longer wearied by this world, the Church Militant still needs to be reassured of the Good News. We do not yet see the new creation. Thus, both John and Isaiah set our eyes on Christ. Isaiah writes,

> The wilderness and the dry land shall be glad; the desert shall rejoice and blossom like the crocus; it shall blossom abundantly and rejoice with joy and singing. The glory of Lebanon shall be given to it, the majesty of Carmel and Sharon. They shall see the glory of the LORD, the majesty of our God.
>
> Strengthen the weak hands, and make firm the feeble knees. Say to those who have an anxious heart, "Be strong; fear not! Behold, your God will come with vengeance, with the recompense of God. He will come and save you."
>
> Then the eyes of the blind shall be opened, and the ears of the deaf unstopped; then shall the lame man leap like a deer, and the tongue of the mute sing for joy. For waters break forth in the wilderness, and streams in the desert; the burning sand shall become a pool, and the thirsty ground springs of water; in the haunt of jackals, where they lie down, the grass shall become reeds and rushes. (Isaiah 35:1–7)

Jesus miraculously restored eyes, ears, legs, and even tongues to declare His praise. These miracles give us a foretaste of the new creation that will be fully realized in the resurrection of the body. Yet, in this life, we wrestle with what we know and see physically and what we know and see spiritually.

By the Spirit the prophet promises many grand things concerning the church, things which under the form of the cross are hidden from the world; and therefore the promises must be understood under the guidance of the Spirit. . . .

The church flourishes inwardly, not in power, in the wisdom of the flesh, in the gleam of splendid works; but it walks along in a simple form, not in ostentatious holiness, and therefore appears to be quite forsaken and without any glitter. Yet there are internal flowers and delights there, but these are not visible, namely, confidence, peace, life, a cheerful conscience, things that are not seen. But it does shine outwardly with obedience, love, humility, etc., which do not seem great in the eyes of the world. . . . Therefore the shape of the church must be discerned by the Spirit, not in the wisdom of the flesh. For here the church is in the wilderness, though it is compared with tilled and happy fields, tilled, that is, not by our merits, but by the grace of God. . . .

They shall see the glory, that is, the church consists in this that it sees the majesty and glory of God. The disciples are joyful in the Lord alone. For the church boasts only of the knowledge of the Lord, as we read in 1 Cor. 2:16. So Peter says, "Grow in the grace and knowledge of our Lord Jesus Christ" (2 Peter 3:18), that is, the church has the knowledge of Christ. . . .

The afflicted must be comforted with such spiritual consolations of the Word, not with any fleshly comfort which does nothing for troubled consciences but with spiritual comfort and with the living Word of God they must be ruled and strengthened. (16:299, 300, 301)

The conscience on its own cannot tell you about Jesus. Only the external Gospel brings the knowledge of the Savior from sins. He fulfilled the righteous requirements of the Law in our stead. He was crucified, buried, and died to satisfy the condemnation of the Law. To see Christ crucified for your sins is to gain a good conscience before God and a joyful conscience because in Him is victory over sin, death, and the devil.

Isaiah writes,

> Out of the anguish of His soul He shall see and be satisfied; by the knowledge of Him, the Righteous One, My Servant, He will justify many, and He shall bear their iniquities. (Isaiah 53:11; author's translation)

He Himself gave His life as an offering for the transgression. "Transgression" is properly called "guilt" in Ps. 32:5. And they do not commit sin. "To commit sin" properly means that someone has done something and remains guilty. Thus we are unable to remove our guilt. Therefore only Christ can do it. . . .

By His knowledge He will justify. As to the manner in which the course of the Kingdom will proceed, how will this King progress? This will be the manner: *By His knowledge.* This is a very lovely text. *By His knowledge He will justify many, because He shall bear their iniquities.* Those who confess that their sins have been borne by Him are the righteous. The definition of righteousness is wonderful. The sophists say that righteousness is the fixed will to render to each his own. Here he says that righteousness is the knowledge of Christ, who bears our iniquities. Whoever will, therefore, know and believe in Christ as bearing his sins will be righteous.

Many servants. Thus the Gospel is the means or vehicle by which the knowledge of God reaches us. Hence the kingdom of Christ does not consist in works or endeavors, since no rule and no law, not even the law of Moses, can lead us to that knowledge, but we arrive at it through the Gospel. A Christian cannot arrive at this knowledge by means of any laws, either moral or civil, but he must ascend to heaven by means of the Gospel. Therefore he says here *by His knowledge.* There is no other plan or method of obtaining liberty than the knowledge of Christ. For that reason Peter and Paul are constantly saying that we must increase in this knowledge, since we can never be perfect in it (cf. 2 Peter 3:18; Col. 1:10). The knowledge of Christ must be construed in a passive sense. It is that by which He is known, the proclamation of His suffering and death. You must therefore note this new definition of righteousness. Righteousness is the knowledge of Christ. What is Christ? He is the person who bears all our sins. These are unspeakable gifts and hidden and unutterable kinds of wisdom. (17:228–30)

Yahweh cries out through the mouth of the prophet Isaiah,

Therefore my people go into exile for lack of knowledge; their honored men go hungry, and their multitude is parched with thirst. (Isaiah 5:13)

However, in the kingdom of Christ,

> The earth shall be full of the knowledge of the LORD as the waters cover the sea. (Isaiah 11:9)

This knowledge is not simply an intellectual entity; rather, it is the knowledge of salvation that comes through the preaching of the Gospel. Jesus gave His soul, His life, as an offering for our transgressions. To know Christ is to know Him rightly as the Lamb who bears our sin. By this knowledge, we are justified—that is, pardoned of all sin and declared righteous in God's sight. This is not a onetime event; rather, it is a lifelong learning and growing in the knowledge of salvation.

Luther states,

> I have said that the individual words must be pondered in supreme faith, and they must be read and considered with the most watchful eyes, so that it is not simply any kind of knowledge or understanding but a knowledge that justifies, in opposition to other kinds of knowledge. Thus you see this remarkable definition of righteousness through the knowledge of God. It sounds ridiculous to call righteousness a speculative knowledge. Therefore it is said in Jer. 9:24: "Let him who glories glory in this, that he understands and knows Me." Therefore this knowledge is the formal and substantial righteousness of the Christians, that is, faith in Christ, which I obtain through the Word. The Word I receive through the intellect, but to assent to that Word is the work of the Holy Spirit. It is not the work of reason, which always seeks its own kinds of righteousness. The Word, however, sets forth another righteousness through the consideration and the promises of Scripture, which cause this faith to be accounted for righteousness. This is our glory to know for certain that our righteousness is divine in that God does not impute our sins. Therefore our righteousness is nothing else than knowing God. Let the Christian who has been persuaded by these words cling firmly to them, and let him not be deceived by any pretense of works or by his own suffering, but rather let him say: "It is written that the knowledge of God is our righteousness." (17:230)

By nature, we are all enslaved to anxiety of the conscience and the fear of death—the parchedness of the conscience that Isaiah 41:17 describes. But Luther does not want us to be deceived by suffering; instead, he wants us to meditate on Christ's suffering for us. Thus, pastors must preach Christ crucified, the one who became thirsty for us in order that we might never be thirsty again.

Christ is the one who turns His tree of death into a tree of life for us, resulting in a forest. As Isaiah 41:18–20 describes, Jesus replants cedars, acacia, myrtle, olive, cypress, plane, and pine trees to make a new garden—a picture of the new creation, the new heavens and the new earth. He opens rivers, fountains, and pools to bring an endless and abundant supply of water and life. In paradise restored, there will be no more droughts and no more death. Likewise, in the restored conscience, there no longer will be doubts or anxiety of death. The refreshed conscience has a shared seeing and shared knowledge with God regarding the renewal of creation. The life-sustaining and life-giving Gospel brings pardon and peace to the heart.

Conclusion

For Luther, the doctrine of justification praises the glory of Christ and gives true comfort to the terrified conscience. Thus, true pastoral care is rooted in justification. The message of the Gospel tells the heart, "Fear not! Behold your God." The image of God is restored to the conscience. He is not an angry judge. He is a gracious God. Whereas the Law shows God without Christ, the Gospel reveals the incarnate God, Immanuel—God with us. Christ is the God of our salvation. He is the Prince of Peace. Jesus is the visible image of the invisible God. The Gospel imprints His image—the image of the Lamb of God—on our hearts. Furthermore, the Gospel restores us into the image of God, in which we know God and believe that He is good. With a good conscience before God, we need no longer have any anxiety in our conscience or fear of death. We see things differently, because we have a shared seeing with the God who created us and redeemed us. Therefore, we rejoice in our sufferings, knowing that the Lord is re-creating all things and will bring it to completion.

> For thus says the LORD: "Behold, I will extend peace to her like a river, and the glory of the nations like an overflowing stream; and you shall nurse, you shall be carried upon her hip, and bounced upon her knees. As one whom his mother comforts, so I will comfort you; you shall be comforted in Jerusalem. You shall see, and your heart shall rejoice; your bones shall flourish like the grass; and the hand of the LORD shall be known to His servants." (Isaiah 66:12–14)

It is as if He were saying: "In place of unrest I will give them a most abundant peace, as if some river were overflowing its banks." This peace of the church is spiritual. It flows in through the forgiveness of sins, which is peace toward God. It extends so far in depth and length that neither death nor Satan nor powers, etc. (cf. Rom. 8:38–39) can be against Him. Therefore you know very well: The believers are lords of all, because they are established in heaven through Christ. Hence he uses the finest comparison to describe this peace which is like an overflowing river. The world's peace, on the contrary, is barely a drop. This peace is not a rivulet, not just a river, but a river at flood stage.

Behold, I will extend, that is, "I will enlarge." The river implies continuity and long duration; it flows all the time. The extending denotes breadth. That is, Christian riches are continuous and endless, high, deep, broad, long. Against all afflictions they will publicly have consolations. Inwardly there is perpetual peace, spread abroad and widely scattered in the conscience. This is the reign of Christ. In this wealth of peace and glory I, Martin Luther, am a disciple. (17:408–9)